38th Annual Pacific Northwest Software Quality Conference 2020

2020 Vision – Quality > Looking Forward

Portland, Oregon, USA
12-14 October 2020

ISBN: 978-1-7138-1865-6

Printed from e-media with permission by:

Curran Associates, Inc.
57 Morehouse Lane
Red Hook, NY 12571

Some format issues inherent in the e-media version may also appear in this print version.

program@pnsqc.org
www.pnsqc.org

Additional copies of this publication are available from:

Curran Associates, Inc.
57 Morehouse Lane
Red Hook, NY 12571 USA
Phone: 845-758-0400
Fax: 845-758-2633
Email: curran@proceedings.com
Web: www.proceedings.com

Monday, October 12, 2020 Schedule

8:45-9:00 AM	Welcome and Highlights for the Day
9:00-10:00 AM	Keynote **TestOps** with **Jason Arbon**
10:00-11:00 AM	**Iron Chef Cucumber: Cooking Up Software Requirements That Get Great Results** with **Chris Cowell**
11:00-Noon	**Human Centric User Acceptance Testing** with **Rebecca Long** & **Software Performance and Load Testing Utilizing JMeter** with **Anna Sharpe**
Noon-1:00 PM	Virtual Lunch with Networking
1:00-2:00 PM	**Capacity to Execute** with **John Cvetko**
2:00-3:00 PM	**Of Machines and Men** with **Iryna Suprun**
3:00-4:00 PM	**Communication is Key: Lessons Learned from Testing in Healthcare Technology** with **Rachael Lovallo** & **Full Stack Testing is a Culture: Drive your team to Embrace Change** with **Christina Thalayasingam**
4:00-5:00 PM	Keynote **Rethinking Test Automation** with **Paul Gerrard**

Tuesday, October 13, 2020 Schedule

8:45-9:00 AM	Welcome and Highlights for the Day
9:00-10:00 AM	Keynote **Breaking Down Biases and Building Inclusive AI** with **Raj Subrameyer**
10:00-11:00 AM	**Generator-Based Testing: A State by State Approach** with **Chris Struble**
11:00-Noon	**Testing COVID-19 Models: Getting Important Work Done in a Hurry** with **Christian Wiswell**
Noon-1:00 PM	Virtual Lunch with Networking
1:00-2:00 PM	**Teaching Testing to Programmers. What sticks, and What Slides Off? A Journey from Teflon to Velcro** with **Robert Sabourin** and **Mónica Wodzislawski**
2:00-3:00 PM	**Quality Focused Software Testing in Critical Infrastructure** with **Zoë Oens**
3:00-4:00 PM	**Testing Floating-Point Applications** with **Alan Jorgensen**
4:00-5:00 PM	Keynote **Quality Engineering** **Dr. Tafline Ramos**

Wednesday, October 14, 2020 Schedule

<table>
<tr><td>8:45-9:00 AM</td><td colspan="4">Welcome and Highlights for the Day</td></tr>
<tr><td>9:00-10:00 AM</td><td colspan="4">Keynote
Test Engineers are the Connectors of Our Teams
with **Jenny Bramble**</td></tr>
<tr><td>10:00-11:00 AM</td><td colspan="2">**Staying the Course: How Rigid Processes Create Flexibility** with **Leona Grzymkowski**</td><td colspan="2">**Let's focus more on Quality Engineering and less about Testing** with **Joel Montvelisky**</td></tr>
<tr><td>11:00-Noon</td><td colspan="2">**TestCafe: Grinding Automation Issues (End-to-End Web Testing Approach)**
with **Juan de Dios Delgado Bernal**</td><td colspan="2">**Are You Ready for AI to Take Over Your Automation Testing?**
with **Lisette Zounon**</td></tr>
<tr><td>Noon-1:00 PM</td><td colspan="4">Virtual Lunch with Networking</td></tr>
<tr><td>1:00-2:00 PM</td><td colspan="2">**The New Role of the Agile Tester – The General Contractor**
with **Melissa Tondi**</td><td colspan="2">**Towards a Culturally Inclusive Software Quality**
with **Jack McDowell**</td></tr>
<tr><td>2:00-3:00 PM</td><td colspan="4">Panel: **Diversity in Testing & Technology**</td></tr>
<tr><td colspan="5">Workshops</td></tr>
<tr><td>3:00-5:00 PM</td><td>**Grow & Show Your Security Knowledge with Shadow Bank Chad Holmes &** Security Innovations</td><td>**Adding Some Accessibility to your Day Michael Larsen**</td><td>**Who We Are at Work Shapes Everything Jean Richardson**</td><td>**Write Right Agile User Story Acceptance Tests Robin Goldsmith**</td></tr>
</table>

38th Annual Pacific Northwest Software Quality Conference 2020

2020 Vision – Quality > Looking Forward

Portland, Oregon, USA
12 - 14 October 2020

Table of Contents

Iron Chef Cucumber: Cooking Up Software Requirements That Get Great Results

Chris Cowell
Christopher Cowell, LLC

christopher.w.cowell@gmail.com

Abstract

Gathering requirements with behavior-driven development (BDD) tools like Cucumber seems simple at first, but at Cambia Health Solutions we discovered how hard this tool can be to use correctly and how quickly teams can sour on it when they don't understand its nuances. After two years of experimenting with Cucumber and learning how to harness its power, Cambia has successfully made it an essential part of the company's software development process. Based on this experience, I'll share best practices, anti-patterns, and real-world examples to help you use Cucumber and other requirements-gathering tools more artfully and effectively.

This discussion is aimed at QA people, developers, UX designers, product owners, and development managers who use Cucumber or other BDD tools to gather software requirements. You'll learn how you might be using Cucumber in unhelpful ways, how to write crisper and more understandable requirements, and how to make it a pleasure for everyone on your development team to write, read, and implement those requirements. Although the talk looks at requirements through the lens of Cucumber, most of the content is relevant to anyone who reads or writes software requirements no matter what tools or processes they use.

Biography

Chris Cowell is an independent technical trainer, writer, and coach based in Portland, Oregon. He developed and tested software for two decades at Cambia, Puppet, Jive, Oracle, and Accenture, and in a previous life wrote for the Let's Go travel guidebook series. Since realizing that he likes people more than computers, he now focuses on technical training. His specialties are Cucumber, behavior-driven development, and helping less-technical folks conquer impostor syndrome and feel comfortable and confident as they onboard at software companies. Chris studied computer science at Harvard and philosophy at Berkeley, but really learned to teach by showing his aging parents how to use email.

1. Introduction

If you grew up in the '70s or '80s, you might remember the classic board game Othello (also known as Reversi). My childhood Othello box had the slogan "seconds to learn, a lifetime to master," which, I discovered as my brother beat me again and again, was a good description of the game's deceptive depth.

Cucumber, a tool for supporting behavior-driven development (BDD), can be described the same way. Because you can learn the basics in 60 seconds, it's easy to be lulled into thinking you fully understand it.

But after working with Cucumber for a year as a QA person at Cambia Health Solutions, and then for another year as a Cucumber consultant, I find myself constantly learning more about it and changing my mind about how best to use it. I'm not alone in this regard: even the people who designed Cucumber are evolving their understanding of how to use it most effectively.

In this paper I'll give a lightning-fast introduction to Cucumber for people who have never used it, and then walk through some of the best practices that I've developed. Most of these best practices are relevant to anyone who gathers business requirements regardless of whether they use Cucumber to do so. But I'll explain these strategies through the lens of Cucumber, and all examples will use Cucumber's syntax (which you may see referred to elsewhere as "Gherkin"). Off we go!

2. What is Cucumber?

I said that you could learn the basics of Cucumber in 60 seconds, so start your stopwatch now.

Cucumber supports BDD in two ways. First, it gives a formal structure for writing and organizing software requirements. Second, it allows development teams to write code to turn those requirements into executable tests. The end result is magical. You get an organized list of requirements that all the software's stakeholders can understand, and you have a constantly updated view of how many of those requirements have been delivered by the development team. It's a dream tool for anyone who wants to write software using BDD, but is also fantastic if you use a more traditional write-code-first, write-tests-later approach.

Cucumber calls its requirements "scenarios." Each scenario has a title and a set of Given, When, and Then statements: given some state of the system, when the user does something, then something else happens.

For example, here's a typical scenario for a web app. It specifies that users must log in before they can use the app:

```
Scenario: Require login
      Given Anne is not logged in
      When she navigates to any page
      Then it redirects her to the login screen
```

Scenarios can get more complicated than this, but some really are just this straightforward.

One additional complexity: you can use **And** or **But** keywords to allow multiple **Given** or **Then** statements in a single scenario:

```
Scenario: Require login
      Given Anne is not logged in
      And the system does not recognize her IP address
      When she navigates to any page in the app

      Then it redirects her to a login screen
      And it gives her the option to create a new account
```

Believe it or not, you now know enough to use Cucumber! But because of its Othello-like hidden complexity, you don't know enough to use Cucumber effectively. Let's see what we can do to fix that.

3. Best Practices

I mentioned that Cucumber has two parts: the requirements-gathering part and the executable test part. The best practices I'm presenting here all have to do with the first of these: they are about how to write good requirements. A discussion of the best practices for turning those requirements into tests deserves a whole separate paper.

Out of all the techniques I've learned from using Cucumber, I'll present the seven that have had the biggest impact on me and my teams. These tips will help you write thorough requirements that are understandable by all the software's stakeholders and will help your team deliver high quality software quickly.

For each of these best practices I'll explain a technique and include a made-up but realistic example. The best practices are presented in no particular order.

3.1 Context

Imagine that we're writing a web app for ordering high-priced, unnecessarily fancy custom-made ice through a startup called Rose City Artisanal Ice.

We want to use Cucumber to write high-level, feature-focused requirements for this web app, and we need to share those requirements with both technical and non-technical stakeholders. We intend to have each requirement understood and approved before developers write a single line of product code to satisfy that requirement. In other words, we're following strict BDD procedures.

3.2 Write like you talk

The first best practice is to write requirements using a natural, normal tone and everyday vocabulary. In other words, write as if you were explaining the requirement to a friend in a casual conversation.

This might sound obvious, but it's a common problem. People often write specifications using a style they'd never use when talking with a colleague. Sometimes they write in a compressed, almost cryptic way, probably thinking that this seems more "high tech" or is more efficient. At other times they write too much, using convoluted, unnecessarily complicated prose. This probably comes from a belief that more language is better language, or that specifying every last detail is a necessary condition of good requirements. But when requirements are either too compressed or too verbose, they're hard to read and understand.

Let's illustrate this principle with an example. Say we want to let a web app user filter their ice options based on the source of the water it's made from. Here's a scenario that captures that requirement but is too compressed:

```
# bad example: too compressed
Scenario: filter source
```

```
Given Barbara searches ice
When filter set to spring water
Then only spring water ice
```

Here's a scenario that goes too far in the other direction, expressing the requirement with unnecessarily complex language and too many words:

```
# bad example: too complex
Scenario: filter the results of a search for ice, using the source of the
      water from which it is made
   Given Barbara is searching for ice but would like that search to exclude
         ice made from any water source other than her preferred source of
         spring water
   When Barbara activates the filter functionality within the list of
        results returned by the search feature
   Then the only ice that is presented to Barbara within the search results
        is ice made from spring water, which is her preferred water type
```

Finally, here's a well-written scenario that falls somewhere between the two previous examples. It uses a conversational style and proper but succinct English:

```
Scenario: filter ice by water source
   Given Barbara is searching for ice
   When she filters out ice not made from spring water
   Then the results show only spring water ice
```

Now that sounds like something you might actually say out loud in a conversation.

3.3 Be careful with your logic

The next best practice is to double- or even triple-check any requirements that use logical terms like "and," "or," "not,", "all," and "only". Even though programmers are used to thinking carefully about logic as they code, it's easy for them—and anyone else who writes Cucumber scenarios—to overlook logical nuances in ways that break their requirements.

Consider this scenario about selecting the region that the ice comes from:

```
# bad example: incorrect logic
Scenario: filter ice by region of origin
   Given Claire is searching for ice
   When she requests only Alaskan ice
   Then the results show all the Alaskan ice options
```

Do you see the problem in this requirement? There's a logical fault that could potentially cause the scenario to fail (if run as a test) when it should pass, and pass when it should fail. And even if it's not turned into an executable test, it might lead a programmer to implement the feature in a way that's not what the authors of the requirement intended.

The problem lies with the word "all" in the **Then** step. Say there are only two ice options made in Alaska. If the app returned both of the two Alaskan-made ice options but also returned 98 ice options that are made elsewhere, this scenario would be satisfied even though only 2% of the results are relevant to Claire. She asked for *only* Alaskan options, after all. The person writing the requirements probably intended the **Then** statement to look like this instead (notice the single-word change):

```
# correct logic
Then the results show only Alaskan ice
```

With this rewritten statement, the product code is only correct if it returns Alaskan ice and nothing else. That's almost certainly what users expect to see when they try to filter the results in this way.

Logical mistakes like this are easy to make and commonly found in the wild. They make it impossible to know whether your software does what you want it to. So always double-check your usage of logical terms and make sure the scenario accurately captures your intention.

3.4 General scenario titles and concrete steps

Scenarios are most easily understood when their titles are general and their steps are concrete. This means that titles should steer clear of including specific details, whereas steps should include lots of those sorts of details.

For example, say our web app must validate the ZIP code of the customer's shipping address. Here's a good way to capture that requirement:

```
# good example of general title and detailed steps
Scenario: validate well-formed shipping ZIP
      Given Diana is ready to check out
      When she enters "97201" for her ZIP
      Then the system accepts her ZIP

# good example of general title and detailed steps
Scenario: validate malformed shipping ZIP
      Given Diana is ready to check out
      When she enters "ABCDE" for her ZIP
      Then she gets an error asking her to correct the ZIP
```

The scenario titles describe the feature without getting into specifics of how the feature might be tested. These titles are all you need if you want a quick glimpse of the system's intended behavior. It's easiest to understand the behavior if you're given a high-level overview of what it should do instead of concrete examples.

The scenario steps, on the other hand, serve as examples of how the feature actually operates. If you enter a specific ZIP code, specific behavior should result. Including concrete details in the steps provides extra color to scenarios, improving them in several ways: they become more vivid, more powerful, easier to read, and easier to remember. This is important when a stakeholder is trying to read and understand 200 scenarios without falling asleep. You won't break your scenarios if you omit specific details and instead use general descriptions in your steps, but your scenarios won't be as effective as they could be.

For example, this **When** step is not as good as the **When** step in the previous scenario:

```
# bad example: no concrete details
When she enters a malformed ZIP
```

Just referring to a "malformed ZIP" makes this a less powerful example of the ZIP-validation requirement than referring to a specific malformed ZIP.

Note that the concrete ZIP values included in the "good" scenarios above are relevant to the main point of those scenarios. Including concrete details about what kind of ice Diana is buying, explaining that she has logged in three times today, or including her login credentials in the steps would add harmful clutter to these scenarios since those details have nothing to do with the scenarios' main focus, or what aspect of the requirements they are trying to illustrate. So while details are important in to include in steps, only include *relevant* details.

3.5 Don't overuse Cucumber

It's tempting to write a Cucumber scenario for everything a user might do with your software: describe every error condition, every odd workflow, and every possible operation and permutation. But well-written scenarios are expensive to write, share, edit, and maintain, and creating a mountain of scenarios that cover every conceivable situation is almost always more expensive than it's worth.

Just as the "runnable tests" feature of Cucumber isn't meant to provide your only layer of testing (you still need unit and integration tests!), the requirements-capturing feature of Cucumber isn't meant to be your only means of writing formal requirements. To avoid moving beyond the point of diminishing returns with Cucumber, it's generally best to write a scenario for each happy path (i.e., the most common sequences of clicks and data entry that result in the software being used the way it was intended) and only a handful of unhappy paths (user actions that produce warnings or errors). Include just the unhappy paths that are likely to happen, that are catastrophic when they occur, or that exercise code that developers are nervous about. While the other, less-critical unhappy paths should of course also be captured in requirements, it's more sensible to put them in plain English paragraphs or whatever non-Cucumber format your team agrees on. In short: save Cucumber for the most important stuff.

Besides the expense involved with writing and maintaining a a large number of scenarios, there's another reason to limit the scope of your Cucumber usage. Even well-written scenarios can be hard to read, understand, and compare. The whole point of Cucumber is to make software requirements as easy as possible for all stakeholders—technical and non-technical alike—to understand, discuss, and approve. It does that well, but it's exhausting to read hundreds of scenarios and it's hard to notice the details and logical subtleties that distinguish one scenario from other similar scenarios. After a while, they all blur together and the usefulness of Cucumber is lost. Keeping your scenarios short and the number of scenarios small is the best way to retain their impact and usefulness.

Imagine that we want to capture requirements around changing a user's password. A happy path scenario might look like this:

```
Scenario: change password
      Given Elizabeth is logged in
      When she changes her password to "p@ssw0rd$"
      Then she's redirected to the login page
      And she can log in with the new password
```

We might decide that the only unhappy path that's likely to occur around password changes is when a user enters an invalid new password. There are many ways the new password could be invalid, but in the interest of keeping our collection of scenarios to a manageable size, it's reasonable to capture just one type of invalid password in a Cucumber scenario:

```
Scenario: change password to invalid new password
      Given Elizabeth is logged in
      When she changes her password to "ABC"
      Then she sees a warning that it's too short
      And she is prompted to enter a new password
```

Again, we still need to establish requirements around all the other ways a user could enter an invalid new password, but it makes more sense to write these specs in a non-Cucumber format (and to test them at the unit test level instead of with Cucumber scenarios). We've captured one example of invalid password behavior in Cucumber, and that's enough to give stakeholders an idea of how that feature should generally work. Describing all the ways a password could be invalid–and testing that those invalid passwords are flagged properly by the system–are jobs best left to other tools.

Note that the first scenario above has a short, general title, whereas the second scenario has a longer title that includes more details. This is a recommended approach: happy path scenarios should have titles that assume that everything works as expected, while unhappy path scenarios should have titles that include details about why they trigger an error condition.

3.6 Focus on features, not controls

BDD works best when it describes how people use your software's features, not how they interact with its GUI controls. So Cucumber scenarios should rarely, if ever, refer to buttons, text fields, drop-down menus, or other GUI elements.

For example, here's a badly written scenario that captures the check-out process by referring to what the user clicks and types rather than what she is trying to do:

```
# bad example: refers to GUI elements
Scenario: check out
      Given Francis has finished adding items to her cart
      When she clicks "checkout"
      And she enters her address in the "shipping address" fields
      And she enters her billing info in the "billing info" fields
      And she clicks "pay now"
      And she clicks the "confirm payment" button
      Then she is shown the "order complete" page
      And she sees "thank you for shopping with Rose City Artisanal Ice"
      And she sees "your FedEx tracking number is <TRACKING NUMBER>"
      And the "continue shopping" button is highlighted
```

One problem with this is that referring to all the GUI elements makes the scenario way too long to read comfortably. Another problem is that it might capture Francis's specific actions, but it doesn't capture the *spirit* of her actions. If you asked her what she was doing, she wouldn't say "I'm clicking on this button and entering text in that field." She'd say "I'm checking out" or "I'm paying for the items in my shopping cart." And that *user intention* is what the scenario should capture.

This better-written scenario explains what she's trying to do, not how she's trying to do it:

```
Scenario: check out
      Given Francis has finished adding items to her cart
      When she checks out
      Then she an order confirmation message
      And she sees a shipment tracking number
```

This second scenario is shorter, easier to understand, and more relevant to stakeholders because it captures the behavior of the software's feature rather than its controls.

If you're using Cucumber scenarios as executable tests, don't worry: the scenarios will still test most of the GUI controls in the normal course of using the feature. Any controls that Cucumber misses can be covered with JavaScript unit tests.

3.7 Use personas

A persona is a fictitious person who serves as the user in one or more of your Cucumber scenarios. It's easy to think of a persona as nothing more than a gussied-up test user, and in a sense that's true. But a well-crafted persona is defined using a formal syntax (which I'll explain below, but maybe you can already guess what that syntax is?) and is shared with all the stakeholders so everyone has a common understanding of who the user is and how they're likely to use the software.

For example, we might need two personas to populate the Rose City Artisanal Ice scenarios. Let's call them Gretchen and Hannah. Gretchen is security-conscious: she pays only with Bitcoin, changes her password daily, and opts not to store shipping information in her user account. Hannah, on the other hand, is a typical user with the one quirk of frequently changing her email subscription settings.

Instead of referring generically to "the user" or "you" in our scenarios, we can refer specifically to Gretchen and Hannah:

```
Given Gretchen is logged in
```

or

```
When Hannah sorts ice by cost, ascending
```

It's important to keep personas streamlined, and not burdened with confusing, extraneous details. A great way to ensure that they are as minimal as possible is to define the personas only after you start using them in scenarios. Figure out what traits a persona needs in order to participate in a scenario, and then add those traits to the persona's definition as you write the scenario. By doing this, you make sure that every part of a persona's description is relevant to at least one Cucumber scenario.

Are you ready to learn about the mind-bending, *Inception*-like way that we define personas? It's best to define them in... more Cucumber scenarios. Granted, these are weird scenarios because they only have **Given** statements (no **When** or **Then** statements), but they're still scenarios.

```
Scenario: define persona of Gretchen
      Given Gretchen has a Rose City Artisanal Ice account
      And she has the password "Swizzle$"
      And she has stored Bitcoin info
      And she has not stored shipping info


Scenario: define persona of Hannah
      Given Hannah has a Rose City Artisanal Ice account
      And she subscribes to the email newsletter
```

Why would you go to the bother of defining personas in Cucumber scenarios instead of using plain English paragraphs or something less formally structured? Because if you use Cucumber's optional feature of treating the requirements as executable tests, these scenario-defined personas can themselves be run as tests, and will give you a warning (by failing) whenever the configuration information for the personas drifts away from what you and your tests expect.

For instance, if you execute the scenario that defines Gretchen's persona, it will make sure that she still has Bitcoin info in her account, that she doesn't have any shipping info stored, and that her password is set as expected. If someone accidentally changes any of these pieces of information in the database that stores her user account info, the scenario that defines Gretchen's persona will fail and you will know that scenarios further down the line that rely on Gretchen's Bitcoin info might also fail. So you should ignore the other failing tests until you fix Gretchen's user info in the database, at which point her persona definition scenario will pass again.

Alternatively, you could write your test code so that instead of validating Gretchen's user account info, it instead is responsible for *configuring* her account information to conform to the persona definition. This is an effective brute-force way to avoid configuration drift problems for test users.

There's a nice fringe benefit to using formal personas: they make it simple to follow the best practice of using the active voice in each step. If you think back to high school English, using the active voice means that you have a clear subject performing some action. For example, without personas you might write a scenario using the less effective passive voice, like this:

```
# bad example: passive voice
When the email newsletter is received
```

As your high school English teacher probably told you, switching to the active voice makes your writing more direct and powerful. Fortunately, using the active voice is almost effortless when you include a persona in your steps:

```
When Hannah receives the email newsletter
```

3.8 Use present tense

Let's end with a best practice that's easy to understand and easy to implement: use present tense in all of your steps. If your brain works like mine does, it's almost impossible not to write **Given** steps in past tense, **When** steps in present tense, and **Then** steps in future tense:

```
# bad example: inconsistent tenses
Scenario: view cart
        Given Isabelle added ten items to her cart
        When she views her cart
        Then she will see those items alphabetical order, ascending
```

Fight the urge to do so! Or go back afterwards and change all tenses to present tense:

```
Scenario: view cart
        Given Isabelle adds ten items to her cart
        When she views her cart
        Then she sees those items in alphabetical order, ascending
```

There are two reasons to keep everything in the present tense. First, using a consistent tense within and across scenarios makes those scenarios easier to read and understand, especially for a bleary-eyed reader who is looking at the 50th scenario in a row. Second, by writing everything in the present tense you simplify the process of re-using any code you've written to turn these steps into executable tests. For example, in the future you might write a scenario that includes this step:

```
When Jessica adds ten items to her cart
```

Even though the persona has changed and this step is a **When** instead of a **Given**, the "adds ten items to her cart" text is the same, which means that Cucumber can execute the same underlying code for either of those steps.

3.9 The most important best practice: use your best judgment

There are very few black-and-white issues in life, and that includes Cucumber usage. The most important best practice is: *it's OK to break any rule that doesn't make sense in a particular context.* If one of the rules I've described makes your scenario clunky, complicated, or difficult to understand, ignore that rule! These recommendations are sensible starting places, but you shouldn't hold yourself strictly to them. Writing Cucumber scenarios is as much art as science, so trust your instincts about what makes a scenario clear, succinct, and unambiguous. Consistency is more important than any of the other rules we've discussed, so if your company or team prefers a way of writing scenarios that bends or breaks any of these rules, follow that direction.

4. Conclusion

Cucumber is a transformative technology for software development teams. It allows all stakeholders, regardless of their level of technical sophistication, to understand, share, and discuss software requirements. It provides a constantly updated view of how many of those requirements have been satisfied. To top it off, Cucumber makes behavior-driven development not only possible, but a pleasure.

It's not cheap to use. Writing, revising, organizing, and sharing scenarios takes a lot of time. It can be hard to keep a development team focused on gathering requirements instead of jumping ahead to writing product code. But the payoff is worth it both in terms of development speed and software quality.

It can be tough to convince management to try Cucumber, given the potential disruption to their teams' established workflow and the amount of up-front time that it demands before actual product code starts showing up. But if you think Cucumber might work for your team, these best practices might help you convince your management that Cucumber is worth a try. It's a mature technology with a supportive ecosystem, active practitioners, and a proven track record. I hope these ideas will help you use Cucumber so effectively and efficiently that you'll become as enthusiastic an evangelist for the technology as I am.

Human Centric User Acceptance Testing

Rebecca Long

rebecca.long1@engie.com

Abstract

Software is built by people to solve problems and make lives easier for other people. As quality professionals, we understand the importance of ensuring our software is properly and fully tested before getting shipped. Often our testing efforts require a User Acceptance Test (UAT) step to get final sign-off before a release. This step, unfortunately, can be messy due to communication barriers that may exist between the engineering team and the users which can lead to misses, frustration and other strong emotions for all involved. Overcoming these barriers requires strong up-front organization, clear expectations, and keeping the human aspect of this testing step in focus. I will share with you some best practices to keep our UAT sessions human centric, setting you up for success with better communication and greater trust between teams.

Biography

Rebecca Long is the Quality Assurance Manager at Engie Impact in Spokane, Washington. She has 15 years' experience in software engineering focused on quality assurance and DevOps and holds undergraduate and master's degrees in computer science. Rebecca has been a leader in the local tech community for most of the last decade running the QA user group SpoQuality and in 2018 launching the non-profit Future Ada to support and advocate for diversity and inclusion in STEAM (science, technology, engineering, art, and mathematics). She lives with two cats, who are the true masters of the household.

1. Introduction

Software development goes through many phases to get from inception into users' hands. Testing throughout each phase is critical for producing a high-quality software product. Each testing phase has a different focus and different purpose. Many software projects include a User Acceptance Testing (UAT) phase before releasing the software into a production system. UAT is defined as testing "from the perspective of the users and other stakeholders for whom [the software] has been built or acquired" with the goal of managing risk, building confidence, assessing business processes are correct, and confirming that the software is ready for release (Hambling and Goethem, 2013).

The UA testers are often not engineers and are instead a representative of your end-user base. This base may be the general public, a specific industry or group, or internal business consumers. These testers should be treated as your customer when it comes to all feedback provided back to the engineering team. This feedback can give insight into problems needing to be fixed and gaps that need to be addressed. Setting up a positive environment where this feedback can be quickly received, logged, tracked and actioned on is important.

2. Human Elements of UAT

Given humans are involved in the entire software development process, considering the human-element is equally important to paying attention to technical details when building and testing applications. Unlike technology, humans come with a lot of characteristics like emotions, lives, families, baggage, hopes and dreams plus different communication styles, backgrounds, educations, and experiences. All of which play into the success of everyday interactions as well as activities like UAT. These human-elements should be kept upfront during UAT sessions to avoid pitfalls in communication, minimizing frustrations and maximizing the effectiveness of the process.

2.1 Communication and Trust

Trust is a human-element that has a tight relationship with different levels of communication. Stephen Covey diagrams this relationship in his book, "The 7 Habits of Highly Effective People" (Figure 1) that the lower the trust the lower the cooperation level (Covey, 1998).

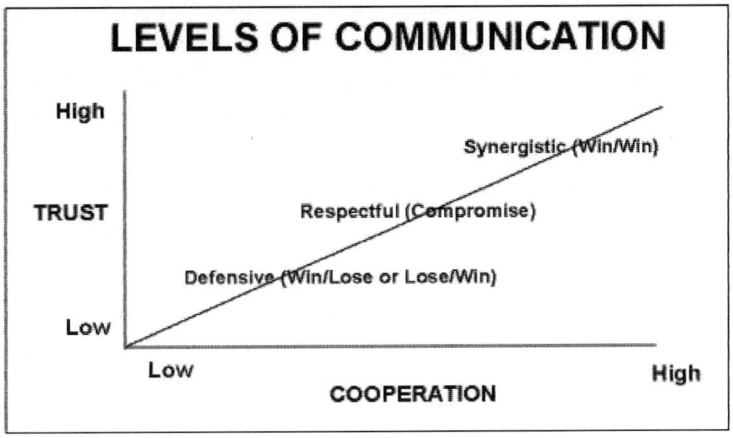

Figure 1: Levels of Communication, Stephen Covey, 7 Habits of Highly Effective People]

It states in "The 7 Habits of Highly Effective People" that "*the lowest level of communication coming out of low-trust situations would be characterized by defensiveness, protectiveness, and often legalistic language*" and leads to only Win/Lose or Lose/Lose situations causing even further reason to be defensive (Covey, 1998). Operating from this place will not create a positive space for an effective UAT session. We want to focus on building trust between members within our engineering team as well as with our UA test team to allow us to reach that high-trust/high-cooperation level of communication.

There are several behaviors that we can work on and be mindful of to build up our "Trust Accounts" (Covey, 2006). Trust Accounts, like bank accounts, can have deposits when behaving in ways that build trust and withdrawals when behaving in ways that break trust. These can look different to different people and often a withdrawal is going to be larger than a deposit. We want to maximize our deposits between our software team and our UAT group as well as minimize withdrawals as much as possible to quickly build up and maintain trust. In "The Speed of Trust" there are 13 behaviors called out as trust building (Covey, 2006):

Straight Talk	Demonstrate Respect
Create Transparency	Right Wrongs
Show Loyalty	Deliver Results
Get Better	Confront Reality
Clarify Expectations	Practice Accountability
Listen First	Keep Commitments
Extend Trust	

Table 1: Trust Building Behaviors, Stephen M. R. Covey, Speed of Trust

We can instill these behaviors into our interactions during UAT by being open and honest with the reality of our software and processes, recognizing gaps and actively working to improve them, owning up to mistakes, stick to commitments, being transparent if things need to shift, and extending trust to others involved in this process by assuming everyone else is doing these same things.

Getting to a high-trust environment will also allow individuals to avoid blame and shame sessions when reviewing feedback provided by UA team. It will also help avoid judgement if confusion arises. High-trust environments allow information to flow freely, mistakes are tolerated as learning opportunities, issues raised can be dealt with directly, and collaboration and innovation thrive (Covey, 2006). This is where we want to operate in and be mindful as we run any User Acceptance Test session.

2.2 Inclusive Environment

Inclusivity is another human-element to take into consideration to create a positive space for effective communication during a UAT. This means your UAT spaces and communication channels should all be welcoming so everyone involved feels they belong, and their feedback is valued. There are many ways to build an inclusive space including using inclusive language, avoiding inappropriate language or humor, defining terms that may not be known by all involved, and answering questions without judgement. Inclusion expert Jennifer Brown writes that people feel included *"when our coworkers affirm that (1) we belong, (2) we matter, (3) what we do matters, and (4) "they" hear what we say"* (Brown, 2017). Creating this inclusive space will maximize engagement and successful communication during UAT.

Part of an inclusive environment is having the engineering team take an empathetic leadership role when running a UAT session. Empathy is about being able to step into someone else's shoes and see and feel what they are experiencing. Merriam-Webster Dictionary defines empathy as "*the action of understanding, being aware of, being sensitive to, and vicariously experiencing the feelings, thoughts, and experience of another of either the past or present without having the feelings, thoughts, and experience fully communicated in an objectively explicit manner*" (Merriam-Webster).

Author and TED Talk speaker, Simon Sinek, is quoted as saying "*My success hinges entirely on the people I work with—the people who enlist themselves to join me in my vision. And it's my responsibility to see that they're working at their best capacity"* (Levitt, 2017). This is the mindset the engineering team should take -- doing everything they can to ensure UA team is able to test and provides feedback at the best of their ability. Having empathy on their experience as testers includes withholding judgement for "mistakes" or "user error", checking your biases about users (and testers and anyone else) at the door, and not getting frustrated when problems are reported. All this feedback is valid and what your users are likely to experience. We need to have empathy for these experiences, take them seriously and ensure they can provide these experiences back to the engineering team.

3. Best Practices

There are some standard best practices that should be used for a successful UAT session while also considering the human-element explained here.

3.1 Clear Expectations

The first step is always getting a commitment from leadership on doing a UAT session. Then you can work with your software team to define the purpose, goals and timeline needs for your UAT. Before scheduling anything with UA testers, you should have answers to the following questions:

- What environment will be used for testing?
- Who is responsible for setting up the test environment?
- What feedback are we looking for out of this test session?
- Will there be formal test scenarios? If so, who will create them?
- What are the test data requirements?
- What kind of data set will be used? Production replica or generated data or something else?
- Where will UAT results be documented?
- How will problems be communicated, vetted, logged and prioritized?
- What is the timeline for running this testing session?

Once these questions are answered, communicate them to everyone involved in the UAT. Clearly and transparently define roles and goals for those involved. It's important to explicitly set the appropriate expectations around the session up front to keep everyone on the same page. People will come into the UAT session with their own implicit expectations which they will use to judge things by. Not clearly setting expectations around process, roles, responsibilities and goals at the start leaves people to their original expectations and "*if they feel like their basic expectations have been violated, the reserve of trust is diminished*" (Covey, 1998).

Creating and maintaining a high-trust environment for these test sessions is important to maximizing their success. As "The 7 Habits of Highly Effective People" calls out, "*when expectations are not clear and shared, people begin to become emotionally involved and simple misunderstandings become compounded, turning into personality clashes and communication breakdowns*" (Covey, 1998). All those communication breakdowns lead to an inefficient, stressful and frustrating UAT experience for all involved thus lowering the value produced by this important testing phase.

3.2 Feedback Loops

Feedback loops of different types are important in any testing phase. These loops "*have different costs and response times and return different types of information*" all focused on getting feedback around quality to the engineering team as fast as possible (Cummings-John and Owais, 2019). According to Hubspot:

"*A feedback loop is a process in which the outputs of a system are circled back and used as inputs. In business, this refers to the process of using customer or employee feedback (the outputs of a service or product), to create a better product or workplace*" (Hubspot Blog, 2018).

We often see feedback loops in software development through our continuous integration systems and automated testing processes. Many of our development and test tools can quickly provide automated feedback to the development team to be actioned on as needed in a timely manner. These are highly valuable and necessary for teams to utilize.

Building in intentional human-centric feedback loops will aid in a fast flow of communication back and forth with the development team during the UAT phase. Human-centric feedback loops for UAT should include structured and clear communication channels. Planned meetings such as a kickoff and close out session along with daily touchpoints provide consistent known channels for communicating with the overall UAT team on feedback and get concerns addressed. These meetings can be in a scheduled room, over a conference call, and/or via a designated group chat for all UAT participants to be in for support and discussion. A UAT coordinator should be designated to facilitate all the meetings and formal discussions. Having a coordinator also makes it easy for anyone to reach out for immediate assistance or updates on status.

All feedback loops and communication channels should be inclusive and safe for participants. The human-element must always be considered for fostering trust and collaboration. The UAT coordinator is responsible for ensuring there is no blaming when feedback is reported back to the development team. The UAT coordinator is also responsible for ensuring there is no judgement when working with UA team or when questions arise. Everyone participating should be doing this as well, but the UAT coordinator needs to set the tone and call out bad behavior, keeping everyone focused on the shared goal of producing a high-quality product.

Every team and every UAT is different in what they need and what the preferred feedback loops are. We should be working to continuously improve these processes and learn from what works for our groups and what doesn't. At the end or following UAT, capture lessons learned and actively work to incorporate improvements in future UAT sessions. This is one of the core trust behaviors, "Get Better":

"*Get Better is based on the principles of continuous improvement, learning, and change. It is what the Japanese call kaizen, and it builds enormous trust. ... When people see you as a learning, growing, renewing person—or your organization as a learning, growing, renewing organization—they develop confidence in your ability to succeed in a rapidly changing environment, enabling you to build high-trust relationships and move with incredible speed*" (Covey, 2016).

3.3 Documentation

In a similar vein, having clear documentation up-front and throughout the UAT process is critical to keep everyone on the same page and maintain a human-centered focus. Even within an Agile Development environment, creating good documentation upfront on direction and instruction for how UAT is to be run will save you time and frustration. This initial documentation should include answers to the questions you had at the start of UAT: the purpose, goals, roles, responsibilities, scope, assumptions, constraints, environment information, risks, etc.

Take advantage of checklists to keep track of vital setup and teardown procedures for UAT. Checklists "*remind us of the minimum necessary steps and make them explicit. They not only offer the possibility of verification but also instill a kind of discipline of higher performance*" (Gawande, 2009). You can find a variety of UAT checklist examples to help get you started in User Acceptance Testing: A Step-By-Step Guide (Hambling, and Goethem, 2013). Create ones for your unique needs and modify it as needed with each run to continuously improve.

The scope of what is under test and what is not, which parts need UAT focus and feedback, need to be documented and provided to the UAT team before starting. This information can be sent to the team to review ahead of time and/or reviewed together at the UAT kickoff. Scope could be items to test from a high-level view or feature focused on what's ready for test. Test scripts of specific test scenario to run should be provided and ready at the start of the kickoff for UA testers to use.

UAT should also produce artifacts (e.g. bug reports) which are clearly documented for easy troubleshooting and prioritization. Templates should be provided for UAT team to use for filling out their reports. UAT testers should work with a QA representative to assist in quickly vetting problems and getting them properly logged.

Avoid making this documentation part of UAT tedious or inconvenient as it can "*[discourage] … recording of found bugs*" (Weinberg, 2008). Additionally, it will be important to stay committed to a blameless environment when issues are discovered and reported back to the development team. Be mindful of tone in written reports and how problems are presented to the UAT group. There is "*no benefit … gained by adopting a blaming or patronizing tone*" and it only leads to eroding trust (Kaner and Bach, 2001). All issues are opportunities for the quality of the product to improve which is everyone's shared goal.

At the end of UAT, make sure to clearly and explicitly document the outcome. What passes? What fails? What gaps were discovered? What items are critical to be addressed before getting a release sign-off? Put front and center in the top-level UAT documentation a summary of everything with the overall outcome stated and any release recommendation to go with it.

4. Success Template

Considering everything discussed here so far -- creating a human focused and inclusive environment – here is a baseline template to get you started on setting up a successful human-centric UAT.

4.1 Preparation Work

1. Understand your testing needs from users
   a. What questions are you asking from them?
   b. What feedback are you looking for?
2. Get leadership commitment
3. Create documentation for test session
   a. Checklists
   b. Test scripts
   c. Defect reporting process & template
4. Setup UAT environment for testing
   a. Confirm correct builds / releases are deployed and configured properly
   b. Run a build verification test on environment to validate it works
5. Identify & document test data requirements
   a. What can / should be used?
   b. What cannot / shouldn't be used?
   c. Does any of it need to be generated special for this test session?
   d. Is data already loaded in the system which can be used?
6. Identify UAT team
   a. Are they actual users of the system?
   b. Are they representatives of actual users of the system?
   c. Do they already have access to the system?
   d. Do user accounts / access need to be set up?

4.2 User Acceptance Testing

1. Kick Off
    a. Include UAT team & key engineering support resources
    b. Explain testing plan
    c. Walk through documentation and test data requirements
    d. Discuss feedback loops & communication ground rules
    e. Identify & share facilitator / key engineering point-of-contact
    f. Provide any known issues to UAT team
    g. Be thankful for everyone's time in helping with the test session
2. Testing Session
    a. Stay in constant contact with UAT team
    b. Answer questions and address problems quickly when brought up
    c. Be grateful for issues raised & take note to avoid them in the future
    d. Report defects in issue tracking system (confirmed or not)
3. Daily touchpoint
    a. Include UAT team & key engineering resources
    b. No-blame and no-judgement zone
    c. Discuss status and defect found
    d. Get a pulse on the emotional impact of the test session on users
    e. Clear any roadblocks blocking the UAT team
    f. Express gratitude in meetings and thank everyone in attendance
4. Close Out
    a. Collect any final feedback from UAT team
    b. Confirm everything was properly documented
    c. Document lessons learned
    d. Get sign-off or recommendation from UAT team on go/no-go for release
    e. Thank everyone for their help

5. Conclusion

The human-element is always the most complicated to account for and manage. However, considering human factors when designing a User Acceptance Test session can prove extremely fruitful resulting in minimal frustration and stress and maximum effective communication and collaboration. The template and suggestions in this paper will help get you setup on a path for success. Every team and individual are different so you will need to take that into account, adapting as you go. Just like with Agile Development, working with humans is an iterative process where you want to fail fast, acknowledge and learn from your mistakes, and continuously improve.

References

Brown, Jennifer. Inclusion: Diversity, the New Workplace & the Will to Change. Purpose Driven Publishing, 2017.

Covey, Stephen M. R. The Speed of Trust. New York, NY: Free Press, 2006.

Covey, Stephen R. The 7 Habits of Highly Effective People. Provo, UT: Franklin Covey, 1998.

Cummings-John, Ronald, and Owais Peer. Leading Quality: How Great Leaders Deliver High-Quality Software and

Accelerate Growth. Great Britain: ROI Press, 2019.

“Empathy.” Merriam-Webster. Merriam-Webster. Accessed September 7, 2020. https://www.merriam-webster.com/dictionary/empathy.

Forsey, Caroline. “The Definition of Negative and Positive Feedback Loops in 200 Words or Less.”

HubSpot Blog, July 6, 2018. https://blog.hubspot.com/marketing/feedback-loop.

Gawande, Atul. The Checklist Manifesto. New York, NY: Picador, 2009.

Hambling, Brian, and Pauline Van Goethem. User Acceptance Testing: a Step-by-Step Guide. Swindon, UK: BCS, 2013.

Kaner, Cem, and James Bach. Lessons Learned in Software Testing. New York, NY: Wiley, 2001.

Levitt, Shelley. “Why the Empathetic Leader Is the Best Leader.” SUCCESS, March 15, 2017. https://www.success.com/why-the-empathetic-leader-is-the-best-leader/.

Weinberg, Gerald M. Perfect Software: and Other Illusions about Testing. New York, NY: Dorset House, 2008.

Software Performance and Load Testing Utilizing JMeter

Anna Sharpe

Asharpe213@gmail.com

Abstract

Software of any type requires users to interact with it and depending on the business requirements, the software needs to perform with a certain number of users. A company which expects to sell its software to 100 customers for example needs to understand how often their platform is going to be used. If each customer is expected to use the software once during each business day, the software needs to be able to perform when 100 people are logged in at any given time.

The software company has the obligation to its customers to guarantee their software can perform at a certain level with 100 people logged in each day. Management at any software company should decide what level of performance is adequate and relay those expectations to the customers and development teams.

Utilizing JMeter by Apache is a cost-effective method for evaluating the current performance of the software and exposing errors to the development team which can be fixed. Routine performance testing with JMeter will also show performance over time, exposing how new functionality has affected the performance of the software.

The goal of this presentation is to demonstrate how to set up a JMeter project for the first time and understand the results. There are other ways of utilizing JMeter, but this is my preferred method and I challenge you to expand off it. I will not be going into detail on how to fix any errors found from performance/load testing as I do not expect QA engineers to be fixing code nor server settings.

Biography

Anna Sharpe is a quality assurance engineer located in Spokane, WA. She currently is employed with RiskLens as their first quality assurance engineer. Sharpe graduated from Whitworth University in 2014 with a BS in computer science. During college she began her career as a quality assurance engineer working as an intern and was quickly hired as a full-time employee. When she is not glued to a computer, she spends her time swimming with the local Masters swim team. She is currently working on renovating her first house.

1. What is the problem?

Software development is very expensive. Finding an engineer who understands how to performance/load test software is difficult. This leads to a lack of performance and load testing before software goes to the hands of customers. An unproven platform in the hands of customers can have devastating side effects. One of which is when engineers must drop what they are doing to babysit production servers and help customers. If the performance of the application is not improved quickly, customers could feel the need to shop the competitors and find a more reliable platform. The reputation damage and fallout of this is huge.

When a new software is being developed, timelines put pressure on management and the engineering team. Both want the software to be complete and in the hands of customers. This can lead to shortcuts being taken and performance/load testing is an easy step to put on the sidelines. However, procrastinating on performance/load testing means any bugs found could be more difficult to fix.

2. Why is this difficult?

Every company wants quality software to sell and stake its reputation on. To achieve this quality software status, managers and engineers must work together to prioritize expectations, including expected performance metrics. It is a substantial undertaking to performance/load test software because a knowledgeable engineer must be allocated who can write the performance/load tests (in any tool) and the systems team responsible for the environment being tested must be available to monitor and fix bugs found. Deadlines always force limitations on what resources are available which could mean even if a bug is found, no one has time to fix it. An added complexity is performance/load tests are most effective when run against the production environment. Any bugs in lower environments may be due to server configurations, which are important to find, but not as important as issues specific to production. The only way to guarantee performance/load metrics in production for customers is to run the tests in production. Even a duplicate of production is not a 100% guarantee because an exact duplicate of production is almost impossible to create.

3. How I solved it

I prefer to use free software which has a lively community of support. I have noticed paid for software is too rigid to be useful and having to contact their support team is often too slow for a QA Engineer under a deadline. I also look for software which has a plethora of detailed documentation to influence my design decisions so I don't have to learn the software by trial and error. JMeter by Apache has been my favorite tool for performance/load testing to date. I can write performance/load tests very easily through a GUI and if I have a particularly tricky feature to test, I can create custom functions to meet my needs. I went to my lead and informed them of the importance of performance/load testing so they could help me relay the importance to all necessary management. I was able to discuss with the appropriate teams responsible for the servers what I needed from them and what impact they should expect.

4. JMeter by Apache

JMeter is an open source application which mimics users to put stress on an application to reveal the performance. To achieve this, it offers a plethora of functions from sending JSON requests to native commands or shell scripts. JMeter works at a protocol level to look like a browser, but never executes the JavaScript in HTML pages. The only real limitation is the speed of the internet available. Apache maintains a wonderful website documenting all available features and a large community of users who work together.

5. Getting Started

The following information is intended to walk a first-time user through the basics of JMeter and give confidence to explore the capabilities further. JMeter has a surfeit of features which are documented on their website to facilitate performance/load testing any application[7]. In addition, I recommend reading the first few pages of the Apache JMeter website to give you more inspiration[1].

5.1 Gather a flow

Once the team, company and management agree to the development of performance/load tests, I begin by gathering a flow through the software which includes all major functionality. A good flow through the platform should include features such as logging in, creating new items, loading a list page, editing an item, etc. The performance/load tests should consider as much database functionality as possible, especially if a list page has a large amount of data it is returning, as these can expose failures in the database connections. Another area to include is any icons being loaded as overly large icons can be the reason a specific page is slow to load. Once the flow has been established, it is time to set up the JMeter project and prepare the application to be tested.

5.2 Create the flow

I recommend first time users of JMeter use the GUI for development as it can be easier to understand since it is a visual representation of what is happening in the tests. The easiest way to get started is to add a recording node to your JMeter project and record the flow through the application. To record interactions, add a HTTP(S) test script recorder node[9] to your project and configure the proxy[3] on a browser. Then simply perform the flow in the browser and the requests will automatically be created as HTTP request nodes in your JMeter project.

If the software being tested requires a login, multiple users need to be available in the environment where the performance/load tests are going to be run. I prefer to use a CSV file to contain the users' data. I organize it such that each row is a unique user and each column represents a specific value for that user (username, password, etc) as shown in the figure below. In the JMeter project, add a CSV data set node8 and configure the settings appropriately.

	A	B	C
1	asharpe@gmail.com	P@sswOrd1	Red
2	asharpe0@gmail.com	P@sswOrd1	Blue
3	asharpe1@gmail.com	P@sswOrd1	Yellow

A basic test plan should contain a thread group10, HTTP cache manager[11], request default node[2], cookie manager[6], and one or more HTTP request nodes[12]. At the end of the test plan, I recommend using the summary report[13], results tree[14], and aggregate graph[15] to decipher the results. Other result processors are available, but these three are easy to read and detailed enough to investigate any subsequent errors. These graphs are also excellent for distributing to the team so they can also be informed of the results.

5.3 Variables

Variables are extremely useful throughout the test plan. It is rare to have HTTP requests exactly the same for each thread due to some values in a response are necessary in future requests. One example would be, if I create a new item, that item will probably have an ID value which is unknown until I send the request. In this instance a variable is needed to scrap the ID from the response to insert it into the request to view that new item. Use a JSON extractor[5] inside the new item request node to gather the ID value from the response to an appropriately named variable. Then on the request to view that new item, simply use the variable created: ${itemID_1}. I prefer to rename any variables extracted to ensure I can easily understand my requests. Another type of variable I use frequently is the user defined variable[17]. I use this type of variable primarily to determine which environment I am testing so I can easily change which environment the tests run against. I develop the tests in my local environment, so when I eventually run them in production, I can easily change one value in the user defined variable node to the production URL.

5.4 Using Fiddler

HTTP request nodes can be developed in several ways, my preferred method is using Fiddler as the guide to understand my application under test rather than the recording tool mentioned above. With Fiddler open and recording interactions, I manually perform the flow in the application to understand the format of the requests and any values which may be dynamic for each user. It may be necessary to include variables such as any random numbers, environment values which might change, values read from a CSV, files to be uploaded, etc. Look for values which are dynamic in the requests, for example item IDs or date values which change for each thread. If a value is dynamic or should be different for each iteration, a variable needs to be defined. In other situations, the value can be read from an external file, for example using a different user for each iteration, the user credentials can be read from a CSV file.

For each request observed in Fiddler, I take note of the expected response for validation purposes. By default, JMeter will show a request failed if the response is not 200, however, all other validation must be done by the engineer. Adding validation nodes is very important for each node as false positives will render the test useless; the response assertion[18] child node should be added to each request to avoid this. The response body might contain an error parameter and I always validate that the error parameter is empty. The assertion can be more specific and search for exact text in the response of the request indicating exactly what failed. For example, if the response has the possibility to return validation error text containing "incorrect password", I will validate on that text string so when it fails I know exactly why it failed. This can be expanded to sending a request to create new object, if the request is expected to return an object ID and data specific to the new object, I want to validate those values are present and populated. If the request to create an object returns a 200 but an empty response with a "name must be unique" validation error and I do not check for the expected values, I would never know my request failed. To avoid this circumstance, I add a response assertion to the request specifically checking for an object ID value and any other text indicating the object was indeed created. It can be frustrating to have the last request fail when an issue originated from an earlier request failing silently. Each request I send has at least one assertion to lower the risk of false positives.

6. Running JMeter

I prefer to run the tests using the GUI and there are a few buttons I use routinely. The green play button at the top when clicked will start the test run and while it is running the stop sign button just to the right will become enabled which is used to terminate the test. When running the tests multiple times, i.e. during development, the results node can become crowded and too difficult to read. There is a clear all button in the top with two brooms as the icon, this will clear all results and any error and warning messages. The error and warning messages can be viewed by clicking the yellow triangle sign with an exclamation point located in the upper right corner of the GUI. These error and warning messages are useful in debugging any issues which may arise.

It is important to always run the tests outside normal business hours for when customers are not expected to be using the application. If the production application is expected to be used by customers 24 hours a day and 7 days a week, the company needs to inform customers about a maintenance window when the tests will be run. It is important to minimize customer interaction with the application while the tests are being run because they will not appreciate a slow application. In addition, the test results will be skewed if for example 10 customers are in the application using resources not represented in the tests. The conclusion of any test run should include a manual smoke test of the application being tested to ensure no lasting damage. It is embarrassing to leave an application in an un-usable state for someone else to discover.

6.1 Performance tests

With the same JMeter project, both load tests and performance tests can be run. Performance tests are defined by management and their requirements of how many users they expect to be in the system at once interacting with the application. In a performance test, the number of threads should reflect the number of expected users. I run the performance test for 2-3 hours and monitor the servers for errors which might occur and the task manager performance. The task manager can give useful data on how the server is handling the performance test. The goal of this performance test is to confirm the application can handle the business requirements set by management.

6.2 Load tests

Load tests on the other hand will test the resources of the application and how gracefully the application can recover from being overloaded. I always prefer to start this process by running the test with only one thread and loop through that one thread 10 times. This step gives me confidence the application can handle a minimal amount of load and my tests are written correctly. The next part of this process is to ramp up the number of threads. While watching the CPU usage on the servers, run the test for 10 minutes repeatedly with each run increasing the number of threads until the server(s) show a CPU usage above 95%. I use 95% CPU usage as my benchmark for load testing because the system is working hard and from here it is easy to add a few more threads to then overload the system. Once the number of threads is determined, I let the test run for 1-2 hours and monitor the server(s) under load. Once the test has concluded, I watch as any queues empty and take note of any error messages recorded.

7. Understanding the results

As the test runs, I prefer to watch the results tree node and monitor the requests, mindfully skimming them for any issues. If too many requests are failing, I will terminate the test run to triage what the issue might be. I also will review the summary report node to keep track of how many requests have gone through so far. Usually I am running these tests while a systems engineer is assisting me to monitor the server logs and CPU usage of the application under test, so I like to communicate to them every so often how many requests have been sent.

The most common issue I have run into is my IP address being blocked due to so many requests coming from my one computer. When this happens, all requests in the view results tree node return 401 unauthorized and it is easy to verify by manually opening the application. If I cannot access the application manually, I know I need to ask the network engineer to whitelist my IP address.

The results tree node can be saved to a file for review after the test run is complete. This will yield details on exactly what the request body sent and exactly why it errored out. These error messages are useful in determining if a certain request is unstable compared to the rest of the requests. For example, I have run into issues with too many users logging in at once and 10% of the requests fail; it was obvious in the results file the server returned a 500 error for the 10% failed requests.

Upon the completion of a satisfactory test run, I save any results to a specific location and document the specifics of the run, including the number of threads used and the duration of the test. I also save the graphs generated on the aggregate graph node as this represents the performance for that day. As these tests are run routinely, these graphs can be combined to show a trend of how performance is changing over time. With this data, the QA engineer can relay information to the team if a certain release has increased or decreased the performance of the application.

8. Conclusion

This outline of how I use JMeter is meant to be a stepping stone for other QA Engineers to begin the process of performance/load testing for their company. None of the companies I have worked for believed performance/load testing were important initially. I started from scratch in working with management to get approval and then develop the tests. The important note is the JMeter tests I have created thus far in my career have found bugs in production which the team decided needed to be fixed.

References

1. https://jmeter.apache.org/usermanual/get-started.html
2. https://jmeter.apache.org/usermanual/component_reference.html#HTTP_Request_Defaults
3. https://jmeter.apache.org/usermanual/jmeter_proxy_step_by_step.pdf
4. https://jmeter.apache.org/usermanual/component_reference.html#HTTP_Header_Manager
5. https://jmeter.apache.org/usermanual/component_reference.html#JSON_Extractor
6. https://jmeter.apache.org/usermanual/component_reference.html#HTTP_Cookie_Manager
7. https://jmeter.apache.org/usermanual/test_plan.html
8. https://jmeter.apache.org/usermanual/component_reference.html#CSV_Data_Set_Config
9. https://jmeter.apache.org/usermanual/component_reference.html#HTTP(S)_Test_Script_Recorder
10. https://jmeter.apache.org/usermanual/component_reference.html#Thread_Group
11. https://jmeter.apache.org/usermanual/component_reference.html#HTTP_Cache_Manager
12. https://jmeter.apache.org/usermanual/component_reference.html#HTTP_Request
13. https://jmeter.apache.org/usermanual/component_reference.html#Summary_Report
14. https://jmeter.apache.org/usermanual/component_reference.html#View_Results_Tree
15. https://jmeter.apache.org/usermanual/component_reference.html#Aggregate_Graph
16. https://jmeter.apache.org/usermanual/component_reference.html#JSON_Extractor
17. https://jmeter.apache.org/usermanual/component_reference.html#User_Defined_Variables
18. https://jmeter.apache.org/usermanual/component_reference.html#Response_Assertion

Capacity to Execute

Waterfall to Agile Transition Considerations - a Case Study

John Cvetko

John.Cvetko@TEKasc.com

Abstract

Transforming your enterprise to an Agile SDLC can be an arduous journey. Transitioning any large organization to a new state is a multifaceted problem and takes thought and planning to ensure the desired "intent" is achieved. The goal is to minimize disruptions to business operations and increases the probability of success. Whether the desired approach is incremental or a sea change, understanding the "capacity to execute" is crucial when evaluating the organization's ability to achieve the desired goal. By assessing the capacity of the existing organization, it is possible to determine best how to plan strategically and systematically to move the organization to an Agile framework. In this paper we will discuss the assessment of an organization relative to the Agile principles, and how to develop a strategy that maximizes the Agility of the organization in the new paradigm. Using a case study, this paper will explore common issues with the transition to an Agile SDLC, and how, if not done with care and forethought, could result in significant risk for the organization.

Biography

As a Principal of TEK Associates, Mr. Cvetko works with companies and government agencies to improve their organizations by helping them manage the IT challenges they face. He applies state of the art solutions to evolve business processes, creating more efficiency and productivity, all while improving quality. His previous work as a CIO was enabled by a variety of program, system and product management positions held throughout his career. The last 12 years have been primarily focused on assessing and transforming large enterprise software systems for state governments. He has worked with the state governments of Colorado, Washington, Oregon, North Carolina, North Dakota, Mississippi, Utah, Kentucky, and Oklahoma. Earlier in his career he worked as a management/technical consultant for firms such as NIKE and Boeing, and in product development and program management for Tektronix, PGE/Enron and ASCOM.

1. Introduction

All too often, outside consulting firms or internal Agile champions position Agile to be a solution to deeply rooted organizational issues, or worse, as a philosophy that will bring dramatic flexibility to a rigid system. Overemphasizing Agile as the solution to all problems does a disservice to the organization being served, and erodes the Agile brand when expectations are not met.

The Agile SDLC has some unique qualities that can be useful for organizations to varying degrees; however, it should be thought of as a tool in a company's tool bag and scrutinized using the same return on investment rigor applied to other business initiatives. Developing a business case that outlines the purpose, business context, perceived limitations and culture is paramount to understand the problem being solved and establishing pragmatic expectations. The coupling of realistic expectations with rigorous business analysis, enables the leaders to envision and articulate their intent (a.k.a., the end-state). Understanding the end-state will then help to establish the key performance indicators (KPIs) needed to monitor the progress being made towards the business objective. By having this level of visibility, the leaders can help remove obstacles and course correct as needed to improve the chances of success. Using a thoughtful and purposeful approach to transformation will, in the end, create a more robust Agile implementation that will propel the business toward its objective. [Brosseau 2019].

This paper is structured in three distinct sections: The Case Study will provide information on an organization that is struggling to implement Agile. The Transition Considerations section will discuss fundamental elements important to organizations implementing Agile. The third section is the Transition Analysis, which will review the Case Study implementation relative to these considerations.

2. Case Study

The case study presented here is of a large IT enterprise in an organization that will be referenced as the XYZ company in this paper. The XYZ company has five main lines of business (Programs) that are dependent on each other. Each Program has complex workflows and many regulatory and compliance obligations. The enterprise has 6 feature releases a year that are delivered on a fixed schedule and with a fixed capacity, thus creating a "release train" [Leffingwell 2007]. Each release contains upwards of 30-40 intertwined Waterfall and Agile projects that ranged from 100 to 8K development hours and are from all Program areas.

The IT senior management structure has more of a facilitation function, connecting governance, Programs and IT executive management to IT functional managers and vendors. This approach could be considered a laissez faire management style, with a high degree of decision making done by consensus.

2.1. Shared Resources and Competing Priorities

The Program areas compete for development resources and often have their projects bumped from a planned release, due to a higher priority project. Often a lower priority project is rescheduled multiple times until the organization risks being out of federal or state compliance, which then elevates its priority by default. Once a project becomes a high priority, additional scope is added by the Program because of the uncertainty of future development resource availability. The constant scheduling challenges for shared resources and competing priorities create dysfunctional behaviors that are a continued source of friction between the Programs and IT.

To address the friction, the IT management recommended moving all projects in the releases to the Agile SDLC. This recommendation was touted as providing a faster, more flexible development approach that could provide higher quality at a lower cost, all while reducing risk for the organization. The underlying assumption was that the software development was inefficient and that by implementing an Agile SDLC, the Programs would increase their chances of getting a project done more quickly.

2.2. Stalled Agile Transition

At the time of this writing, the transition to Agile by the organization was in its third year. On initial implementation, the organization had conducted Agile training, employed coaches, identified tool replacements, and delivered Agile projects successfully alongside of the Waterfall projects in the same release. This moved the organization from a pure "Waterfall release train" to the "hybrid release train" mentioned above. The Agile projects were considered small in scope and isolated, i.e., not a critical path for other projects, free of dependencies and could be pulled from the release at any time. Conversely, the large Waterfall projects crossed many programs and could not be pulled from the release without a significant delay in the schedule.

The hybrid releases worked well initially, however the need for more flexibility was required. For example, a large Waterfall project had a few moderate changes that were added one month prior to the release date. These late changes significantly increased the risk of defects being introduced into production. The risk was mitigated through additional testing, which ultimately delayed the schedule. The delayed schedule did not affect the project with the last-minute changes; however, it did impact the delivery of a time sensitive, critical project in the same release.

The need for the late changes was legitimate, and the organization held a series of meetings to discuss available options to mitigate this issue in the future. The first option suggested was to move the larger projects to Agile. It was at this point the Program heads noticeably baulked at the idea and their general skepticism of Agile became known. It was clear the Programs had not realized the value they were promised and had developed a level of distrust of IT management. The expectations of Agile were set so high and in such a shallow way, that the skepticism and reluctance with using Agile for the larger projects is understandable.

The final solution implemented is known as the "soft requirements" approach. The idea being that 99% of the Waterfall requirements are correct, but occasionally the business needs the flexibility to make moderate changes to a project after the initial requirements cutoff date. To support this approach the process was changed to allow for two requirement cutoff dates; the first date was set at four months prior to the release (soft change cutoff), and the second date at one month prior to the release (final cutoff).

The "soft requirements" approach was a change of the Waterfall SDLC to compensate for the perceived deficiencies in the implementation of the Agile SDLC. This effectively stalled the implementation of Agile for the foreseeable future.

3. Transition Considerations

3.1. Business Case

It is often the case that when moving to Agile, several adjectives are used to sell the idea, e.g., Agile is more flexible, provides faster delivery, improves quality, etc. While these statements may be true, it would be foolhardy from a business perspective to base such a transition on adjectives alone, especially if your organization is not delivering well with its existing SDLC. If the enterprise is managed poorly using Waterfall, why would one believe that it would be any better with Agile? Why would Agile make bad management good? Sadly, it is not uncommon to see organizations make changes based on superlatives alone.

Agile consultants are sometimes inadvertently tarnishing the Agile brand by not addressing the underlying organizational issues first. It is not uncommon to hear management consultants touting the magic of Agile to fix" insert whatever the company issue is here". For example, in the XYZ case study above, the IT management did not understand the cause of the Program's dissatisfaction of the IT department pre-Agile. Albert Einstein once said, "If I were given one hour to save the planet, I would spend 59 minutes defining the problem and one minute resolving it." Presenting Agile as a solution to an ill-defined problem may create unwanted second and third order effects in the organization.

3.2. Management Intent

All too often, Agile is implemented in organizations without an understanding of the business context, structure of the organization and culture [Ramesh 2018]. In post-Agile implementations it is common to hear staff complain that their company did not implement "true" Agile and they consider themselves "Agile-ish", "Agile-fall" or worse, they have implemented "fake Agile". This in part, can stem from a lack of appreciation by the staff of the business context limitations, i.e., highly regulated industries, unions, existing contract obligations, organizational risk tolerance, centralized management structure, etc. These conditions can be hard boundaries for implementing an Agile framework and can result in limiting the degree of flexibility desired.

Unlike Waterfall, Agile couples a set of prescriptive qualitative characteristics with quantitative development techniques. The Agile manifesto core values and the 12 principles are collectively an intent statement. The difference between a goal versus an intention is that a goal is focused on achieving a specific objective, whereas an intention is more concerned with the mindset and end-state [Mattis 2020 44-45].

Consider the following Agile principle: "The best architectures, requirements, and designs emerge from self-organizing teams" [Agile manifesto 2001]. The end-state of this principle is "the best architecture". The mindset of "self-organizing teams" in this principle is vague and can be interpreted in a thousand different ways. The intent of this principle, if read by a line employee, functional manager, and executive staff will be interpreted based on the fears, desires and expectations that are top of mind in the context of their current environment. As an example, a line employee in a highly regulated industry with a strict management hierarchy, may interpret this as freedom from micromanagement and the ability to select the development team of his choice. However, management may interpret this principle in a much more conservative way. This interpretation gap can have the unintended consequence of increasing frustration and lower morale in the organization, i.e., it could do harm.

Taking time to examine the organization relative to the Agile principles will help identify potential issues and limitations of the implementation. This analysis will help articulate the contours of the Agile end-state and can be used as a feedback loop to test the level of decentralized decision making desired by executive management.

Once the end-state is defined, then developing a "management intent" statement is useful for broad communication to the organization. Using the language of the organization to communicate how Agile will fit into the environment can reduce ambiguity that can cause unnecessary cultural friction and frustration. An intent statement consists of three distinct elements; it describes the purpose, method, and end-state. It is intended to be a living statement that will help shape decision making of the staff when dealing with the obstacles they will address throughout the transition. This statement should also be tested periodically, this will be described in the next section.

3.3. Testing Management Intent

The testing of management intent can be thought of as a feedback loop for managers that is useful to course correct, adjust the tempo of the implementation, or coach teams when needed.

The scope and the modality of the testing can be done in a variety of ways. The testing approach depends on the leadership style and the tolerance of management for criticism. It is important to have in person, face to face discussions at a minimum, this reinforces and models a core tenant of Agile for the teams. Some managers prefer skip level interviews or management by walking around, others may prefer staff huddles. In addition to the face to face discussions, it is also highly recommended to conduct an anonymous survey. An anonymous survey will provide unfiltered feedback that may be useful to detect hidden, non-obvious issues. Additionally, depending on the size of the organization, it will provide a much larger sampling which can provide an understanding of the general morale of the staff.

3.4. Implementation Performance

The only way to determine if a return on investment or some level of success was achieved, is by measuring the performance of a previous state to the new state. If performance measurements cannot be conducted, then the investment should be considered high risk.

How do you measure two seemingly very dissimilar things, in this case, Waterfall and Agile performance? A starting point is to separate the qualitative from the quantitative components of the SDLC. Agile is ladened with co-mingled quantitative/qualitative statements which can make it seem difficult, however, if it can be counted or expressed using empirical data then it is a quantitative element. The table below shows a crosswalk of common performance metrics for the SDLC's. Not all elements in the table need to be measured, but at a minimum, unit of work, time, and money (scope, schedule, and budget) must be measurable and measured as key performance metrics (KPI's).

Table 1 SDLC Metric Crosswalk

Measurement Description	Metric Terminology*	
Quantitative	**Agile**	**Waterfall**
The proposed features, enhancements, upgrades.	Backlog	Requirements
Ranking of the most desirable features.	Ordered backlog	Requirement prioritization
Incomplete or inconsistent requirements.	Recidivism rate	Changes to requirements
The completion of projects to schedule and budget.	Agile Earned Value[4]; Epic and release burndown	Earned value, Schedule variance[3]
The average work a team does over time.	Velocity	Earned value
Consistency in workflow across the teams.	Cumulative flow	Resource leveling
Overall bugs/defects found in user testing	Defect rate	Defect rate
Defects found in production.	Escaped defect rate	Leakage rate
Average time it takes to fix a defect.	Defect resolution rates	Defect resolution rates
Indication of technical debt (application level) [2]	Increasing defect resolution times; reduced accuracy in time estimation, increasing time estimation, etc.	Increasing defect resolution times; reduced accuracy in time estimation, increasing time estimation, etc.
Cost to deliver all requirements.	Total epic costs	Total project costs
Qualitative Measurements		
User experience	UX studies, surveys	UX studies, surveys
Client satisfaction	Surveys	Surveys

1. Not exhaustive

2. Technical debt can be difficult to accurately measure easily. There are a variety of tools that can simplify the task in a more precise manner. For the purposes of this paper however, some high-level measurement approaches are listed.

3. PMBOK 2004

4. Sutherland 2014

3.5. Quality

Unlike scope, schedule and budget, quality is more difficult to measure since it can be both quantitative and qualitative. Quality means different things to different people, and time should be taken to understand what is most important to the organization. Using a car as an example, quality could mean luxury, style, and prestige for some, while reliability, cost and longevity are valued for others.

Understanding the complete breadth of software quality characteristics with a common language for communication is important. The software quality standard ISO 25010 systematically outlines software quality from 8 different dimensions, see figure 1 below [ISO 25010].

The ISO standard is comprehensive, and it is only presented here as a reference to depict the breadth of elements that can be considered for measurement. The organization would select the highest priority elements to be monitored before, during and after the transition. Selecting a few elements to monitor does not mean that all other elements are not important or will not be tracked, it only means that these are the key elements that must not be affected negatively by the transition. The measurement could be at the high level, i.e., Usability, Security, etc., or it could be a specific element like that of Operability and Fault Tolerance. Measuring the high valued quality characteristics provides the ability to identify issues, and to determine if the Agile implementation is having the desired effect on the final product.

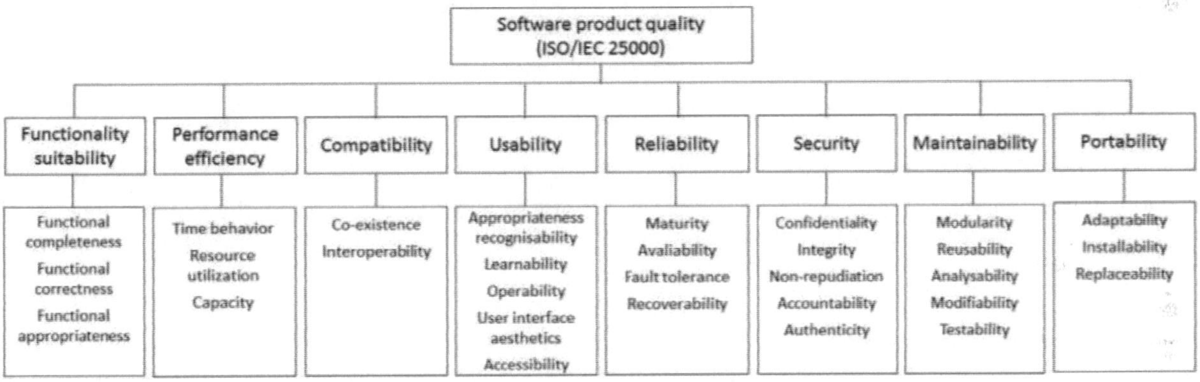

Figure 1. ISO 25010, Quality Software Standard

3.6. Value

Value is often mentioned as a focus of Agile and is touted as a differential between Agile and other SDLC's. Some organizations that employ Agile, struggle with the concept of value, to the point of it being overthought and hindering performance. Software value is not a new concept; the only difference between the two SDLC's with respect to value, is that Agile heavily emphasizes this characteristic, keeping it top of mind.

Like quality, value means different things to different people at different levels, which is why some may struggle with it. Using the basics of scope schedule and budget, i.e., the "iron triangle", coupled with the fourth element quality, a case can be made that these four elements determine software value. See figure 2 on the next page.

In layman's terms, this means that the software development group is delivering what is desired, when it is desired, within budget and with the quality characteristics expected. By identifying and tracking metrics along these four dimensions, value is inherently being measured.

Figure 2. Value Triangle

4. XYZ Agile Transformation Analysis

When a plane falls out of the sky due to a design issue, the subsequent investigation and analysis will often identify systemic failures across many complex processes. Like a plane crash analysis, a failed, or in this case, a stalled implementation of Agile has many bad assumptions, missed opportunities and failures across several functional areas. A more detailed understanding of some of the issues and failures of the transition are provided below.

4.1. Business Case Assessment

A formal business case with an analysis of the existing organizational issues and how they would be mitigated using Agile was not conducted. While it is hard to imagine that an initiative of this importance would not have some rigor supporting the effort, it is not uncommon. The responsibility for this error lie with both the IT and Program senior managers.

The primary method utilized by IT to convince the Programs to move to Agile were anecdotal examples laden with superlatives. The Programs accepted this information at face value and did not request any due diligence on the claims being made. This was a missed opportunity to formally address the heart of a structural issue of having to reorder projects in the backlog because of the shared development resource as mentioned in section 2.1.

4.2. Planning and Implementation Assessment

There are three recognized approaches to transition an organization to Agile [Mckinsey]. The first approach is the big bang, ironically it is a Waterfall approach to implementing an Agile framework. The thinking behind this approach is that the transition will be disruptive using any approach, so it is best to minimize the disruption time and do it all at once.

The second approach is to transition in waves, tackling key horizontal and vertical components iteratively over time. For example, wave one might be to reorganize a specific isolated product line to Agile. Wave two may be to implement new tools that will better support Agile processes, etc.

The third approach is termed as "emergent" and is a bottom up approach, meaning that the transition is largely driven organically by the line staff and functional managers. This approach minimizes the risk of business interruption; however, it can take much longer to fully implement. Given the laissez faire management style, consensus decision making, and low risk tolerance, the XYZ organization naturally gravitated toward an emergent approach.

Staff was provided with formal outside training, in conjunction with an Agile coach to assist the teams through their first set of projects. Small, relatively easy projects were selected to limit business risk and ensure early success. During this process, discussions occurred about upgrading to more modern tools that better supported the Agile processes. Tools were identified but would only be implemented when time in the development schedule permitted.

In lieu of any extensive planning, it was assumed by the IT senior managers that once Agile was introduced, all the projects would naturally want to move to the Agile methodology. The pace of the transition, along with the limited realized value that Agile was providing, left the transformation initiative open for comparison and constant criticism by the Programs.

4.3. Development Vendor and Program Experts

The software development was outsourced to a capable vendor with all development staff residing onsite. The contract could handle both Waterfall and Agile development, this was accomplished by providing a “wrapper” around an Agile development to integrate it with the organizations project structure. This approach is referred to as an “adaption layer” and is common for organizations that do not have a high degree of contracting flexibility.

Even with this contract protection there was still reluctance by the vendor to fully embrace Agile for the following reasons:

1. The Programs had a limitation of providing knowledgeable resources on a consistent basis for requirements elicitation and demos. Given the system had five major intertwined Programs, it was often required to have all five Program Subject Matter Experts (SMEs) available for decision making. The Programs could sustain scheduled, short bursts of intense requirements elicitation and then minimal contact for follow-up if needed.

   This fire-and-forget environment was more easily accommodated by the traditional Waterfall process. In these specific types of systems, the Program SMEs were often the final decision makers and they were stretched thin for a variety of reasons. This is an issue that is commonly known in this vertical market. Finding and training a SME to a point where they are effective could take years. The development vendor, not being assured of having the right business resources in a reliable and sustained manner, viewed this as a risk that could be better mitigated by using Waterfall for large projects.

2. The services delivered by the organization were heavily regulated, and fiscal accountability and transparency was required. All projects had a 10% cost overrun flexibility against the final estimate given by the vendor.

   For Waterfall projects, change orders could be managed by the vendor in a more formal and traditional fashion. With Agile there is an inherent expectation of broad flexibility, where changes are continually expected and embraced for the duration of the project, however, providing this level of flexibility without additional money was a financial risk for the vendor. This was a source of continual frustration for the Agile teams.

4.4. User Testing Analysis

For these types of systems, User Testers began workflow testing after sufficient software functionality was delivered to the test environment. One would expect that Agile would be more advantageous in this model, however User Testing was only conducted on the Waterfall and not Agile projects during the development process. While counterintuitive, the Sprint incrementalism did not provide sufficient end-to end workflow to make it efficient for the User Testers until all the Agile project code was delivered to the test environment.

The Waterfall projects on the other hand, were being developed in an iterative fashion with major pieces of code delivered into the test environments at predetermined times. This approached enabled the testing to be done efficiently during the development cycle. This enabled the User Testers to conduct all or portions of the end-to-end tests in parallel or slightly lagging the developer's system integration test (SIT) team, prior to the final release. It should be noted that the inefficiency of testing the Agile code was not due to a limitation of the Agile SDLC, but rather, it could be attributed to the length of the Sprints (2-3 weeks) and the size of the Agile projects. A larger project with longer Sprints could easily be structured to deliver a greater amount of functional code for User Testing during the development period.

4.5. Desired Quality Metrics

Using the ISO 25010 terminology, the XYZ organization identified Functional Completeness, Modifiability, Usability and Security. Many more metrics were monitored as a matter of course for all projects; however, the organization highlighted these elements for the reasons described below.

The definition of these terms by the standard, and the reason for the organization's focus on these metrics are described as follows:

"**Functional completeness** - Degree to which the set of functions covers all the specified tasks and user objectives."

The organization focused on functional completeness because they were unsure if user stories could accurately capture the intertwined program requirements to the level needed. Functional completeness was measured and monitored in User Test by tracking the number of changes or updated user stories required by the Programs.

"**Modifiability** - Degree to which a product or system can be effectively and efficiently modified without introducing defects or degrading existing product quality."

This was selected because they were interested to see if the defect rate was comparable to their existing defect rates, which was currently monitored by the test team.

"**Security** - Degree to which a product or system protects information and data so that persons or other products or systems have the degree of data access appropriate to their types and levels of authorization."

Security was highlighted because they were unsure how the security requirements were captured using user stories. Security was measured by the number of changes requested during the Security Testing, and if the documentation was sufficient for the governing compliance body.

"**Usability** - degree to which a product or system can be used by specified users to achieve specified goals with effectiveness, efficiency, and satisfaction in a specified context of use."

The XYZ organization, as a matter of course, conducted quarterly surveys to their internal staff with respect to user satisfaction. This existing measurement tool was adjusted to delineate between project types without identifying the SDLC utilized. This blind survey approach was intended to mask the SDLC used from the client to not skew the results.

4.6. Quality Analysis

The post Agile implementation quality measurements above, indicated that Agile did not significantly degrade or improve the organizations output. Below are some notable improvements and issues found by the quality elements that were being tracked.

4.6.1. Usability and Functional Completeness - The Programs valued the periodic demonstrations provided by the Agile process; they were presented not only to Program SME's but to the line staff as well. This approach fostered a level of inclusion that was well received. It allowed the organization to get feedback from line staff which was not done with the Waterfall projects until User Test. The feedback provided typically resulted in minor changes that would impact efficiency and usability. It should be noted that the discussions that occurred during the demonstrations were informative to the engineers beyond just the features that were presented. This increased communication flow was noted in some of the user survey comments.

As mentioned previously, the surveys were adjusted to elicit feedback on specific projects, this enabled the comparison between like sized Agile and Waterfall projects. The scores were reviewed pre and post implementation and indicated a slight increase in user satisfaction with the Agile projects.

4.6.1.1. Documentation - The level of initial documentation was considered insufficient and was updated to reflect more details in the user stories. When the handoff occurred to operations, the documentation for the project was lite, however it did not contain key information that was considered essential by the organization.

Example: An Agile project tasked with the creation of a dashboard that monitored the processing of a large amount of documentation flow for the Programs was commissioned. After the release to production, an operations supervisor noticed some anomalies that were thought to be from incorrect calculations. When operations asked for design documentation for review, the user stories were provided which were inadequate to determine the data and calculations that were used to derive the dashboard information. To further investigate the issue, engineers would need to be consulted, while meeting with engineers is not an issue per se, it did highlight an increased dependency on the vendor.

This also indicated that the accuracy of User Testing may be affected, meaning that the testers were testing the dashboard functionality to the level of the user stories provided and not to the underlying business logic. Lastly, when the issue above surfaced, the development vendor became concerned that the reduced level of documentation had increased their risk and potential liability.

While this documentation example may seem insignificant, the dashboard was court mandated due to a death of an individual, caused in part by incorrect system processing. These issues were addressed by providing additional pertinent information within the user stories. This had the effect of increasing the overall number of user stories.

4.6.2. Security - The organization implemented a variation of Scrum called "Secure Scrum" (S-Scrum) [Pohl 2015], which provided a technique for identification and tagging of user stories that have a security component. This approach not only provided security requirements management and traceability for testing; it also was helpful in raising general security awareness among the team.

4.6.3. Modifiability - The Agile teams could handle minor last-minute changes easily, in some cases too easily, i.e., during the final release certification period. This had the potential to disrupt testing, training, and since the projects were part of a project release train, a change this late in the process could be a risk to the build process. The teams agreed that no changes would be done prior to the last Sprint.

4.7. Value Analysis

In general, the XYZ organization at the highest level is receiving significant value because each project being delivered a has fixed scope, schedule, budget, and quality requirements. As the needs shift for the organization, the projects are reordered in the backlog to reflect the changing business circumstances. This natural structure provides a macro level of value attainment for the organization.

At the individual project or micro level however, the reshuffling is perceived by the Programs as a value deficiency. When individual projects are reordered in the backlog, the time component of value is not being satisfied for these groups, i.e., the project is not delivered when it is desired.

Implementing Agile will not fix this fundamental problem, however the act of transitioning to an Agile SDLC was an opportunity to review existing issues within the organization, as mentioned in section 4.1. Identifying this issue prior to the Agile implementation would have highlighted the source of frustration and, more importantly, set the correct expectations with respect to the limitations of Agile in the context of the organizational structure.

5. Conclusion

This paper has demonstrated some of the many different aspects to consider when implementing an Agile framework in an enterprise. These aspects, if not understood or addressed prior to the implementation can result in a stalled, chaotic, or even failed Agile implementation. This case study highlights the confluence of misaligned expectations for Agile, lack of preplanning analysis, and laissez faire management style. These conditions, in combination with management's decision to utilize an emergent Agile implementation approach, resulted in an unintended negative consequence of creating a level of distrust between the Programs and the IT department.

Understanding the problem to be solved by conducting analysis of the context and structure of the organization relative to the Agile principles, will help characterize the desired end-state which is key to setting expectations. Further, this form of modeling can be useful to determine where structural changes can increase the probability of success, and ultimately, a more Agile organization.

References

Brosseau, Daniel, 2019. "The journey to an agile organization" Mckinsey May 10, 2019
https://www.mckinsey.com/business-functions/organization/our-insights/the-journey-to-an-agile-organization#

Leffingwell, Dean 2007. Scaling Software Agility: Best Practices for Large Enterprises. Addison-Wesley.

Mattis, Jim N., and Bing West. 2019. Call Sign Chaos: Learning to Lead. New York: Random House.

Beck, K., et al. (2001). "The Agile Manifesto." Agile Alliance. http://agilemanifesto.org/

Project Management Institute. 2004. A guide to the project management body of knowledge (PMBOK guide). Newtown Square, Pa: Project Management Institute.

Sutherland, Jeff, 2014. "Agile Defense - The transformation of how wars are fought, how logistics are delivered, and how the Department of Defense does business." Scrum Inc 2014.

International Standards Organization (ISO). 2011. ISO/IEC25010 Systems and software engineering — Systems and software Quality Requirements and Evaluation (SQuaRE) — System and software quality models. Geneva, Switzerland: International Organization for Standardization.

Ramesh, Balasubramaniam, et. al. 2018. "Consider Culture When Implementing Agile Practices." MIT Sloan Management Review posted Oct. 03, 2018
https://sloanreview.mit.edu/article/consider-culture-when-implementing-agile-practices/

Pohl, Christopher, Hof, Hans-Joachim, 2015. "Secure Scrum: Development of Secure Software with Scrum". The Ninth International Conference on Emerging Security Information, Systems and Technologies 2015.

Of Machines and Men

Iryna Suprun

iryna.suprun@gmail.com

Abstract

Artificial Intelligence (AI) and Machine Learning (ML) are everywhere. Smart thermostats, self-driving cars and virtual assistants are changing our lives. AI and ML help people to make decisions and process information. They are used in medicine, education, retail, advertising and in many other industries, including software development and testing. Some even predict that soon AI will replace software programmers and testers. Nobody knows if these predictions will become true and if so when. There is no doubt although that AI will impact the way we test and will require a new set of skills.

Testing tools that use AI and ML are emerging and become more mature. Ready-to-use AI solutions are available on the market today and can be integrated into the testing process now. Paid and free AI and ML classes are offered by most of the online learning platforms.

In this paper, we are going to overview the state of AI in software testing and how it impacts the software development industry. Finally, we will take a brief look at AI-powered testing tools and discuss how we can use them to enhance testing.

Biography

Iryna started her career as a software engineer in 2004 in Ukraine, where she was born. She received her master's degree in Computer Science in 2006, and in 2007 she got her first position as a quality analyst. She moved to the USA in 2008 and continued her career in Quality Assurance (QA), focusing on the telecom industry and testing real-time communication systems and products such as the audio platform for the GoToMeeting application. Three years ago, she decided it was time to try something new and moved to AdTech. She is presently working as a QA architect at Xandr. Her primary job responsibilities building automation frameworks and implementing testing processes from scratch.

1. Introduction

During the last fifteen years, QA as a profession went through many transformations to adapt to changes in technologies and in the software development process. Many predicted that QA as a profession would be eliminated by switching to agile, test automation, Test Driven Development (TDD) and Behavior Driven Development (BDD). It did not happen. Now there are concerns that AI/ML will succeed where others failed.

The most difficult task for Quality Analysts (QA) since the first test was written is executing and automating end-to-end tests. End-to-end tests (sometimes referred as system level tests) are tests that validate application flows from start to finish simulating real world scenarios. They validate the system under test and its components for integration and data integrity. They include communication of the application with hardware, networks, databases and other applications.

Even for a single application where all components are designed to work together, automation of end-to-end scenarios is a challenging, time and resources consuming task. These tests are often very complex and require a lot of maintenance, especially if the application is new and grows rapidly.

Automating end-to-end tests for a software platform where all components were designed independently, using different technologies and implemented by multiple teams, working in many locations and time zones, is a task that requires, based on my experience, quadruple time and effort investment due to increased complexity

The platform end-to-end flows are difficult to execute even manually, because they require complex thoughtful data setup, deep understanding of the platform, and knowing technical details. Add limited QA resources and challenging deadlines, and you have the problem I needed to solve.

The software platform for which I need end-to-end automation for consists of three UIs, over 50 APIs, data processing pipelines (queues, databases), and has multiple dependencies on external data. Teams are located in five geographical locations and four time zones. We mastered testing individual components using unit tests, traditional testing tools (Cypress and home-grown tool built form Cucumber and Java Script), mocks and simulators for external dependencies. Platform level end-to-end tests were our pain point and I needed a way to automate them as fast as possible.

Most AI test automation tools claim that users can automate the very complex scenarios without a single line of code, so the test automation process is really fast and can be easily done by anyone in the team.

Another big promise is the low maintenance. By collecting and smartly using numerous data points about flows, UI elements and user behavior, AI tools claim they are able to update tests without human interaction.

Will these two AI tools features, and others, enable me to create much needed end-to-end tests in days (instead of weeks) and decrease maintenance efforts at the same time? That's the question I wanted to find an answer.

There are many AI testing tools. The maturity of these tools, the usability, and the promises delivered vary. I reviewed the state of the AI-based tools market and tried some of the tools to find answers to two important questions: are tools that use AI as good as their marketing materials claim, and will human QA teams be replaced by these AI testing tools?

2. State of AI in Testing

There is no standard definition of what AI is. In general AI is software that can mimic human intelligence. Based on this definition, even a simple if-else statement can be considered as AI. Usually when people talk about AI today, they are really talking about ML algorithms that use large amounts of data to learn how to perform complex tasks. Hence, for the future discussion let's agree that AI-based testing means a tool that uses ML algorithms to solve one or another testing related task.

There are four big groups of ML algorithms: Supervised Learning; Unsupervised Learning, Reinforcement Learning, and Deep Learning.

- Supervised Learning is based on providing a large number of examples with known output.
- Unsupervised Learning is used to find patterns in the datasets, where outcome is not known.

- Reinforcement Learning and Deep Learning behave more like humans and use neural networks algorithms to be trained to solve specific tasks.

There are six (some say four) levels of Test Automation Autonomy.

- **Level 0** is manual testing. Even when everybody aims to automate as much as possible, it is around 70% of all testing[1] (this percentage varies from 50% to 85% and depends on the source and calculation methods). No AI/ML used.
- **Level 1** is traditional scripting and automated tests. It was introduced more than 20 years ago and still only 25% of testing. No AI/ML used.
- **Level 2** is codeless script generation or recording. It is 5% of testing today.
- **Level 3** is self-healing scripts and bots. The Supervised Learning algorithms are often used to improve self-healing or the existing regression suite.
- **Level 4** is an automatic generation of scripts with no human intervention, scripting or recording. Unsupervised Learning algorithms can be used in this case. For example, for data-mining of production logs and automatic creation of new tests according to those logs.
- **Level 5** is fully self-generating tests that are able to validate complex systems and do so autonomously. Some AI-based automation tools claim that they provide instruments to achieve this level of autonomy. Reinforcement Learning and Deep Learning can be used in this case to generate automated tests based on data analyses of clicks, links and GUI elements.

The overall percentage of Level 3 – Level 5 testing is very low, but it slowly and steadily grows replacing Level 0 – Level 2 automation.

3. AI-Based Test Automation Tools

3.1. AI-based test automation tools vs traditional testing tools

The most visible difference between traditional and AI-based tools from the start is in test authoring. It is a manual process when a traditional tool is used. It starts with defining test cases, validation and assertions and, finally, coding and testing that the test script actually works. Most AI-based test automation tools record an actual user (test engineer or customer) manually executing the test case as the method to create the automated tests. Some testing tools that do not use AI also provide recording as a way to create automated tests. The main differentiator in this case is that AI tools collect tens of data points during recording that later are processed and used for improving/generating automated tests and their stability. Other, more sophisticated, AI-based tools use different ML algorithms to auto generate assertions and tests using logs, collecting real user clicks, or just software under test itself.

The test maintenance is a common pain point when we use traditional automation tools; it is manual and laborious. Tools that use ML algorithms offer self-healing features where tests automatically are updated to reflect changes. AI-based tools automatically adapt to UI changes, such as xpath, tag or other attributes. They use data collected during test creation to identify the same element on the page. User still can decline test change and roll back to the previous test version.

[1] The percentage of automated, manual and self-generated script provided based on World Quality Report 2019-20, PractiTest State of Testing™ Report 2020, Appvance "AI Driven Test Automation.
A Transformational Breakthrough for Software Development" e-book [12] [13] [14]

AI tools are not mature or widely used compared to traditional testing tools, so if users encounter a problem, they most likely need to go to the tool vendors support team. There is less available information about AI tools in general: comparison charts, use cases, real reviews and experience of real users are hard to find. So, if you are considering adapting an AI tool, be ready to do a lot of leg work by yourself.

There are plenty of open source or free versions of traditional test tools. The open source AI-based test tools, as well as free tools, are rare.

There are plenty of traditional testing tools for every type of application, most of the AI tools only support automation of the Web applications. There are just a couple AI tools that provide automation support for mobile apps.

3.2. AI Automation tools market overview

Almost every modern test tool available on the market claims usage of AI to some degree. AI-based tools can be put in three main categories. First, intelligently designed tools that can help to solve some automation issues, but they do not use any ML algorithms. These tools have AI only in promotion materials. It does not mean that these tools cannot solve some testing challenges, or they are worse than AI based tools. It only means that there are no ML algorithms used in their code. These tools are not a subject of this paper, so they are excluded from the future discussion.

The second category is tools that use AI/ML in a supporting role. These tools are used to help QA to perform certain tasks that are hard to do manually due to the limitations caused by human nature, for example, tools that are used for visual testing. Another use-case is to perform testing that if done by people would use subjective measurements instead of a set of objective parameters (video/audio quality).

Tests authoring in such tools is done with active involvement of end-users (test generation based on collecting, extracting and processing logs, clicks and events) or members of the engineering team (test recording).

Last category of AI-based tools are ones that take software under test as their main and only input and generate bug reports as output without any human interactions (Level 5 of autonomy). There are no tools on the market right now that are Level 5 tools. There are some tools, not many although, that have Level 5 features, but most of their offering consists of Level 2 – Level 4 features.

As the majority of tools use AI/ML in a supporting role nowadays we will focus on them and discuss features that make them very solid competitors to traditional tools.

The first big group of such features, ones that help decrease time spent on tasks that people can accomplish and probably do better than any non-AI algorithms, including the following:

- Codeless script generation. Writing code for complex end-to-end scenarios can take as long as development of a new feature; with codeless script generations even non-technical people (for example, end-users during User Acceptance Testing) can record their actions and a smart tool will convert those into automated tests. An automation engineer most likely still will not be able just add these recordings to the test suites. There will be some work required, like setting up users, make object names to comply with naming conventions, etc. Nevertheless, it still can significantly decrease time spent on initial automation of test cases and expand coverage.
- Self-healing. Test case maintenance is probably the most hated task among the developers and QAs. It takes a lot of time; it slows down everybody. AI tools can collect a lot of information about every element on the webpage, so if one attribute is changed, the tool can still recognize this

element and proceed with execution. Some tools also collect information on how applications are used, like user flows, errors, etc., and are able to recognize insignificant changes and adapt.
- Converting test documentation to automation. Using natural language processing mechanisms, it is possible to convert tests written in English to automated tests. Some tools advertise that they can do it with both structured test plans and unstructured user journeys.

The second group - features that perform tasks that are very challenging or almost impossible to do by human beings – including the following:

- Autonomous building of test cases based on usage traffic from real users. These applications collect analytics data from an application clickstream, analyze it and create tests cases based on real system usage. They identify core patterns (sequences) and then run them in the test environments to improve scripts using ML algorithms (remove not required steps, duplicated flows, etc.)
- Autonomous building of test cases based on the analyzing code of application under tests. Bots build the map of software by exploring each path through it and then create set of use cases based on it.
- Visual Testing. Visual testing evaluates the visible output of an application and compares that output against the results expected by design. Some may think that it is a task better performed by humans, but it is just time consuming and we often miss things that a computer would not. Often humans do not pay attention to the things they see many times a day, sometimes people don't see obvious differences (think spot 10 differences between two pictures), and finally, humans cannot go through all screens multiple times a day and notice every difference. Visual testing allows to test the whole UI. Using ML algorithms helps to decrease number of false positives by identifying changes that do not impact user experience and ignoring them.
- Audio/Video Quality Testing. Before it was a highly manual task that required listening to the audio or watching video and giving it a subjective score. Today AI can collect multiple data points about audio/video and how their variations impact audio/video perception by humans. They can perform testing faster based on this data, make it more objective and ignore variations that are not important for humans.

4. AI-Based Testing Tools - Field Study

4.1. Promises Delivered

4.1.1. Quick Start

Recall that (1) automation of complex platform-level E2E tests in the shortest possible time and (2) decreased time spent on their maintenance were the two problems that led to this research. I read a lot of documentation, white papers and watched video lessons for many AI-based automation tools. You can find the comparison table of most popular and most promising AI-based tools in Appendix 1. I selected three of them (Testim, Mabl, and TestCraft) and automated one complex test scenario using each of these tools.

As time was my most valuable resource, I concentrated mostly on the time-saving features. The first most pleasant discovery was how easy it is to start using these tools. All of them have easy to use web-interfaces and provide extensive documentation. It took me just a couple hours from opening a tool for the first time in my life to having my first automated test running. Of course, one should invest way more time to use any of these tools to full potential. Using advanced features like adding code snippets, reusing steps, adding variables, setting up test data, managing test suites and execution requires more training and practice.

4.1.2. Codeless Script Generation (recording)

The next feature I explored is codeless test generation. This feature is implemented in all tools I tried with different levels of maturity. I found that Mabl is the most mature one. Recording of the test using this tool was easy. It was able to handle some challenging navigation tasks, such as switching between different web-applications, finding and selecting checkboxes in dropdowns, and hovering.

Recording tests in TestCraft is slower and requires an extra step to record each action. This might be a showstopper if you plan to involve anyone outside the engineering team into test creation. The real advantage of test recording that anybody can do it. You can ask the product team to record the user acceptance tests, support team to record flows where end-users noticed issues, or even real users to record their action. QA engineers can modify these recorded flows and add them to the regression test suite later. It should not require anything except hitting the record button and forgetting about it to be able to engage non-technical part of the team or end-users in the test recording. If there is anything extra, chances are that they refuse doing it. Unfortunately, in TestCraft it is not possible. I also found that navigation between different modes (recording, execution, editing) is a bit confusing in this tool. On the other hand, I should mention that tests recorded in TestCraft were very stable from the get go and required very little editing after recording.

Test recording in Testim (community version) is least mature. I was able to record the tests easily but they failed in multiple places when I tried to re-run it immediately after recording. To be able to do such actions like switching between different applications, selecting an item from dropdown I needed to add some delays, re record specific action, etc. I did not face such challenges with other tools.

4.1.3. Decrease of maintenance time

It is hard to estimate the advertised decrease in maintenance time during the evaluation period, especially if one has a limited number of automated tests (which is usually the case for Proof of Concept). There is also a need to have the same tests automated using traditional tools that are used in parallel to be able to compare time spent on maintenance of the same tests.

Tests automated by me using different AI-based tools were executed on multiple builds and releases. Every tool I tried handled insignificant changes in the UI, such as text, size or other attributes well. If the change was something that cannot be handled by a tool (introduction of new elements, major redesign of UI) it was much easier and faster to fix automated testcase by re-recording steps than introducing the same change using code.

4.2. Challenges and obstacles

4.2.1. Codeless script generation

Although the creation of tests using recording features is much easier and faster than using traditional tools, it rarely went absolutely smooth. Sometimes I needed to re-record steps or part of the script. Sometimes I needed to manually add delays. Creating custom object names that follow naming convention, having dates in the names was a challenging task in most cases. I believe that when QA looks at the data generated by automated tests she should be able to figure out what test created this data, when, and probably what build was used without opening logs or doing anything extra. There is always the possibility to add JavaScript code snippets (all tools I tried have this feature) to implement this or other custom behavior but in this case, it is not codeless anymore. If code is added all disadvantages of maintaining it come into place, including not easy debugging. As we see despite all achievements in the AI industry, recording tests is still a bumpy process for complex UIs and scenarios even today.

We also should remember that the ability to record tests does not magically solve all common issues of automation. It does not matter if you use code or recording to create tests you still need to make sure that you automate what matters. Tests should be well designed and automated at the correct level. One should also think about test data management, including setup and tear down.

Recording tests can speed up automation by providing an initial set of raw scenarios to work on. Still, automation engineers need to work on defining and reusing steps that are common for many tests, setting up and maintaining testing accounts, selecting test subsets to execute on different stages of the software development lifecycle. Recording all this is not a magic bullet. Engineers still should work to have robust, easy to maintain automation tests.

4.2.2. Self-healing feature is a double-sided sword.

Self-healing is a great feature, but it does not mean that all your tests will be magically fixed every time. Yes, insignificant changes are fixed automatically, but when your UI is mature, you don't have these changes introduced often. I would say such changes are rather rare after a couple of major releases. Definitely collecting multiple data points about each element and using them for element location improves stability of tests. It rather impacts robustness (tests do not fail if text on element changes depending on the time of day, for example) than decreases maintenance time(tests needed to be updated because of some changes in code). I found that self-healing saves way more time if the application has brand-new UI that changes often.

Different tools handle self-healing in different ways. Some of them require approval of every change, at least at the beginning while the system learns, so it is still a time investment. Others just make changes and proceed without notification, which I think is dangerous. For example, a currency sign in the platform I test and the number of digits after decimals is important but if they are missing - the self-healing systems will "auto-fix" such cases. Fortunately, most of the AI-based tools are starting to add the ability to review auto-fixed tests, accept or decline these changes, track history, and rollback to previous version. Don't forget that reviewing changes still requires time. I also suggest that you need to double check what is the mechanism of handling auto-changes before selecting one or another test tool with self-healing features.

To overcome the "auto-healing" problem for the small but important changes that should not be ignored, tests can always be built in a very specific way, where every sign, every comma has its own assertion. The result of this? Huge, slow and challenging to maintain automated tests. We can also make tests smaller and increase the number of tests, but if each test requires its own time-consuming setup having hundreds of such tests will lead to the increased time of test execution. We cannot wait hours each time we build the software.

Every big change in the application, like introducing a new element, removing tabs or anything else, will still result in the test updates that should be done manually. Of course, QAs will be able to do it faster because re-recording steps is faster than adding code. We should remember that it will be faster if QAs use any tool that provides the recording, not only AI-based tools.

4.2.3. Self-generated tests: improve the test coverage, what about quality?

The AI-based automation tools can generate tests in different ways. Some of them generate tests by collecting information on how real users use the software in production. This information can be extracted from logs, clickstream, or both. This probably works for software that uses the Business-to-Consumer model, then there are many users that produce a lot of data for ML algorithms. In the case of Business-to-Business model there are often less users and it is harder to collect enough data to train ML models. There are also many applications/features that do not have "users", for example, different reports that are generated as a result of data processing algorithms and calculations. There is another big drawback of generating tests in such a way – the application or the feature should be in production, and there should be users, so what about new functionality. That said, test generation based on the usage of application can only be used to add missing regression cases.

Another type of self-generated tests are tests generated by link crawlers. These tests check that every link in the app works. This is definitely a useful tool, but a working link does necessarily mean it's the right link, or that its a functioning application.

The auto generated tests only cover what can be easily tested. They find shallow bugs, like not working buttons, particular values, broken links. They will never help you find the requirement that was missed, logic flaws, the error message that was not generated to help the user to overcome the problem, or spot usability issues. Moreover, auto generated tests might give you a false feel of security and allow major issues that escape to production after thousands of automated tests have passed. Such auto generated tests are great to supplement QA efforts, but not a full replacement.

Another concerning thing is that marketing materials for these tools claim that using one or another way of autonomous tests generation will give you 100% of coverage. This raises the question of 100% coverage of what and more important do you even need to achieve these mystical 100%.

5. Summary

The usage of AI and ML in the testing tools is increasing daily. Almost every tool claims that there are some AI powered features that help improve testing. The key word here is "help".

The test recording was introduced a long time ago, but even introducing AI and ML did not make it perfect. It is much better than it was, it saves time, but it still requires human intervention, sometimes for simple cases.

Fully autonomous test generation although sounds cool, is not mature enough to leave all your testing in its hands. It can be useful to reveal gaps in coverage and easy to find bugs. Testing of complex systems cannot be done using only autonomously generated tests. These tests will never ask "what if".

The same goes to self-healing tests. It allows QAs to save time and removes a lot of mechanical, mindless work, but it is not a magic bullet of a fully autonomous task. Users still need to review changes. Moreover, QA Engineers need to design tests using best test automation practices and techniques and incorporate self-healing into design, so actual issues are never auto fixed (add explicit asserts, for example)

I may sound old school but the test that passes even after a change was introduced sounds to me more concerning than exciting. Isn't the purpose of the most automated tests to uncover changes that were accidentally introduced and else would go to production unnoticed? Why do we want to hide these changes?

The AI tools are great in the areas where a lot of information should be collected and quickly processed, like visual testing, video/audio quality, log parsing, collecting real usage information, performance testing.

Visual testing was not covered much in this article only because they do not fit my particular use case, but there are many success stories across industry. It is impossible for a human to detect any single visual change in UI, so using software is justified and pays off. AI in this case helps to find only differences that are perceptible to end-users. They do not use simple pixel-to-pixel comparison, but instead they use class of AI algorithms called computer vision, that helps to keep signal to noise ratio high.

To have the robust, stable, effective, lightweight, trustworthy and easy to maintain automated tests, one should not only select the right tool but also invest in test design. Someone still needs to find out what should be tested, when and how to do it in the most efficient way. AI tools' test designing abilities are very limited, almost non-existent. Mechanical clicking on everything clickable and extracting test scenarios from logs or clickstream can hardly count as a test design technique. AI can automatically generate a lot of tests that can be easily skipped and do not bring any business value or improve quality. Running thousands of tests is either time-or resource consuming so it is still QAs job to find the right balance between increasing coverage and speed of execution.

Tests often require complex data setup in software platforms or just large applications and none of the tools I've seen have features that help solving this task. Data seeding, maintenance and cleanup still should be done with some external tools or workarounds. I found this task sometimes most challenging when we talk about testing software platforms, solutions and software that uses a business-to-business model.

Finally, to have an effective automation the software itself should be designed with testing in mind, and no tool will be effective if application is untestable.

To summarize, AI-based testing tools in the current state cannot fully replace QAs. They can be used in a supporting role and decrease the time spent on mechanical, boring tasks. They are great as a supplement to the QA team, to automate time consuming activities, such as checking that every link in application is working, or tasks that are impossible for a human, such as spotting every visual difference between current and previous build. AI-based tools can be used to collect data about users' behavior to generate production like test scenarios. They also provide the ability to generate tests from existing test documentation.

Existing AI-based testing tools are mainly aimed at web or mobile apps. Nevertheless, these tools continue to evolve and decrease human involvement into checking while at the same time increasing human productivity and giving them more time to concentrate on testing[15].

Will we lose our jobs? Well, any process automation results in the disappearance of one or another job function. Do we need to adapt? That is definitely so, but we already did it many times before, didn't we?

6. Appendix 1. AI Tools Comparison Table

The table below is comparison table of five most popular and most promising, in my opinion, AI-based tests automation tools. The "+" indicates that tool has or claims to have one or another feature or capability but does not indicate the maturity of that specific feature. The information for TestCraft, Testim and Mable provided bases on hands-on experience and research. Information about Appvance and Functionize features provided based on research only.

		Testim	Mabl	Appvance	Functionize	TestCraft
1	Codeless Script Generation/Recording	+	+	+	+	+
2	Autonomously Generated Scripts	-	-	+	+	-
3	Visual Testing	*Integration with Applitools and Test Rail	+	-	+	
4	Auto-healing	+	+	+	+	+
5	Mobile Testing	-	-	+	+	-
6	Code Snippets	+	+	+	+	+
7	Test Plans written in Simple English to Automated tests	-	-	-	+	-
8	Support of cross browser tests	*Integration with Browsestack, SauseLabs	+	+	+	+
9	Performance and Load Testing	-	-	+	+	-
10	Security Testing	-	-	+	-	-
11	API steps	+	+	+	+	+
12	Version Control Systems (VCS)	GitHub Bitbucket	GitHub Bitbucket	Git repositories	Github	Gitlab
13	CI tools	Jenkins Circeci TeamCity Travis Ci Codeship	Bamboo Jenkins CodeShip Azure Pipelines	Circeci Bamboo Hudson Jenkins	Bamboo CircleCI Jenkins Travis CI Spinnaker Go AWS CodePipeline Heroku TeamCity	Jenkins Visual Studio Team Services TeamSity
14	Collaboration Tools	Trello Jira Github issues Slack Email	Jira Slack	Rally Chef	Jira PagerDuty	Jira Slack
15	Big Data		BigQuery			
16	IDE	JetBrains, Visual Studio				

7. References

1. Nick Health. What is AI? Everything you need to know about Artificial Intelligence. https://www.zdnet.com/article/what-is-ai-everything-you-need-to-know-about-artificial-intelligence (accessed June 26, 2020).
2. James Le. A Gentle Introduction to Neural Networks for Machine Learning. https://www.codementor.io/@james_aka_yale/a-gentle-introduction-to-neural-networks-for-machine-learning-hkijvz7lp (accessed June 26, 2020).
3. Introduction to Artificial Intelligence (AI) Microsoft – DAT263x. https://www.edx.org/course/introduction-to-artificial-intelligence-ai-2 (accessed Jan 9, 2020).
4. Testim https://www.testim.io/
5. Mabl https://www.mabl.com/
6. Appvance https://www.appvance.ai/appvance-iq
7. Functionize https://www.functionize.com/
8. TestCraft https://www.testcraft.io/
9. Vu Nguyen. Test Case Point Analysis http://www.qasymphony.com/media/2012/01/Test-Case-Point-Analysis.pdf (accessed July 20, 2020).
10. Javier Ferrer, Francisco Chicano and Enrique Alba. Measuring Testing Complexity University of Mlaga, Spain http://citeseerx.ist.psu.edu/viewdoc/download?doi=10.1.1.188.6343&rep=rep1&type=pdf (accessed July 20, 2020).
11. Michael Bolton. Blog: It's Not About The Typing https://www.developsense.com/blog/2020/08/its-not-about-the-typing/ (accessed August 15, 2020)
12. World Quality Report 2019-20. Quality underpins the key business drivers of every major enterprise https://www.microfocus.com/en-us/assets/application-delivery-management/world-quality-report-2019-2020
13. State of Testing™ Report 2020 https://www.practitest.com/resource/state-of-testing-report-2020/
14. AI Driven Test Automation. A Transformational Breakthrough for Software Development https://www.appvance.ai/portfolio-post/ebook-ai
15. Michael Bolton. Testing vs. Checking. https://www.developsense.com/blog/2009/08/testing-vs-checking/

Communication is Key: Lessons Learned from Testing in Healthcare

Rachael Lovallo

rachael.lovallo@gmail.com

Pulsara

Abstract

Pulsara is a healthcare communication and telehealth platform connecting medical teams across organizations. Since we serve the emergency healthcare industry, software defects could endanger real human lives. Consequently, quality is central to our development process. What is our secret to maintaining high quality in a fast-paced, growing start-up atmosphere where product areas are broad and include mobile, web, and a public API? Communication.

In a healthcare emergency, poor communication can literally mean death, and time cannot be wasted. In software testing, poor communication can mean a drastic decrease in both product functionality and team productivity. Effective communication across teams is key to producing quality products efficiently, and in this paper I share three actionable ways for individual testers to increase communication in their companies.

First, write your bug reports with bulletproof steps to reproduce, so that anyone can not only read and understand them, but also see the problem for themselves. Second, talk to your teammates writing the code you test. Lastly, get a second set of eyes on your work.

Biography

Rachael Lovallo is a software tester driven by a passion for using technology to create positive social change. She currently puts her skills to work as a Senior Test Engineer at Pulsara, a software company that connects healthcare teams to improve patient outcomes and bring acute healthcare into the 21st century.

Rachael is a tester to her core, persistently seeking software defects and rigorously documenting methods to reproduce them. She finds daily fulfillment collaborating with Pulsara's development team to build an intuitive healthcare communication platform that safely handles patient data and truly improves patient outcomes.

1. Introduction

In the mountains of Montana sits a healthcare technology startup called Pulsara. The company's goal is to improve patient care in emergencies via a platform facilitating medical communication. Testing at Pulsara includes unique challenges, as the platform consists of mobile applications for iOS and Android, a browser application and a public API, with a small team of testers ensuring quality.

The following pages focus on something central to Pulsara's mission and purpose: communication. Picture an emergency such as a stroke, or trauma event, where time passing directly corresponds to tissue lost. Medical data indicates that poor communication can waste time and drastically decrease that patient's chances.

Strong parallels exist between communication in an emergency and communication on a development team trying to ship a high-quality product under time constraints. When good communication occurs, not only do customers receive the product faster and with fewer defects, but the development group builds respect for each other and a greater “sense of team” emerges. This paper will provide the reader with three actionable ways to improve quality through communication in the workplace: 1) write each bug report with bulletproof steps to reproduce, 2) open the door to communication with your co-workers and 3) get a second set of eyes on your work.

2. Write Defects with Bulletproof Steps to Reproduce

2.1. Introduction

If a tester writes bug reports that anyone can read, quickly understand, and reproduce, it saves time. It also improves the chances of the defect getting fixed as opposed to closed as "not reproducible," or "works on my machine."

2.2. Some History

When I began testing software, my developer co-worker and I would often talk through defects as we sat near each other. When I switched jobs, I suddenly felt I was starting from scratch learning to work with new developers at a bigger company. Some co-workers were not even in my building, state, or country, much less a cubicle away. It took trial and error to learn to interact effectively with a new team. Now, at Pulsara, how and when bugs get fixed is a decision that requires more than just my co-worker and I. New issues go to a triage team that decides which defects get fixed and when. The triage team is not made up of people I work with directly, and sometimes the group changes. It can be a communication challenge. I experienced frustration at first because the triage team was regularly asking follow-up questions on my defects and I felt I was wasting my team's time. Worse, bug reports requiring lots of questions can lead to misunderstandings, code churn, and even project delays. I started to ask myself: how can I get any teammate to understand my defect reports without needing to ask follow up questions?

2.3. Standardize Defect Report Structure

I found some simple ways to make bug reports easier for anyone to understand. The first is baked into Pulsara’s test process. We have a standard defect report template. We all list steps to reproduce, the problematic result, the result we expected to see, and any other pertinent information, such as build number or environment. Since our defect write-up format is familiar to the wider team, those doing triage can increase efficiency because they know where to look to understand the issue quickly. Some read the whole report, but some may read the result first, then the environment details and do not need further information.

Example Bug Report:

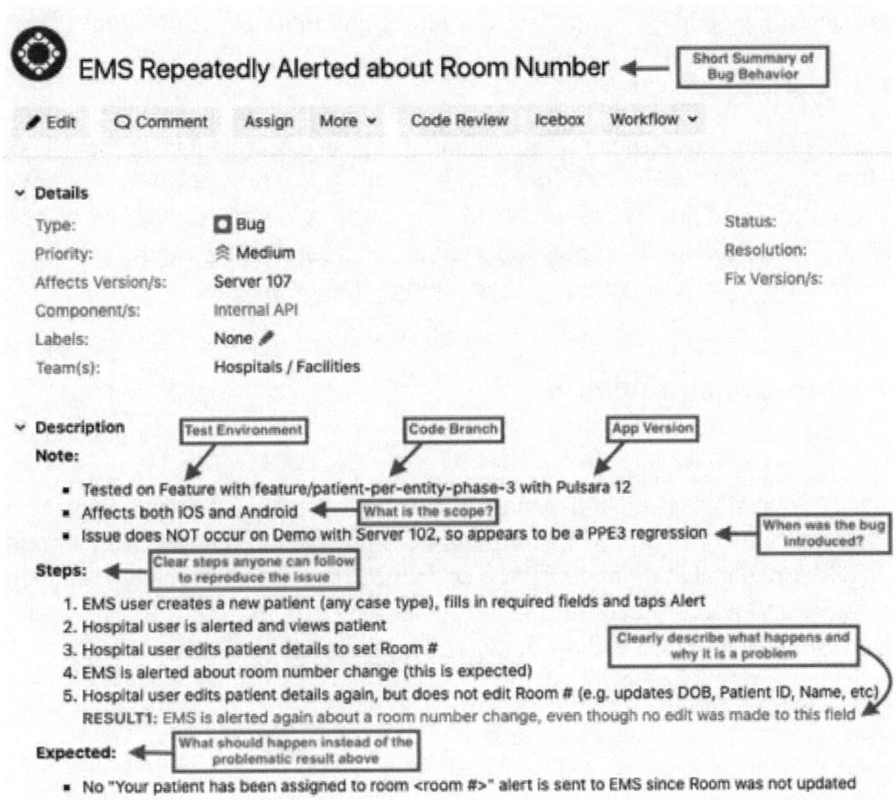

2.4. Tying it to Medicine

The idea is similar to how medical teams run standardized diagnostic tests when trying to diagnose a patient. For example, a stroke score is a common way to quickly diagnose and determine the severity of a stroke. The EMT might look at a patient's balance, eyes, facial droop, arm drift, and speech one by one and assign each a value of normal or abnormal. The process is quick and gives a result any medical professional can understand and use to determine treatment. Similarly, getting well-defined bug reports into developers' hands increases efficiency and likelihood of the issues getting resolved and shipped. All of this ultimately means a higher quality product in customer's hands.

2.5. One Step Further

In addition to considering structure, try adding color, images, or even videos to your bug reports. For example, make the problem result bright red and bold, or add a video of a clunky UI animation. Researchers have found that people tend to differ in the ways they best assimilate information. The main types are defined as Visual, Auditory, Reading/Writing Preference, and Kinesthetic, or the VARK learning styles[1]. Interestingly, leveraging VARK to help students excel has been debunked. However, few dispute that people have a distinct preference for one style and take in information most efficiently if it is presented to them that way[2].

This means that going beyond words when documenting a defect makes it easier for recipients to understand. Odds are small that everyone on a team learns best through reading. Aside from using descriptive words within the bug description, play with color, make text bold, and add images or videos to draw attention to important results. The goal is experimentation to see what helps more defects get fixed right away instead of prompting questions from teammates. Additionally, if a tester makes a bug report easy to understand, the developer will appreciate the effort, and that helps build your team.

2.6. Conclusion.

To review, use a standardized structure for writing bug reports, similar to how medical staff use conventions like stroke scores. Additionally, get creative with color, or add an image or video of a defect to a ticket to help get the issue clearly presented to any team member, regardless of how they mentally process information. This will lead to your bug reports making sense to the whole team, getting them fixed more quickly and ultimately lead your company to shipping a better product.

3. Open the Door to Communication

3.1. Introduction

One of the biggest time-wasters in testing occurs when testers never directly interface with the people writing the code they test. Imagine grain silos standing side by side in a field. Each stands independently from the others. While functional in a grain storage scenario, silos are inefficient in technology companies where teammates must share information to get a high-quality product out the door fast. Breaking down silos while testing means talking more to the people writing the code you test.

3.2. Bedside Manner in Medicine

The most intelligent and skilled doctor will likely be unsuccessful without “bedside manner”. A doctor without good manners might not listen well to the patient’s symptoms and get the diagnosis wrong. Or the doctor might not be able to communicate to the patient about how to best mitigate symptoms. Established ways exist for health professionals to interface with patients to help them feel heard and open a door for trust. These include talking face to face with open body language, eye contact, and pauses to let the patient talk, among others[3].

3.3. The Science

What’s the science behind talking face-to-face? It turns out communication in person (or on video) is superior to methods like email because, like writing good bug reports, communication is more than words. If teammates talk while in the same room, or in a video call, they see each other’s’ body language, hear tones of voice, and look each other in the eye. This interaction results in a phenomenon called “cooperative communication,” which helps get two talking people on the same page because the shared space and experience leads to similar mental states [4]. That can go for better or for worse. If a tester goes into a discussion showing defensiveness and tension, it is likely the other person will mirror their attitude back, and it will not be a productive conversation. However, if a tester goes into a discussion with confidence, but a willingness to listen, they are likely to get the same treatment from their teammate. Both will leave the conversation feeling a sense of team. Beyond work-related conversations, the development team at Pulsara regularly schedules “Beer Friday” where shop talk is minimized and we build deeper connection over a beverage of our choice.

3.4. Techniques

3.4.1. Pair Development

At Pulsara we practice talking to each other in a few structured ways. The first we refer to as Pair Development, and we apply this to tedious test scenarios where we know the functionality will take a few tries to perfect, or to "boomerang bugs" that have been reopened repeatedly. In Pair Development, a tester and developer sit in the same room, or get on a video call. The developer makes a code fix, and the tester pulls the change into their local test environment. By testing then and there with the developer present, another code fix can be made on the spot if defects are found, and the two can test again. They iterate until the functionality looks shippable to both. This means the defect gets fixed within hours as opposed to at least another full day. The process also helps with empathy, as the tester sees the challenging code the developer is augmenting, and the developer sees the testing goals.

3.4.2. Test Parties

Another structured way of talking at Pulsara is via Test Parties, a concept my manager developed. At a test party, we sit down with other testers, but also developers and stakeholders like customer support. We test new functionality in real world scenarios where we take on the roles of EMTs, Doctors and Nurses and try to use our product as they would. The feedback from both the developer, who wrote the code and knows where defects could be hiding, as well as people who have emergency medical backgrounds regularly yields bugs. We also learn more about real-world workflows which then get incorporated into future test efforts. Test parties impact both 1) the short term quality of the upcoming release, and also 2) the quality of future projects.

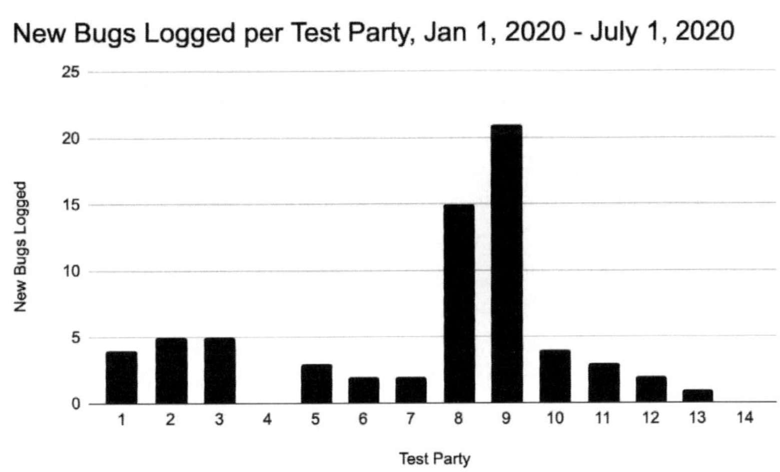

Notes:

- *Outliers with 0 defects found (Parties 4 and 14) were repeated parties for large projects nearing release*
- *Outliers with >5 defects found (Parties 8 and 9) were initial parties for large projects*
- *Average = 4.78, Median = 3, Mode = 2*

3.5. Conclusion

As Daniel Goleman, author of Emotional Intelligence, states: "The social brain is in its natural habitat when we're talking with someone face-to-face in real time." [5]. When challenging questions arise, or when a slack thread or email chain has continued for a while without resolution, start a conversation face to face, whether in the same room, or over a video call. Behavioral research suggests that going into the conversation confident and with well-baked questions make it likely co-workers will reflect the tester's attitude, understand, and help. If testers have more information on a problem, tool, or project, they can test more thoroughly. This contributes to a higher quality product with the current work, as well as in future projects.

4. Ask for Feedback

4.1. Introduction

A common story compares working at a startup to paddling one's own canoe, whereas working at a big company is like attempting to paddle a cruise ship. The story does reflect reality, but the mental image appears overly idyllic. Startup work can feel like pushing a loaded canoe upriver with one's teammates. To make it work, each person must set aside their ego, lean on their teammates, and take constructive criticism. At Pulsara I learned to accept coworker's help, and in turn noticed an improvement in the quality of my work, as well as the quality of the product shipped. The third action item distills the lesson I learned on feedback into a simple daily task: ask for a second set of eyes on testing work.

4.2. Do It Yourself Surgery?

Imagine a surgery. You probably picture a team of people clustered around a patient, each person performing specific tasks. However, in 1960 during a Soviet Antarctic Expedition, Doctor Leonid Rogozov performed self-surgery and managed to successfully extract his own appendix [6]. Comparing the mental image of typical surgery with his experience, most would not want to be in Dr. Rogozov's shoes even with his surgical skills, and no one would recommend self-surgery as a best practice. Surgery takes a group of doctors and operating room staff working together to ensure the best outcome for the patient. Most importantly, the standard surgical team consists of one surgeon and one assistant surgeon. The assistant provides another set of hands, and if complications arise the two discuss the best path forward. In other words, the patient has increased chances of a better outcome because there is more than one person's expertise going into the procedure. This is so well known that best practices tell us there should be two surgeons in the room.

4.3. Research Outside of Medicine

Research on teams outside of medicine supports the idea that collaboration between people leads to better outcomes. A concept gaining popularity when developing teams is called "cognitive diversity." It means seeking out team members with different knowledge, or who approach problem solving differently than others. A study from the Harvard Business Review measured how different teams handled a complex problem within a time limit, comparing the minutes taken to solve the problem against measurements of the cognitive diversity of the group. They specifically looked at knowledge processing, which is the extent to which individuals prefer to use their existing knowledge, versus generating it in the moment. They also analyzed perspective, which is whether individuals prefer to use their own expertise or lean on others. The study found high correlation between the teams with high cognitive diversity, and the teams which performed the challenge correctly the fastest [7], suggesting it is beneficial to have differing experiences and thinking patterns collaborating to ship a successful product.

4.4. What Does it Mean for Testing?

Two heads are better than one when facing a testing challenge. How can this information be applied to testing to help improve quality? One way is for testers to individually take initiative to ask for a second set of eyes on their work. Even better, bake regular feedback into the test team's best practices.

4.5. Concrete Examples

4.5.1. Test Review

At Pulsara my manager implemented a "Test Review" practice. My team spends part of our time reading co-workers' testing notes and offering ideas for additional scenarios to cover or bringing up missed areas. Nothing moves to the done status until this happens and being the reviewer and the reviewed are both challenges that help us grow as testers. We have also found defects through test review that would have otherwise made their way into production, as it is customary to ship the product right after QA is complete. Test review is one additional gate ensuring a release is ready.

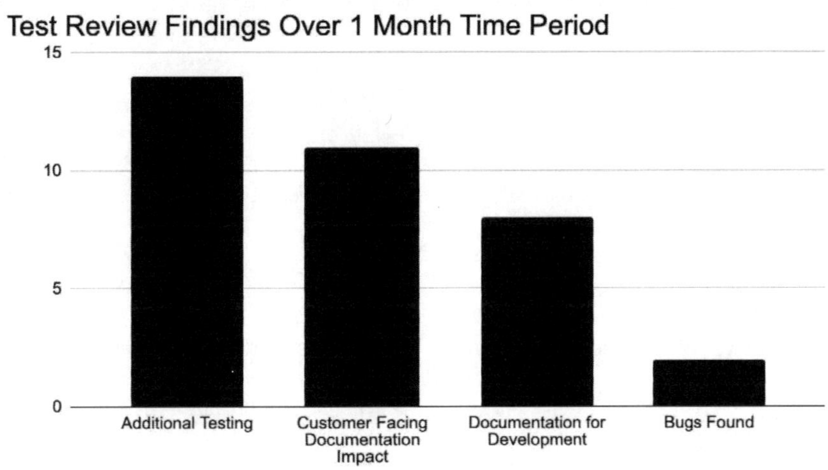

Note: 119 tickets test reviewed in total

4.5.2. Teamwork

A more informal feedback loop is our test group instant messaging channel. We ask questions there, and offer help if others make an inquiry. Additionally, we leverage past test plans and our test management tool when questions arise about product behavior or testing scope. Lastly, we rarely test projects alone, instead splitting the work with at least one teammate. This helps ensure subtle defects are caught by someone viewing the project with fresh eyes. Additionally, more people learn new functionality and are ready to test future releases without a learning curve.

4.5.3. Pair Development and Testing

Pair Development, as described above represents another collaborative test tool regularly leveraged at Pulsara to keep the feedback loop tight between testers and developers. Similarly, we can implement Pair Testing in which testers collaborate in the same time and space. The practice proves especially useful for collaborative features such as video calling, where sound quality or other issues can be easily missed by a sole tester. Lastly, letting one teammate write tests, and another execute them helps us think of more scenarios, and more comprehensively ensures the quality of the product.

4.5. Conclusion

If a person requires surgery, no one questions the need for a competent team. Similarly, testers should rely on their team for feedback and a second set of eyes. Together they will find more defects and will be more efficient in the future since everyone learns to test the different parts of the product.

5. Conclusion

Communication is like a muscle, and studies indicate that improved skills lead to higher quality products that ship faster. Three concrete ways to improve communication include: 1) writing each bug report with bulletproof steps to reproduce, 2) opening the door to communication with co-workers and 3) getting a second set of eyes on work.

The more testers incorporate these actions, the more they can leverage good communication to get a higher quality product into the hands of their customers, faster. At Pulsara that means helping emergency medical workers communicate better, and ultimately improving patient care.

References

1. Toppo, Greg. 2019. "'Neuromyth' or Helpful Model?" Inside Higher Ed, entry posted January 9, https://www.insidehighered.com/news/2019/01/09/learning-styles-debate-its-instructors-vs-psychologists (accessed June 5, 2020).
2. The Atlantic. 2018. The Myth of Learning Styles. April 11. https://www.theatlantic.com/science/archive/2018/04/the-myth-of-learning-styles/557687/ (accessed August 8, 2020).
3. Renter, Elizabeth. 2015. "Why Nice Doctors are Better Doctors," U.S. News & World Report, entry posted April 20, https://health.usnews.com/health-news/patient-advice/articles/2015/04/20/why-nice-doctors-are-better-doctors (Accessed June 5, 2020).
4. Vasil, Jared. 2020. "A World Unto Itself: Human Communication as Active Inference," Frontiers in psychology, entry posted March 25, https://www.frontiersin.org/articles/10.3389/fpsyg.2020.00417/full (Accessed June 10, 2020).
5. Goleman, Daniel. 2013. "Focus on How You Connect With Others," Huffpost, entry posted November 12, and updated January 23, 2014, https://www.huffpost.com/entry/focus-on-how-you-connect_b_4261185 (Accessed June 10, 2020).
6. The Atlantic. 2011. Antarctica, 1961: A Soviet Surgeon Has to Remove His Own Appendix. March 14. https://theatlantic.com/technology/archive/201103/antarctica-1061-a-soviet-surgeon-has-to-remove-his-own-appendix/72445/ (accessed June 10, 2020).
7. The Harvard Business Review. 2017. Teams Solve Problems Faster When They're More Cognitively Diverse. March 30. https://hbr.org/2017/03/teams-solve-problems-faster-when-theyre-more-cognitively-diverse (accessed June 10, 2020).

Full Stack Testing is a Culture: Drive your team to Embrace the Change

Christina Thalayasingam

niro.tina2k@gmail.com

Abstract

Many teams aim only to have a bug free system. Seldom do they believe in delivering true quality. Rarely do they realize that skipping nonfunctional testing like performance and security testing could lead to the breach of your product quality. Many teams still do not understand the importance of Continuous Integration or Continuous testing. This paper will discuss how you could pour the passion into your team to look in all accepts of quality. Move into Full-Stack Testing. Build up a team that values the essence of quality is a culture rather than focusing alone on reporting bugs.

We will discuss ways on making your team walk in the path of Full Stack Testing so that the team knows their vision and the mission. The team should move into a position where any member of the team can understand the testing requirements of the application and execute them. Drive the entire quality team to understand the skills that each of them possesses. There are several skills to assure Quality: Testing, Test Automation, Performance, etc. Generally, there are teams specialized in each of these areas executing each of these test types. Here we need to be able to pick anyone from the quality team to be able to cover any of the above test types.

Full-stack quality engineers are individuals capable of working on all aspects of quality across all the application's layers, using different testing methods. They will think about the many different aspects of product quality, such as functionality, usability, performance, security, and will also be familiar with test automation strategies and technologies. The full-stack QE will have a rich mix of domain knowledge, technical skills, and testing expertise. This is the trend that quality engineering is flowing into today, and we shall discuss on how to get there.

Biography

Christina Thalayasingam has more than 6 years of experience in both functional and non-functional testing. She possesses a development background. Since she has worked on PHP Web Development and Android Mobile Development before taking up Quality Engineering. She has worked in automate testing content management systems for the UK government, point of sales applications, eCommerce application, and clinical trial applications. She was worked on-site in the UK on projects with the UK government sector and major food supply chain management company. Christina is currently working as a Senior Test Engineer at Medidata Solutions by Dassault Systèmes®, an award-winning company that develops and markets software as a service (SaaS) for clinical trials. Also, she has been part of various prestigious conferences, technical meetups and webinars. She is a software testing evangelist.

1. Introduction

Testing is very important for software development companies. Most of them need to guarantee to their clients that their products are multiplatform, multidevice, and that they will work correctly and efficiently. It is always important to perform all quality checks during the entire development cycle. Conducting all quality checks from a very early stage is essential. Such a requirement demands the quality team to be able to drive, administer, and set all vital quality check. They cannot only limit themselves to the traditional skill sets and techniques to achieve this.

The World Quality Report 2018-19[1] states that "*Agile, DevOps, automation and artificial intelligence not only require newer skill sets but also make it necessary for Quality Engineers to have multiple technical competencies*". This continuous introduction of new methodologies and technologies makes it a necessity for a corresponding change in the Quality Engineering strategy. To meet the demanded pace and quality requirements of the end-user in today's world quality engineers are transforming to adapt to the industry changes. Digital Transformation (Mobility, Cloud, Big Data, Data Analytics, Customer Experience, etc.) is evolving leads to the need of test engineers to play a major role in checking quality. There is high requirement from test engineers to think of ways to speed processes for timely and swift delivery which leads the use of one the following STLC Automation, in Sprint Automation, Business Process Automation, TDD / BDD, Continuous Testing, etc. Increasing agile and DevOps practices where dynamic collaboration between multiple teams is the key rather than adhering to predefined static quality gate processes which leads the test engineers to acquire capabilities on emerging technologies (AI, ML, Blockchain, RPA, AR, VR, IoT, and others).

The current testing roles are designed to function in silos where manual testers only focus on black-box testing, automation testers are effective only on certain automation tools, non-functional testers only focus on product non-functional without digging deep into product functionality, and so on. To attain the maximum quality the demand of all these skills for a quality engineer has become vital. To adhere to the current pace and to support the transformation and drive organizations to the highest level of maturity QEs require to become Jacks-of-all-trades[2] (who can do many different types of work) in their game, even though a master of some.

This paper narrates how the goal of making a full stack quality engineering team out of a quality engineering team was approached. Make your team believe in full-stack testing. Let them see the benefits that it could bring to them and the way they work. Have the ritual of creating proof of concepts to make your team believe in why it is beneficial. Every transformation to the Full Stack Testing story begins with the realization that the current setup isn't working. This does not only require technical skill set change but a culture change.

2. Need for Full-Stack Quality Engineers

The fundamental urge for full-stack testing is the adoption of agile product development processes. As software updates are delivered more regularly, Test engineers have less time to complete all the testing. There's not much time towards the end of a sprint, and it's certainly too late to do it months after the feature's development is 'complete'.

Therefore, to achieve fast delivery, testing activities must be blended with the agile process and tasks for the sprint. Said differently, testing is not something that should be done before release; it should be done during every sprint. A story/feature should not be considered 'complete' without testing, and rather than being reactive by looking for bugs after development, full-stack testing will focus on proactively looking for defects throughout the planning, design, and development stages. The Quality engineer needs to think up-front about all aspects of quality and how to test, from the start of the sprint's planning phase. Hence quality engineer must grow their skills to match the new technologies, testing techniques, and methodologies currently in trend. Full-stack testing is focused on defect prevention rather than defect detection.

3. Tasks for Full-Stack Test Engineers

A full-stack test engineer should understand the product well to test it from the user's point of view. Test Engineer should be involved from the early stages of the feature's development so that they can share their advice and experience from the testing and user-perspective. Fewer defects are found after initial development if the test engineers are involved from the very beginning, which includes defining the feature's requirements.

It is a must the test engineer works with the developers to understand a feature's architecture, how it's implemented, and the technologies used. This would help them determine the best ways to test the feature, in all aspects of testing. The full-stack test engineer doesn't need to know the actual code of the application, but a comprehension of the implementation can raise some very useful technical questions. This helps the entire team to think extra carefully when implementing the feature and prevent defects from reaching the end-user.

Full-Stack Testing is required more for defect prevention than defect detection. Making sure that a feature/story has gone through quality check in all layers of the application prevents and non-functional check from new defects occurring even in the future. In this manner defect prevented. Therefore, the yearn for defect detection should be to prevent defects occurring in the future. When underlying issues within application layers are fixed there would be very rare possibility to find issues related to old development in the future. This would help will prevent from wasting time in digging the old skeletons out.

In short, having a Full-stack Test Engineer in your team helps with the following.

- **Efficiency –** Gives the team the flexibility to do more. Having a single test team that possesses all test skills removes the need for an automation team, a performance testing team, etc. This means there'll be less wait time between testing cycles. This means dedicating work for teams in silos can be avoided, which saves time in knowledge transfers to those teams, etc.
- **Efficacy –** Full-stack Test Engineer in a team often would have a deep understanding of the product. This means the Test Engineer knows what, where, and how to test. Whereas a traditional test engineer without this knowledge will most likely test a larger portion of the product since they will only have an overview of the product, so doing deep testing in an area might not be within their scope.

Overall, an experienced full-stack QA engineer is also a product expert, quality advisor, and risk analyst.

4. Build Your Test Team into a Full-Stack Quality Engineer Team

Creating a team of full-stack test engineers requires mastering a lot of skills, which may be challenging for many team members to acquire in a short time. Most of the time a team would not comprise of all members being full-stack test engineers. My suggestion is to start with building a full-stack test team first, where the team has the capabilities to handle any task, such as automation, end-to-end functional testing, performance testing, security testing, and so on, collectively.

Following are the stages of building up a full-stack testing team at the beginning:

1. **Clean the mess in the house -** First of all, clean up the existing mess if any in your current testing process. Process should be created in such a way that a feature should be completely tested in all aspects that would affect the user-experience before is considered to be 'complete'. Precise checklists should be created in order to help test engineers discuss on the types of quality effects around the feature being developed. This would lay the initial foundation stone for the test engineer to create the full-stack test strategy for the feature. It would be advisable to include the software architects and lead developers when create this process, so that the test lead can have a standard list of things to look out for in terms of quality. Aim for goodness, not perfection. Derive test plan templates based on the initial experience and continue to gradually update them as the team learns on how they could do things better.

2. **Start small and aim big -** Do not expect everything to fall in place immediately. Therefore, select very basic features to start with going full-stack testing during the sprint testing. Some feature that would have impact if most aspects, for example, auto-complete on a selection list. The Test Engineer will consider issues such as the time delay to refresh the selection after typing a single letter; how to test the event that triggers a REST call to the backend service; how the UI layer behaves if the backend service is broken; etc. In this way most of the user experience related issues can be covered. Discussing every minute thing of the feature construction would help the test team to test full-stack and deliver it as development 'complete' successfully. Therefore, initial practice on basic features rather than complicated stories can help the test team mature on the process. This will prepare the test team to be able face complicated features.

3. **Weigh out the best fits -** Pick the tools for full-stack testing wisely. Your pick will strongly depend on your requirements, the tech-stack you use in your company and how your daily workflow is handled. If you are thinking of integrating various different type of testing, get a platform that can handle most of it. Choose a framework that works well with the team skill sets and help train them to use it without any issues. The tools you choose is crucial, it can impact many factors like efficiency, adaptability and ability get the maximum out of the benefits of full-stack testing.

4. **Have a believing team -** Make your team believe in full-stack testing. Let them see the benefits that it could bring to them and the way they work. Have the ritual of creating proof of concepts to make your team believe in why it is beneficial. Every transformation to the Full-Stack Testing story begins with the realization that the current setup isn't working. Full-stack is key to achieving speed across the pipeline. The commitment is necessary for it to work. Make them believe automation reduces manual errors, and bakes quality into every step of the process.

    a. **Assign good shepherds to lead the way -** Assign leads or senior engineers who can lead the test team in believing and working towards full-stack testing. Let them guide the team, sketch out a meticulous game plan to incorporate the change. Make sure this is followed as a ritual. They should consider the company priority and project allocation when allocating resources and defining the process.

b. **Full-stack testers are jacks-of-all-trades -** The test team needs to be composed of jacks-of-all-trades in the software testing world. A person who has the basic knowledge in all the important quality checks conducted in an application. A jack-of-all-trade would carry the following pros for the growth of the team:

   i. **Diverse Skill Set -** Usually, a person with several skills or a jacks-of-all-trades is widely miscommunicated and misinterpreted because of the highly negative impact of the phrase. There's a misconception that people who multitask, are quite likely to fail. However, a very important fact is ignored while criticizing such people, their versatility, and their diverse skill set. Full-stack testing is all about jacks-of-all-trades in the software testing. Their diverse skill sets would be vital for growth of the team.

   ii. **Can Be a Blessing for Initializing Full-Stack –** A test engineer with skill sets in most of the test types could be a great addition to a team that requires to take its move to full-stack testing. This can help the other team mates to work together to understand the process.

   iii. **Adaptability and Flexibility –** They could be added to various scrum teams to help the other teams to work towards full-stack testing their features at the initial stages. Acquiring a number of skills eventually makes them proficient enough to make complete use of every component of their skillset. The expansive knowledge base of such individuals makes them flexible and just as comfortable in doing manual functional testing as they would be load testing, processing test data.

   iv. **Long-Term Learner –** Being a jack of all trades, individuals don't just learn one thing. They go through multiple learning processes of different levels of complexities and durations. This definitely helps them gain the most important skill that any person can have - knowing how to learn. Jack of all trades is often lifelong learners. This can help the need to learn for full-stack testing immensely. Eventually the team will grow.

   v. **Able to provide basic training to rest of the team –** A full-stack engineer in the team can train the test team with a strong plan to go forward.

   vi. **Great Fit for Leadership –** A leader is always considered to have a lot of experience. A leader who knows almost every aspect of what they do (in this term full-stack testing) will have an edge over someone who rose through ranks doing only one job. They will be best to help show the way to full-stack testing.

c. **Get help from masters of one -** The team needs support from the subject experts since they are going to start treading into new ground in terms of few/many types. They need to get the ideas from the masters of each quality check. If it is possible it is best to recruit someone who has such rare valuable skills, so that she/he could teach/train the team with testing types like maybe performance testing or security testing. Eventually such candidates will grow into becoming full stack testing jack-of-all-trades and create them too.

5. **No more working in silos –** Quality checks do not have to depend on expert silo teams like the API test team or the performance testing team. Now all-important quality checks will be completed by the scrum test team before story/feature is marked as "complete". Therefore, lesser issues will be found when it reaches the silo teams who will be at the end of the SDLC. The team now will be able to exchange roles within them, cover each other, help each other and work together on challenging tasks. This would lead for a more sophisticated full-stack test team.

6. **Continuous learning and scrutiny -** Continuous learning is key to keep improving your full-stack testing practice and culture. Scrutinize from what is new out in the industry and learn and adhere to the approach that helps your team to grow.

7. **Practice what you preach -** Building quality into your SDLC (software development life cycle) requires a commitment to automation to full-stack testing. You know you're on the right track when automation is something you do not just to reduce effort, but to also move faster, and build quality. As you embrace a culture of automation, it's bound to transform your testing efforts and result in high-quality apps that are shipped faster.

5. Full Stack to Continuous Testing

As the team starts practicing full-stack testing on every story after a certain point they will gain expertise in what they do. This is when it is time to think about full-stack test automation. Till this stage it is not necessary for the team to automate all test types. Certain tests should be initially conducted manually or semi-manually till the team gains the in-depth knowledge of it. Once the team has reached a point of expertise and confident, they should look into options to move into the world of automating all regression tests be it functional/non-functional. This would eventually lead the team to continuous testing and that should be the goal from the very start. Continuous testing [2] has immense benefits not only for the test team but to entire scrum/product/project team. Continuously running quality checks will show where the application stands in all aspects of quality.

6. Benefits of Full-Stack Testing

The full-stack testing team would eventually be a versatile test team who would have gain immense knowledge and experience. This experience will help them trouble-shoot an issue with the full-stack test mind set. They would be working not only on the functionality but also on other quality checks which would be an added benefit where quality checks being slipped or forgotten would not be much of a case anymore. Moreover, having them would help with timely delivery which would be budget-friendly. The full-stack testing team would be able to take complete ownership of the quality of the application.

7. Setbacks to Be Mindful Of

Full-stack testing has so many benefits and that is what many test teams are currently working towards today. However, there are certain things that we need to be mindful of to make sure that we get the right output. The time of the team should be managed precisely, and no training nor learning should their affect productivity. There could be confusion on roles and responsibilities in the absence of certain team members. Those need to be clarified and communicated clearly. Finally, as new trends flow in it could be difficult to keep up with them. However, it is best to delegate members to monitor trends on each aspect of quality so that the team can be aware of the latest and eventually scrutinized the current practices.

8. References

1. https://sii-concatel.com/wp-content/uploads/blog_enjoyit/2018/10/World-Quality-Report-2018-19.pdf
2. https://dev.to/katieadamsdev/jack-of-all-trades-or-master-of-one-56b2
3. Continuous Testing - https://www.tricentis.com/products/what-is-continuous-testing/
4. https://huddle.eurostarsoftwaretesting.com/need-for-full-stack-qa-in-2020/
5. https://syscolabs.lk/blog/full-stack-quality-engineering/

Generator-based Testing: A State by State Approach

Chris Struble

cstruble@meteorcomm.com

Abstract

Learning a new software testing technique and applying it successfully in your career is deeply satisfying. What if your organization is heavily invested in a different testing technique? How can you convince your colleagues to try your technique, and help them to adopt it successfully?

Many organizations use Example-based testing (EBT), where test cases are manually designed one example at a time, then executed automatically in a repeatable way. EBT techniques such as Test-Driven Development (TDD), Behavior-Driven Development (BDD), and Acceptance Testing have been widely adopted. EBT falls short because it cannot be used to test examples that no one thought of.

EBT shortcomings had led to development of techniques for automated generation of test cases. In Generator-based Testing (GBT), software behavior is described to a tool that generates test cases in a non-deterministic way, which are then executed automatically. Three examples of GBT techniques are Model-based testing (MBT), Property-based testing (PBT), and Fuzzing. Each of these techniques have found high profile defects that escaped EBT testing. Even so there has not been widespread adoption of these techniques.

This paper will present an approach to doing GBT that makes it more accessible, and easier to progress through states of adoption. The approach is based on more than 20 years of experience using MBT. The paper will also describe an MBT framework developed in Ruby using open source tools in the past year, and the results of introducing it in a workplace where EBT techniques were already widely adopted.

Biography

Chris Struble is a Senior Software Developer in Test (SDET) at Meteorcomm LLC in Renton, Washington. He has 25 years of experience as a software professional, primarily in quality and test automation, with excursions into development, agile team leadership, and continuous delivery. He holds an MS in computer science from Walden University and an MS in mechanical engineering from the University of Houston. In his spare time, he writes music and fantasy fiction, and plays guitar and computer strategy games. He lives in Renton, Washington with his wife, daughter, and two cats. Find him at: chrisstrublewrites.blogspot.com

1. Introduction

When I started my software engineering career in the early 1990s, most software testing was a manual process of trying out a sequence of steps, writing them down, and executing them again.In 2020, automated test execution is widely adopted, with test execution frameworks available in many programming languages, and for every level of testing, from unit testing to system testing, and for functional and non-functional aspects of software. Automated test execution transformed the job roles of software developers and software testers, moving them closer together than ever before. Today testers must be able to write code, and developers must be able to write tests. In some workplaces the distinction has disappeared altogether. For this paper "tester" is used to mean anyone doing software testing, regardless of job role. For most testers, test case design remains a manual process of writing sequences of steps one example at a time. This practice is so common that conventions have been developed to make it easier. Here is an example written in the Gherkin syntax of the Cucumber test framework:

```
Given I have a locomotive travelling at 80-mph
When it approaches a curve with a 30-mph speed limit
Then an overspeed warning message should be sent to the operator console
And the operator does not slow the train within 30 seconds
And I should see the locomotive slow safely to a stop automatically
```

Most testers would immediately recognize the intent of this example, because people naturally communicate and learn by example. Examples are a form of storytelling, and stories needs concrete characters who do concrete things, even when some of the characters are systems and software. The above example describes a scenario that can occur with Positive Train Control (PTC), an automatic safety system for railroads in the United States. The functionality in this example is designed to prevent an overspeed derailment, such as the one that occurred on December 18, 2017 near DuPont, Washington (McNamara, 2019). The above example is concrete, with specific speeds and time intervals. Ideally, we would like to make a general claim about software behavior, more like this:

```
Given I have a locomotive travelling at some speed
When it approaches a curve with a lower speed limit
Then an overspeed warning message should be sent to the operator console
And the operator does not slow the train in time
And I should see the locomotive slow safely to a stop automatically
```

David MacIver (2019) describes test cases that "use a concrete scenario to suggest a general claim about the system's behavior" as "example-based tests".In this paper Example-based Testing (EBT) is defined to mean any practice where:

- Test cases are manually designed one example at a time
- With the goal of suggesting that the software works
- By demonstrating automatically that each example works

EBT practices including Test-Driven Development (TDD), Behavior-Driven Development (BDD) (such as the Cucumber examples above), and Acceptance Test-Driven Development (ATDD) are widely used for software testing today.

EBT has inherent shortcomings. A single concrete example can only suggest that a general claim is true. It takes many concrete examples to have confidence in a general claim. People, including most testers, are not very good at thinking of a thorough set of examples. A consequence is that defects escape the software development process and are first seen by users after the software is released. Some escaped defects occur because of schedule and cost constraints of software projects, but many escaped defects are examples that no one even thought of.What if we could automate test case design, using a computer program to "think of" more examples? That is the goal of Generator-based Testing (GBT), defined as any software testing practice where:

- Test cases are generated automatically from a description of the software behavior
- With the goal of discovering defects in the software
- By demonstrating automatically if each generated test case works, or not

This paper will focus on three practices that fit this definition: Model-based testing (MBT), Property-based testing (PBT), and Fuzzing. Each of these practices have been in use for more than 20 years, enough time to have found many important escaped defects. Here are just three real-world examples:

- Mars Polar Lander crash, 1999
    - The Mars Polar Lander was on lost December 3, 1999, just before touchdown on Mars. After the crash, a NASA team used T-VEC, an MBT test generation tool, to successfully identify the likely cause of the crash. A fault in the Touchdown Monitor system caused the lander to shut down the descent engines prior to reaching the surface (Blackburn, 2002).
- HeartBleed OpenSSL Vulnerability, 2014
    - HeartBleed was a security vulnerability in the OpenSSL cryptographic library. It was independently discovered in April 2014 by Neel Mehta of Google, and a team at Codenomicon (now Synopsis) using a Fuzzing test tool. The vulnerability was undetected for two years. (Synopsis, 2014)
- Volvo AUTOSAR Emergency Braking System Fault. 2015
    - Volvo hired Quviq to perform acceptance testing of the AUTOSAR software on its vehicles. Quviq used its QuickCheck PBT tool to detect over 200 problems, including a serious problem where the emergency braking system could be deprioritized over non-critical functions, such as adjusting the volume. (Hughes, 2015)

Despite successes like these, GBT practices are rarely used. A global job site had over a thousand job listings mentioning EBT practices in the qualifications, while GBT practices were mentioned in only five.

For GBT practices to become mainstream, I believe they must be presented as complementary practices that make up for EBTs shortcomings. EBT and GBT can and should coexist in a tester's toolkit, and in the same software development group. The following GBT framework attempts to support that idea.

2. Generator-Based Testing (GBT)

To practice GBT requires artifacts and tools that work together. In order of appearance, these are:

- A Description of the software behavior the Tester wants to test
- A Generator that generates Test Cases from the Description
- An Executor that executes each Test Case against the software
- An Oracle that determines if each Test Case passed or failed
- A Repeater that tells the Executor to rerun each failed Test Case
- A Shrinker that finds a minimal Repro Case that reproduces each failure

Figure 1 shows a workflow of how a tester would use these artifacts and tools together.

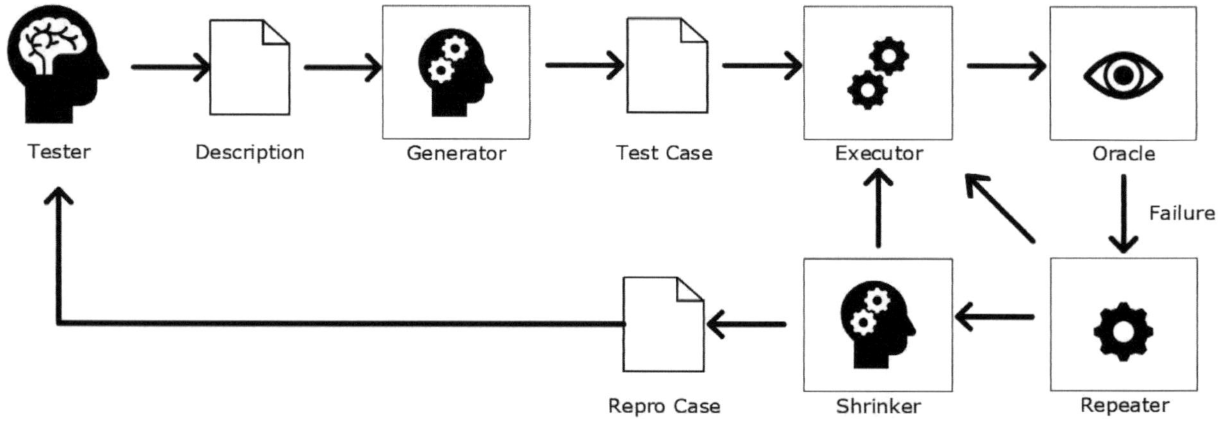

Figure 1 – Process of Generator-based Testing (GBT)

A Description is an artifact such as a file, graph, or source code that formally describes a behavior to be tested. The Description is created by the Tester.

A Generator is a tool with source code tightly coupled to the format of the Description. It processes the Description and outputs Test Cases.

Generators are non-deterministic. Each time a Generator processes the same Description, it may produce a different set of test cases. This is because Generators use search algorithms or random algorithms to generate test cases. This is a strength in GBT since the goal is to find defects.

Executors and Oracles should already be familiar from automated test execution. An Executor runs each test step against the software under test, and an Oracle determines if that step passed or failed.

A Repeater is a tool that reruns the Executor for Test Cases that were failed by the Oracle. If a Test Case fails again, it is considered a defect candidate and sent to the Shrinker.

A Shrinker is a tool that uses a search algorithm to reduce a test case that consistently fails, into a shorter Reproducible (or Repro) Case that reproduces the same failure.

Shrinkers are necessary because Generators can produce very long test cases, with many steps, only some of which may be important to the failure that occurred.

The Repro Case is then analyzed by the Tester to determine the cause of the failure. The root cause might be an error in the Description, Generator, Executor, Oracle, or a mismatch of one of these with the behavior of the software under test. The appropriate action is taken, and the process is repeated.

Any of the steps in the workflow can be done manually. The greatest benefits occur when each step of the workflow is automated, and when the output of one step flows automatically into the next step.

To make these concepts more concrete, the next section will discuss the practice of Model-based Testing (MBT) in more detail, along with a case study.

3. Model-Based Testing (MBT)

Model-based Testing (MBT) is one type of GBT. In MBT, the Description is a "model", such as a finite state machine, UML state chart, process flow diagram, or similar directed graph. The model describes actions that cause changes in the state of the software under test.

In MBT, representing the model visually as a graph is essential. A model graph can be used as a specification, to communicate the tester's understanding of the software behavior to. This requires a Model Editor, a tool to display the graph, edit it, and save it back to a file readable by the Generator.

MBT has been practiced since the 1990s or earlier. Some milestones include:

- First paper using the term "MBT" (Apfelbaum, Larry and Doyle, John. 1997)
- First dedicated conference workshop (A-MOST. 2005)
- First textbook (Utting, Mark and Legeard, Bruno. 2007)
- First certification (ISTQB. 2015)

My first experience with MBT was in 2000, when I used TestMaster, a commercial MBT tool, to generate test cases for a laser printer driver installer, finding over 100 new defects in a six-month project (Struble, Chris. 2004). That project made a lasting impression on me.

I found model graphs to be a natural and effective way to generate test cases, and I never stopped using them, even when automated generators were not available to me. I continued to try new MBT tools periodically or wrote my own.

Here are a few more highlights from my use of MBT in my software testing career:

- I released Hanno, an open source MBT web testing framework in Java (Struble, Chris. 2008)
- I tested .NET web applications using Microsoft Spec Explorer, in 2012
- I evaluated Conformiq Creator, a commercial MBT tool, in 2016

My efforts were successful in the sense that I learned from them, raised awareness about MBT among my colleagues, and in several instances successfully found product defects. None of these efforts led to MBT to become an ongoing practice at the organizations I worked for.

One impediment to software teams adopting MBT is that the mental shift required to make the transition to MBT takes several months. For teams to adopt it, several people need to go through the learning process at the same time, or there needs to be sustained support for it. Few employers are willing to make that kind of investment in tester training.

Once mastered, MBT can be quickly reapplied years later. One tester used MBT early in his career and returned to it 20 years later (Lowry, Benjamin. 2020).

It is easier to get started with MBT now than when I started. Several well supported open source MBT tools exist today (Micskei, Zoltán. 2018). This was helpful when I tried MBT again in 2019.

4. Meteorcomm MBT Case Study

In 2019 I joined Meteorcomm LLC (2020), a telecommunications company headquartered in Renton, Washington.

Meteorcomm develops a messaging system for railroads called Interoperable Train Control Messaging (ITCM). ITCM maintains communication between locomotives, waysides and railroad back-offices via radios and IP networks. Figure 2 shows the major components of the ITCM system.

The main application of ITCM is Positive Train Control (PTC), a safety system that was mandated by the Rail Safety Improvement Act of 2008. PTC is designed to stop a locomotive if it is not able to continuously prove to the back-office that it is safe for it to proceed. Over 90% of the track miles that implement PTC in the United States use the Meteorcomm system.

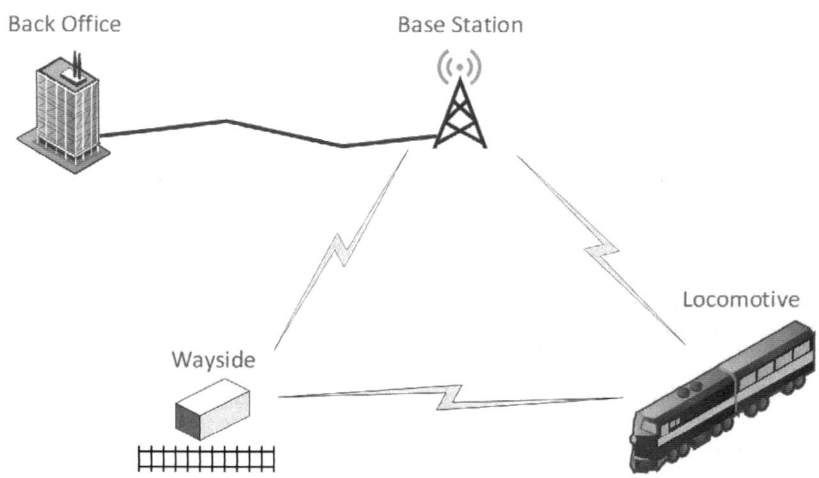

Figure 2 – Interoperable Train Control Messaging (ITCM) System

Meteorcomm is rearchitecting its back-office systems as Docker containers running as "pods" in a Red Hat OpenShift (Kubernetes) cluster. A library of several thousand functional tests, written in the Ruby programming language for the Cucumber BDD test framework, are being rewritten for the new architecture. Sequence diagrams are used extensively to model message flow through the system.

Several times a year development teams get two-week "innovation sprints" to work on projects of our choosing. I used one of those intervals to introduce MBT to Meteorcomm. I wanted an MBT tool in Ruby so it would work with our test code, but I could not find one, and writing one from scratch would have taken too much time.

Instead I used an open source MBT tool called GraphWalker (Karl, Kristian. 2020). GraphWalker has been developed since 2005 and is the most fully featured free MBT tool. It is written in Java but can be controlled with any programming language through a REST interface.

In two weeks, I wrote a Ruby program called Test Generator to generate and run tests for ITCM using GraphWalker.

Here is how it works, using the terms in the GBT framework:

- Description: A finite state machine model is created in GraphWalker JSON format.
- Generator: GraphWalker running as a REST service.
- Executor and Oracle: A Ruby model class with methods for each element in the JSON model file. Edge (transition) methods execute actions, and vertex (state) methods verify that the software is in the correct state.
- Test Case: The sequence of steps generated by GraphWalker can be saved to a "walk file".
- Repeater: Test Generator can re-run a walk file, without using GraphWalker to re-generate.
- Shrinker: Currently a manual process. To be automated in the future.

The overall workflow can be summarized as follows: Test Generator loads the JSON model into GraphWalker, then GraphWalker traverses the model one element at a time. For each element, Test Generator calls the Ruby model class, until GraphWalker reaches 100% edge (transition) coverage.

Figure 3 shows a simple GraphWalker model of AMQP Sender (called "tx" in the model), rendered using the AltWalker Model Editor (Altom. 2020). AMQP Sender is a test pod that runs in the OpenShift cluster. It provides a REST interface to send messages using the Advanced Message Queuing Protocol, simulating messages sent by locomotives or waysides.

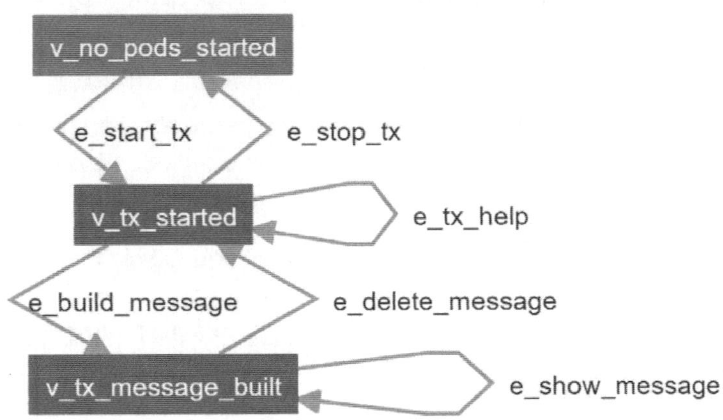

Figure 3 – GraphWalker model of the AMQP Sender test pod

This model has three vertices and six edges. The initial vertex "v_no_pods_started" means the pod is not started. Once the pod is started, it can be stopped, display a help page or build a message. Once a message is built, the message can be displayed or deleted.

GraphWalker typically took 12-16 steps to reach edge coverage using Djikstra's algorithm.

I presented the Test Generator and showed it generating and running tests for the AMQP Sender model, calling the backend test library used by our existing Cucumber test cases. I got positive feedback that encouraged me to keep working on it.

I spent another two weeks enhancing Test Generator with more features, improved documentation, and unit tests. I built a more complex example model. This model (not shown) has three pods: AMQP Sender, MRG3 Broker, and AMQP Receiver. AMQP Sender sends a message to the broker, which stores the message in a queue, until it is read by AMQP Receiver. The model had 10 vertices and 28 edges. GraphWalker typically took 84-100 steps to reach edge coverage on this model using Djikstra's algorithm.

Finally, I set up a half-day workshop with the testers in my department. Six people attended and got to use Test Generator to model and generate tests in a group exercise. None of them had used MBT before. I asked in a survey if they would consider using MBT in their day-to-day work. Here are some responses.

"Learning new approach to testing. Random generation of tests, down different possible paths every time. I felt this approach would be useful for generating every corner case which otherwise wouldn't get done during normal test automation."

"I think this type of testing could be very beneficial if you get the vertices and edges to match up well to parts of the code base. This may require some trial and error. I would be interested in knowing if there's any sure procedure for converting design documents to these graphs."

"I need to think about whether this really adds value in our testing domain. While I see immediate value and application in web/UI testing, I haven't seen adoption of this technique in the back-end systems and integration testing domains I've experienced throughout my career."

After these efforts, Test Generator was added to the list of officially allowed testing frameworks at Meteorcomm. I hope to use it to search for defects in ITCM in the coming year.

5. Property-based Testing (PBT) and Fuzzing

In 2019 I became aware that MBT isn't the only game in town. In a web search I found a video by John Hughes called "Don't Write Tests." He does another form of generative testing called Property-based Testing (PBT).

PBT started in 1999, when Hughes co-wrote a Haskell library called QuickCheck for generating test cases for functional programming languages (Hughes, 2015). Assertions are made on "properties" that functions must satisfy for all inputs, and many examples are randomly generated attempting to falsify the assertion. If a falsifying example is found, QuickCheck automatically tries to shrink the test case to find a minimal test case that reproduces the same failure.

PBT has been described as "a more structured approach to fuzzing". Fuzzing is a generative testing practice where random inputs are entered into a computer program until it crashes. Fuzzing has been used since the 1980s, and today is often used to find new security vulnerabilities, such as HeartBleed (Synopsis, 2014), or to test any software where random crashing bugs are a concern.

PBT is not limited to functional programming languages. QuickCheck has been ported to 35 languages. Hypothesis, a Python library for PBT, was introduced in 2015 (MacIver, David. 2019). It has so far been ported to Java and Ruby. Over 2000 open source projects are already using Hypothesis.

PBT is not limited to unit testing. It is used for integration testing and system testing, and even testing of stateful systems (using what Hughes calls "models", though these are not the models of MBT).

Learning about PBT and Fuzzing made me realize I needed to expand my concept of GBT to encompass them. The "shrinker" concept is used by both, and the term "example-based testing" comes from PBT.

I haven't use PBT yet. I hope to try it in the coming year.

6. What MBT and EBT Could Learn from PBT

Looking at PBT from the perspective of an MBT expert, I believe that MBT could benefit from some of the concepts that PBT has implemented, in particular:

- Model in code: Most testers would prefer to use source code rather than graphs to capture their understanding of test behavior. This avoids context switching between graphs and code which can slow down the test generation process.
- Automate shrinking: MBT generates long sequences of test steps, especially when tests are generated and run at the same time. Most MBT tools do not implement shrinking, leaving it for the tester to do manually. Automated shrinking would make MBT a more efficient workflow.
- Embrace randomness: Randomness is a strength when searching for defects. PBT embraces this. MBT's search algorithms are also non-deterministic, but MBT tool vendors don't always emphasize this. This is misguided. MBT should embrace randomness as a selling point.

EBT could also benefit from randomness. Running manually designed EBT test cases in random order is an easy way to detect test cases in EBT test suites that interfere with each other and remove flakiness.

7. A State by State Approach to Test Learning

Mastering a new software testing practice takes time. Embedding it in a software development group takes even longer and involves passing through a series of states of personal and organization learning. What follows is a model, in GraphWalker format, of such a learning process.

Figure 4 – Personal Learning States

Figure 4 shows the states of personal learning. In the beginning, the tester is unfamiliar with a new testing practice. If they read about it, they become familiar with it. If they try it, perhaps installing tools and working through examples, they achieve personal knowledge. Then they have a choice. They can try to become an expert, by applying it in a real project. This might take a few months. If that isn't possible right then, they can set it aside. After a year or so, neglect sets in. Then to get back to the state of personal knowledge, they would have to try it again.

Once they become an expert, they have another choice. Share the expertise with their colleagues, in a presentation or demo, or neglect it. If they neglect it, they can always apply it again later to get back to be an expert. If they share the expertise, then the tester has reached a state I call "shared familiarity". They are an expert, and their colleagues know they are an expert.

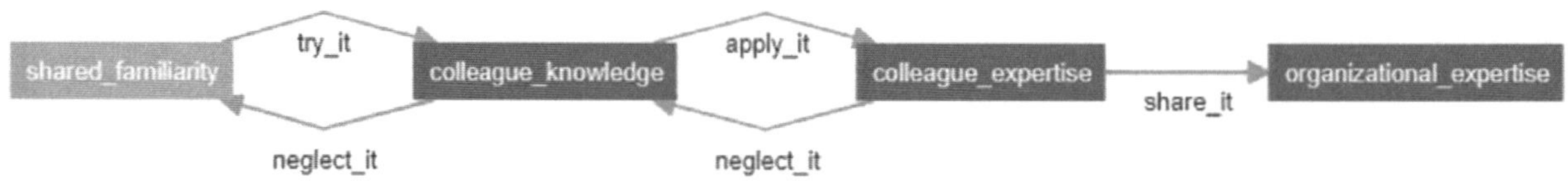

Figure 5 – Organization Learning States

Once the expertise has been shared, the organization then can learn. This process is shown in Figure 5. Each of the tester's colleagues has the choice to try the new technique, or not. The original tester can help by leading a workshop where colleagues get to try it as a group. For a colleague to become an expert, they must apply the knowledge on a real project. Once the organization has at least two experts in a testing technique, they should be able to maintain that expertise in the organization.

Organization learning of a new testing practice can regress from neglect at any point. Ongoing support from management is essential. Dedicated innovation weeks, training weeks, brown bags, internal conferences, and other opportunities for knowledge sharing on a regular basis, encourage testers to learn new practices and to maintain and spread that knowledge in the software development group.

Summary

This paper gave a definition of Example-based Testing (EBT), and a definition of Generator-based Testing (GBT) that encompasses Model-based Testing (MBT), Property-based Testing (PBT), and Fuzzing. It described three major escaped defects that were found with each of these practices. It described the tools needed to practice GBT. It discussed a case study of introducing MBT to a software development group by creating an MBT framework in the same programming language as existing EBT test libraries. Finally, it presented a state machine model for personal and organizational learning, that may help in adopting GBT practices (or any new testing practices) in a software development group.

Acknowledgements

I want to thank managers past and present who encouraged my explorations: Irv Tyrrell, Denzil Dwelle, Rita McCann, and Starr Parker. Thanks to Harry Robinson for inspiration and encouragement. And most of all, thanks to my wife LeAnne Struble for her patience and support.

References

McNamara, Neal. 2019. NTSB Issues Final Report On DuPont Amtrak Derailment. https://patch.com/washington/seattle/ntsb-issues-final-report-dupont-amtrak-derailment (accessed 7/14/2020)

MacIver, David. 2019. "In Praise of property-based testing", Increment.com, Issue 10, August 2019, https://increment.com/testing/in-praise-of-property-based-testing/ (accessed 06/28/2020).

Blackburn, M.R. 2002. Mars Polar Lander fault identification using model-based testing https://www.researchgate.net/publication/4004301_Mars_Polar_Lander_fault_identification_using_model-based_testing (accessed 06/28/2020)

Hughes, John. 2014. Experiences with QuickCheck: Testing the Hard Stuff and Staying Sane https://www.cs.tufts.edu/~nr/cs257/archive/john-hughes/quviq-testing.pdf (accessed 6/28/2020)

Synopsis. 2014. https://heartbleed.com/ (accessed 6/28/2020)

Apfelbaum, Larry and Doyle, John. 1997. "Model Based Testing", Software Quality Week Conference, http://citeseerx.ist.psu.edu/viewdoc/summary?doi=10.1.1.86.1342 (accessed 06/28/2020)

A-MOST. 2005. Advances in Model-Based Software Testing https://conf.researchr.org/series/a-most (accessed 06/28/2020)

Utting, Mark and Legeard, Bruno. 2007. Practical Model-Based Testing: A Tools Approach. San Francisco: Morgan Kaffmann, ISBN 978-0-12-372501-1.

International Software Testing Qualifications Board, Foundation Level Model-Based Tester Certification. 2015. https://www.istqb.org/certification-path-root/model-based-tester.html (accessed 06/28/2020)

Struble, Chris. 2004. Model-Based Testing of Installers in a Development Environment. http://testoptimal.com/ref/MBT_Installers_Dev_Env.pdf (accessed 06/28/2020)

Struble, Chris. 2008. Hanno Model Based Web Testing Framework. https://sourceforge.net/projects/hanno/ (accessed 06/28/2020)

Lowry, Benjamin, 2020. Model based-testing: Gone and back again https://speakerdeck.com/bplowry/model-based-testing-gone-and-back-again-net-perth-march-2020 (accessed 06/28/2020)

Micskei, Zoltán. 2018. Model-based testing (MBT). http://mit.bme.hu/~micskeiz/pages/modelbased_testing.html (accessed 06/28/2020)

Meteorcomm LLC. 2020. https://www.meteorcomm.com/ (accessed 06/28/2020)

Karl, Kristian. 2020. GraphWalker. http://graphwalker.github.io/ (accessed 06/28/2020)

Altom Consulting. 2020. AltWalker Model Editor https://altom.gitlab.io/altwalker/model-editor/#/visual-editor (accessed 06/28/2020)

COVID-19 Model Testing Getting Important Work Done in a Hurry

Christian Wiswell

cwiswell@idmod.org

Abstract

Hitting milestone dates can be challenging even with all of the right planning and scheduling. The COVID-19 work disruptions are unprecedented. Policy decisions about how to respond are informed by sophisticated computational models, which in turn need to undergo scrutiny.

Testing computational models is challenging because the desired behavior is "accurately simulates the real world," but the real world behavior is at least partially unknown or theoretical.

This paper will tell the story of how the Institute for Disease Modeling (IDM) tested its Covasim model, and how that work was divided between Subject Matter Experts and professional software testers. This story includes discussion of collaboration, test methodology, and balancing risk with time constraints.

Biography

Christian Wiswell's career in software testing began as a manual link-clicker in 1999, and proceeded through jobs at web startups, Microsoft, and Google. He started work at the Institute for Disease Modeling in 2013, becoming a test manager in 2015.

1. Introduction

The purpose of this paper is threefold. Firstly, it is to equip people to test specialized software without becoming a subject matter expert. Secondly, it is to discuss testing of computational models of infectious disease transmission. Lastly, it is to tell the story of how a particular piece of software was efficiently tested so that others can learn from the experience.

To these ends, the paper will discuss the Institute for Disease Modeling and its Covasim model, which simulates outbreaks of COVID19. It will also discuss some issues with testing stochastic and scientific software and tell how some tests were developed in the Covasim case. Hopefully, the narrative parts of the paper will also be helpful to people trying to understand some of the soft skills of working with subject matter experts on the testing of software.

2. Background: Institute for Disease Modeling (IDM)

The Institute for Disease Modeling (IDM) is a group working in Washington State on applying the power of computational modeling to the study of infectious disease transmission. The Institute consists of a mix of academic researchers with expertise in computational modeling, and software engineers with experience in designing, building, and testing software.[1]

[1] More information about IDM is available at https://idmod.org/

The Institute has existed with different names and organizational structures for about ten years, and has published dozens or papers in academic journals, and worked with many other institutions (including NGOs and government institutions) to help people understand disease dynamics.

Most of the work of IDM in the past has been on the diseases Malaria, Polio, and HIV, and in more recent years has expanded to include Typhoid, Measles, and Tuberculosis / HIV coinfection.

2.1. The EMOD Model

A large part of IDM's research on these diseases uses IDM's Epidemiological MODeling software (EMOD). The following is a quick overview of EMOD software to give context for the discussion of the Covasim model. For a more thorough discussion of the EMOD software, please see the linked paper in references.

EMOD is a stochastic, agent-based engine for simulating epidemics. Agent-based means that every time an EMOD simulation is run, a separate object in memory is created to represent each person in the simulation who may get infected. Agent-based models are powerful tools for answering modeling questions where each individual is potentially unique. For example, a malaria simulation where some individuals have no bednets, others have new bednets, and others have bednets that are aging and less effective. Stochastic means that some events in the simulation are dependent on a random number draw. This means that before the simulation executes, it is not possible to know the exact state of the simulation at the end. While stochastic, agent-based models can be computationally expensive, EMOD was designed around the concept of transmission pools, which makes some kinds of simulations faster.

2.1.1. Transmission pools in EMOD

EMOD's transmission pool concept is how the model implements agent-based transmission. Consider the following example. In this simple model, we have five agents. Two of the agents are infected, which is represented by lightly shaded people. Three of the agents are susceptible to a new infection, which is represented by being dark. However, the two infected agents are shedding different levels of infection. This could be for any number of reasons. For example, perhaps one of the agents is washing their hands more frequently, which reduces that person's shedding. It is also possible that one of the agents is at a more infectious part of their infection than the other one (in a disease where infectiousness goes up and down over time).

Let's consider how EMOD models transmission.

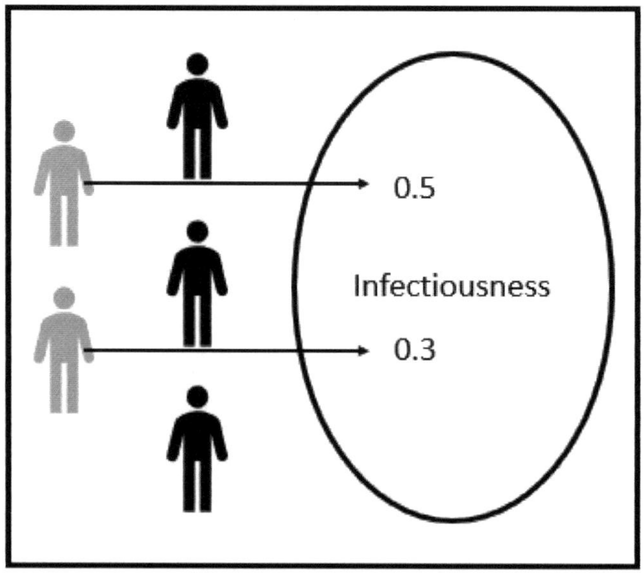

Figure 1: Two people contribute to the infectiousness pool through shedding.

In Figure 1, we see the two infected agents contributing to the transmission pool. This is called shedding. In the case of a respiratory disease like Measles or Tuberculosis, can be caused by coughs or sneezes.

After shedding is complete, susceptible agents are exposed to the total infectiousness, and some of them are selected to be newly infected. In the example, one agent becomes infected during exposure (Figure 2). During the next shedding phase, this individual may contribute to shedding.

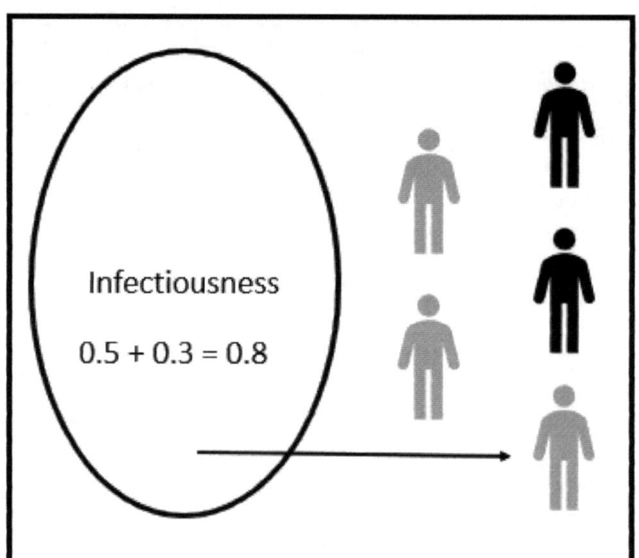

Figure 2: With a total infectiousness of 0.8, one of the three susceptible agents becomes infected.

2.1.2. EMOD inputs and outputs

EMOD requires a configuration file defined in JSON format, where each key is the name of a model parameter and the corresponding value tells the model what to use. For example

```
"Simulation_Duration": 50
```

tells the model to run for 50 time steps before finishing and writing reports.

Most of the model outputs are channelized JSON, where each key is the name of a reporting channel and the corresponding value is a list of results per time step. For example

```
"New_Infections": [0,1,0,3,5,12]
```

Indicates that there was 1 new infection on the second time step, 3 on the fourth time step, and so forth.

2.2. Testing of Modeling Software

Validation of this kind of software is very challenging. Consider the following question:

Does this model correctly determine how long after becoming infected a person starts shedding virus?

Answering this question by looking at the outputs of a normal simulation is impossible.

- Each individual who becomes infected will draw a pre-infectious period from a probability distribution (for example, a bell curve distribution). To see if the distribution is correct, you would need to consider several people at the same time.
- Models that only output total counts at each time step make knowing the state of each person impossible. Consider a simulation with two people. One of them is infected at time 3, the other at time 4. One of them begins shedding at time 6, and one at time 7. Output files similar to EMOD's would contain data to represent these totals like so

```
"Which_Timestep":  [1,2,3,4,5,6,7,8,9]
"Infected_Count":  [0,0,1,2,2,2,2,2,2]
"Shedding_Count":  [0,0,0,0,0,1,2,2,2]
```

  But this data doesn't tell you which of the two infected people began shedding on time 6. When the simulations contain hundreds or thousands of individuals, any chance of getting data about individuals from these reports disappears.

- Lastly and perhaps most importantly, the word *correctly* here is impossible to answer, because the scientists using these models are making estimates based on the best data they can find.

Fortunately, there are techniques for dealing with the first two problems. For testing to see if draws from a probability distribution are correct, there are powerful statistical techniques one can use to see if lists of numbers are likely to have come from a given distribution. In the case of EMOD, we've found that the Kolmogorov-Smirnov[2] and Anderson-Darling[3] tests have proven useful but required a great deal of time and effort to implement them properly. Interpretation of statistical test results is also non-trivial.A discussion of how to use these tests for software validation is out of the scope of this paper.

Resolving the problem with getting the proper outputs can be resolved through additional logging or careful crafting of test simulations. In EMOD, our development teams have enabled specialized logging outputs that can tell us the state of every individual at each simulation time. Creating this required a lot of effort on the part of the development staff and must be disabled in production environments to prevent non-test simulations from overwhelming file storage (these debug logs can be very large).

In some cases, it may be possible to configure a simulation in a way that highlights a specific feature of the model. For example, if we want to find out how long infections last without confounding our results with new infections, we can configure the simulation to force every individual to be infected at the first time, and just measure the total count of infected people at each time to make those durations visible at the whole simulation level.

3. The Challenge

In late 2019, a novel coronavirus was first identified in the Wuhan region of China that produced a very serious respiratory condition, and the disease began spreading rapidly. By early 2020 it had reached the United States and was beginning to cause infections and deaths in Washington State, where IDM is located.

Among the many important areas of COVID-19 modeling were questions around what interventions could be taken to limit the spread of the disease. Among the proposed interventions were the following items.

- **Testing -** Including testing some percentage of all people and testing some percentage of symptomatic people
- **Contact tracing -** After a person is diagnosed, trying to find the people they have been in contact with and testing them for infection
- **Quarantining families -** Keeping the families of infected people away from other people in case they have infections that haven't been detected
- **Isolating infected people -** Keeping people known to be infected away from other people
- **Social distancing -** Closing workplaces, schools, or both, and encouraging policies that would limit disease transmission among people in contact (masks and handwashing)

[2] scipy.stats.kstest, from scipy.org https://docs.scipy.org/doc/scipy-0.14.0/reference/generated/scipy.stats.kstest.html (accessed September 4, 2020)

[3] scipy.stats.anderson from scipy.org https://docs.scipy.org/doc/scipy/reference/generated/scipy.stats.anderson.html (accessed September 4, 2020)

The EMOD model, while very flexible and powerful, had some limitations at the time that would have made modeling these interventions difficult[4]. EMOD's implementation of transmission pools (section 2.1.1) didn't track human-to-human transmission. This meant that the model was unaware from which person a newly infected person got their infection, so contact tracing in EMOD wasn't possible. Also, EMOD did not track families, workplaces, or schools, which made complicated social distancing scenarios (Shut down middle schools and large workplaces, but not elementary schools and small workplaces) not feasible.

4. Our Solution: Covasim

Fortunately, IDM had a new modeler with strong computer science skills who brought a different computational model to help answer these questions. This is the origin of the Covasim model. Covasim was developed specifically for answering questions around COVID-19 and the interventions mentioned above, so it had many features built in to make this easy.

The Covasim model is like EMOD in that it is also a stochastic, agent-based model. A critical difference between the two is in how disease transmission works. Instead of using transmission pools, each person in Covasim can have from one to four contact networks. A contact network for an individual is a list of people in their household, work, school, or community. Instead of shedding into the transmission pool, individuals in Covasim expose some number of their personal contacts. A contact tracing intervention considers the contacts that an individual has and either tests those contacts for COVID-19, puts those contacts in quarantine, or performs some other operation.

Because the model was built with these questions and functionalities in mind, the modeling work began quickly, and researchers were able to begin work on answering questions about COVID-19.

4.1. Testing Covasim

From a software testing point of view, the model was completely new. IDM's software engineering teams had years of experience in developing and testing new EMOD features and disease models but had never seen the Covasim software before. At the same time, IDM's research teams were using Covasim to inform policy decisions. This led to a real sense of urgency in testing the model quickly to ensure that the model produced correct results and provided good policy guidance.

To further complicate matters, IDM had issued a work from home order in March, so in-person collaboration with the research team was going to be difficult if not impossible. My initial attempts at testing the model were not very productive. Based on my experience with EMOD, I expected to find configuration files that I could begin editing, JSON reports produced as default outputs, and the idea of implementing statistical tests for every property of the model was quite intimidating.

The modeling team had created tests of the model that consisted of running it in different ways, enabling different features and then viewing the resulting graphs that were produced. When I reached out to see if I could be of help, they asked if it would be possible for me to generate code coverage numbers for their existing tests.

[4] Many of the limitations of EMOD for Covasim modeling have since been overcome, but this code is not yet publicly released.

To make sure that some professionally designed test coverage could be implemented, I decided to lean on humility by simply following the directions in the README for running simulations. The instructions were straightforward. The software was in pure Python, and could be installed through the pip utility, and the simplest simulation could be run in Python through four lines of code.

Install with `pip install covasim`. If everything is working, the following Python commands should bring up a plot:

```
import covasim as cv
sim = cv.Sim()
sim.run()
sim.plot()
```

Figure 3: Covasim's quick start guide

Once I got simulations running, I began outlining a number of automated tests, using Python's unittest framework. I created skeletal outlines of a number of test areas, creating several test methods as "Not Yet Implemented" (NYI) and building entirely empty classes for each area of the model where I thought some test verification could be added.

This served two purposes. It showed the modeler the areas I intended to investigate. Also, it allowed me to have a sense of scope and progress toward completion. Each time I implemented another one of these tests and got it enabled, I could run the unit tests and watch the number of passing tests increase, and the number of skipped tests (all of the NYI tests were skipped) decline.

Ait this point, I reached out to the Covasim modeler again. Given that we were both working from home, we ended up having an extended conversation on a Slack chat about how to add software test coverage with verification to the model. When I showed the modeler the skeletal tests I wanted to implement, the modeler kindly volunteered to add documentation as comments into the parameters.py file, including suggestions for appropriate tests for each parameter. This allowed me to receive instruction about the observable behavior of each of the parameters, as well as get some excellent suggestions about tests that could be easily implemented.

Perhaps most importantly, agreeing upon the parameters file as a shared responsibility began to build a sense of mutual trust with a new colleague. With this information as a clear point of agreement between us, I was able to write the support classes for my tests using parameter names that were familiar to me. At the time, Covasim's parameters dictionary had a key named "n" and another key named "n_infected". My support layer created a property called "number_agents" that I could use to refer to "n", and "initial_infected_count" that I could use to refer to "n_infected". Using the parameters.py file from the model code and my unittest_support_classes.py file in my test code, I could respond quickly to changing parameter names by only changing my code in the support layer, rather than having to change each of the individual tests every time a parameter was renamed.

4.2 Tests produced

This section contains some examples of tests that were produced for testing the Covasim model.

4.2.1. Testing reproducibility

One of the first tests produced was test_random_seed.

Like a lot of stochastic software, Covasim allows the user to set a random seed. This test is meant to show that the random seed is honored. To do so, it simply runs three simulations. The first two simulations use the same random seed, and the third uses a different one. All other parameters are the same. From a scientific sense, this test is worthless, as it shows nothing about a scientific property of the model.

From an engineering point of view this test is interesting. Consider an outside modeler who wants to reproduce results from a Covasim publication. This modeler may begin by running the exact same simulation that the original modeler did. If they get a different result than the published one, this would make reproducing the results difficult. This test gives reason to believe that reproduction of results is possible, because that modeler has the ability to use the exact same series of random number draws that were used in the original publication.

During model development, this test would fail when something added to the model made draws against the random number table before the seed was set. In other words, this test found defects in regression.

4.2.2. Testing of variance

A good example of testing variance in the model is test_exposure_to_infectiousness_delay_deviation_scaling. While the title of this test is really long, the thing it is testing is very small. The feature under test is identified in the test case title. This test is examining the delay between when an individual becomes exposed to when they become infected. In other words, "how long after a person is exposed to their infection do they begin shedding virus?" Within that delay is a random draw from a probability distribution, and this test is meant to see that the standard deviation of that distribution is honored. Consider several standard deviations here:

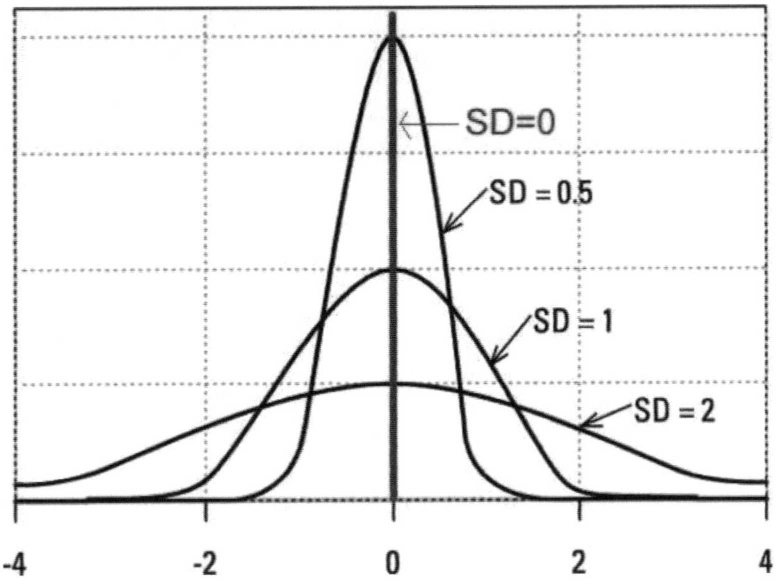

Figure 4: The effect of changing standard deviations on a normal distribution

As the standard deviation increases, the lowest and highest values in the distribution get farther from the mean, and the probability of the mean value decreases. So long as the mean of the distribution and the number of events (people who become infectious) remains the same, all of the cumulative values remain the same: mean period times the number of individuals.

In a realistic simulation, testing this feature is impossible, as discussed earlier (section 2.2). Basically, the information about any individual duration is lost in the noise of the other hundreds of infections reporting as cumulative numbers. This means that the configuration of this test will be very different from a realistic simulation.

A software tester can exercise their craft by configuring the simulation in a way that will illuminate the feature in question. In this case, the initial infected count (how many people are infected at the start of the simulation) is set to the number of agents (the total count of people in the simulation). This does several useful things. Firstly, it prevents any new infections from muddying the data, as there are no susceptible people. Secondly, it gives every single infection the very same start time, so every time a new person becomes infectious, we can tell how much time that took by subtracting the start time.

Consider a single individual, where we can express this as an equation:

Days for person X to become infectious = Day person X is infectious – Start day of simulation

With a simulation configured this way, what the test does is run a series of simulations with increasing standard deviations and stores three pieces of data:

- The first day any person became infectious
- The last day any person became infectious
- The highest number of people who became infectious on a single day

Consider the graph from Figure 4 again. As the standard deviation increases, the first day a person becomes infectious should be earlier. The last day a person becomes infectious should be later. And the number of people becoming infectious on the peak day should decrease, because the curve is flattening out (as the extremes spread farther, there are less people to change on the peak day).

Like the random number seed test, this test doesn't tell us anything really interesting about the science of COVID-19, it merely tells us that the parameter that controls the standard deviation seems to be working.

4.2.3. Testing of duration in the model

Building upon the previous test of variance, we have test_exposure_to_infectiousness_delay_scaling.

Look at the graph from Figure 4 once more. At the center of the graph, it shows that with a standard deviation of zero, the bell curve becomes a straight line, and every event should happen at the mean.

Having already shown that the variance is honored (with the previous test), we run a series of simulations where the standard deviation is zero, and we change the mean to several different days. Since the distribution tells us that all of the events must occur on the same day, the verification is simple. We look at the number of people who are infectious for each time in the simulation. If the current time is less than the mean, that number of people should be 0. If the current time is equal or greater than that time, the number of people should be equal to the whole population.

This is a strong prediction, and when the test confirms this prediction, it gives us a very strong result.

5. Results and Conclusions

5.1. Testing modeling software in a hurry

Earlier in this paper, I considered this question someone might ask about an infectious disease model:

Does this model correctly determine how long after becoming infected a person starts shedding virus?

Without the engineering effort to create voluminous logging, and the test automation effort to use powerful statistical tests and log parsing, we had to find a different way than we did for EMOD. Instead, for Covasim, we can now answer this question this way:

- The parameter that defines the standard deviation of the pre-shedding period is honored. We use relative validation (the results for standard deviation 3 are earlier, later, and broader than for 0, 1, or 2) for this.
- The parameter that defines the mean of the pre-shedding period is honored. We use absolute validation (with standard deviation of 0, and mean time of 13, every human in the simulation becomes infectious on day 13) for this.

Therefore: Whatever distribution of pre-shedding period the modeler specifies is what the modeler gets.

This reduces the concern of "Does this software accurately simulate the real world," because the question changes to "Does this software simulate the world that is specified by the user?" This becomes a question that can be answered through software testing.

5.2. Conclusions

A great deal of work was put into testing the Covasim model, but only part of that came from software engineering teams. One of the lessons learned here was one of humility. When testing specialized software, lean on your specialists to test things you cannot. Some of their methods will be unlike your own, and you need to allow them the space to apply those methods. As someone who writes automated tests, it is hard to wrap my head around "plot a graph and look at it" as a test methodology, but when the final deliverable is a graph that answers a question, having an expert looking at that graph and pondering it may be the most powerful tool in our toolbox.

The second lesson here is of confidence. As Jenny Bramble said, "anyone who has made their career in testing software is an expert in testing software," and that includes you. So even when working on highly specialized, highly sophisticated software solutions, there's always ground to cover from an engineering point of view. Can you install the software, can you uninstall it, and can you run existing examples?

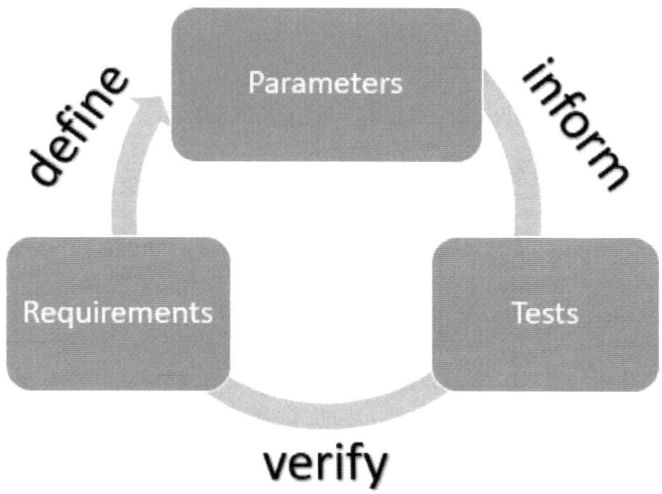

The last lesson is one of collaboration. In working on highly complex, highly specialized software, find some place where the Subject Matter Expert (SME) can tell you about where the knobs in the software are, how you can turn them, and how you should observe them working. For a mailto: link on a web page, you probably don't need any help, but for modeling contact tracing among school age children you probably do. In my case, that was the parameters dictionary that the SME was able to document in about an hour. This took very little effort on their part but was immensely useful for the work I did based on it. The researcher wrote requirements, which described the parameters. I consumed the parameters in tests, and then validated against the requirements.

If you can find this common ground with your SMEin and apply your expertise to the software parts of the problem, you can effectively test specialized software.

References

Anna Bershteyn, Jaline Gerardin, Daniel Bridenbecker, Christopher W Lorton, Jonathan Bloedow, Robert S Baker, Guillaume Chabot-Couture, Ye Chen, Thomas Fischle, Kurt Frey, Jillian S Gauld, Hao Hu, Amanda S Izzo, Daniel J Klein, Dejan Lukacevic, Kevin A McCarthy, Joel C Miller, Andre Lin Ouedraogo, T Alex Perkins, Jeffrey Steinkraus, Quirine A ten Bosch, Hung-Fu Ting, Svetlana Titova, Bradley G Wagner, Philip A Welkhoff, Edward A Wenger, Christian N Wiswell, for the Institute for Disease Modeling, "Implementation and applications of EMOD, an individual-based multi-disease modeling platform" Pathogens and Disease, Volume 76, Issue 5, July 2018, fty059, https://doi.org/10.1093/femspd/fty059

Fok, Luis "What is the shape of normal distribution when standard deviation is least?"
https://www.quora.com/What-is-the-shape-of-normal-distribution-when-standard-deviation-is-least
(accessed August 20, 2020).

Bramble, Jenny "Building Automation Engineers from Scratch"
http://uploads.pnsqc.org/2019/papers/Bramble-Building-Automation-Engineers-From-Scratch.pdf
(accessed August 20, 2020)

The more powerful statistical tests mentioned in section 2 are available in the SciPy library for python and are listed here https://docs.scipy.org/doc/scipy/reference/stats.html#statistical-tests
(accessed August 24, 2020)

- Komolgorov-Smirnov test https://docs.scipy.org/doc/scipy-0.14.0/reference/generated/scipy.stats.kstest.html (accessed September 04, 2020)
- Anderson-Darling test https://docs.scipy.org/doc/scipy/reference/generated/scipy.stats.anderson.html (accessed September 04, 2020)

For more information about the Institute for Disease Modeling, see https://idmod.org/

For more on the Scipy library, see the following paper

Pauli Virtanen, Ralf Gommers, Travis E. Oliphant, Matt Haberland, Tyler Reddy, David Cournapeau, Evgeni Burovski, Pearu Peterson, Warren Weckesser, Jonathan Bright, Stéfan J. van der Walt, Matthew Brett, Joshua Wilson, K. Jarrod Millman, Nikolay Mayorov, Andrew R. J. Nelson, Eric Jones, Robert Kern, Eric Larson, CJ Carey, İlhan Polat, Yu Feng, Eric W. Moore, Jake VanderPlas, Denis Laxalde, Josef Perktold, Robert Cimrman, Ian Henriksen, E.A. Quintero, Charles R Harris, Anne M. Archibald, Antônio H. Ribeiro, Fabian Pedregosa, Paul van Mulbregt, and SciPy 1.0 Contributors. (2020) **SciPy 1.0: Fundamental Algorithms for Scientific Computing in Python**. *Nature Methods,* in press.

Teaching testing to programmers. What sticks, and what slides off? A journey from Teflon to Velcro.

Robert Sabourin
robsab@gmail.com

Mónica Wodzislawski
mwodzis@ces.com.uy

Abstract

Rob Sabourin and Mónica Wodzislawski share many decades of experience with teaching software testing concepts to programmers.

There is a lot of interest in teaching programming skills to testers (Hendrickson, 2010), (van Delft, 2017), but Rob and Monica suggest that it is even more important to teach testing skills to programmers. Corporate initiatives to "shift left" and development "test-driven" approaches are only effective if a skilled programmer is also a skilled tester.

Biography

Rob Sabourin has more than thirty-eight years of management experience leading teams of software development professionals. A highly respected member of the software engineering community, Rob has managed, trained, mentored, and coached hundreds of top professionals in the field. He frequently speaks at conferences and writes on software engineering, SQA, testing, management, and internationalization. Rob authored I am a Bug!, the popular software testing children's book; works as an adjunct professor of software engineering at McGill University; and serves as the principal consultant (and president/janitor) of AmiBug.Com, Inc. Contact Rob at robsab@gmail.com.

Mónica Wodzislawski is an International Consultant in Software Quality and Testing with over twenty-five years of experience in IT. As a software testing pioneer in Uruguay, she has contributed to building a large environment for software testing, both, in industry and academia, with the motto: "test to learn and learn to test." She is responsible for the first fully-online Testing Career (3 years in its complete version) in Spanish offered by the Centro de Ensayos de Software. Mónica has been a speaker at several international conferences. She is also a professor of Software Engineering in the CS Department within the School of Engineering at Universidad de la República.

1. Introduction

This paper will describe several different approaches used by the authors to teach developers about the design and implementation of unit tests.

Training methods explored include test validation training for software engineering undergraduates, onsite short courses in specific unit testing approaches, tools centric training, onsite short courses blending test design, and behavior-driven development as well as online training for short training tutorials versus online training for degree programs.

Custom training based on skill assessment and task analysis will be contrasted with generic courses.

We will compare the training outlines and teaching approaches (target audience, activities, exercises, and grading approaches) applied as well as provide some anecdotal reports of positive and negative outcomes.

The lessons learned may be interesting to organizations and development professionals seeking to identify methods to apply testing skills early in development activities.

2. Big Bang Lecture

Robert Sabourin was approached by SecCo, a digital signature software development company, to teach their team of over 200 programmers how to develop unit tests. The ½ day training was delivered to all the developers at the same time. A show and tell approach was requested. A cheat sheet was provided to participants.

To implement the on-site lecture, Robert prepared coded examples for each test design technique demonstrated. Robert hired contract programmers familiar with the programming language, and technology stack, to prepare the examples. Each example was expressed in a short document, including:

- Test objective
- Visual model
- Design decisions and tradeoffs
- Unit test code
- Assertion code
- Screenshots of test running in the target IDE

The test design approaches were a blend of black box, white box, and non-functional testing, including static analysis and dynamic analysis.

Test design techniques included in the lecture were:

- Variable identification
- Domain analysis
- Equivalence classes
- Boundary testing
- Decision tables
- Control flow path analysis
- Story Boards
- Combinatorics
- Pairwise techniques
- Failure mode analysis
- Performance
- Stress
- Static analysis including inspections, reviews and use of static analysis tools
- Dynamic analysis including CPU, Memory, and Network access
- Code coverage-based techniques
    - Statement

    - Branch
    - Decision
    - Basis paths
- Creative approaches
    - Lateral thinking
    - Mind mapping
    - Heuristic models
    - Taxonomies
- Risk-based approaches

Note that readers can reference Lee Copeland's book "A Practitioners Guide to Test Design" (Copeland, 2008) to learn more about these techniques.

A single leaf cheat sheet was prepared using legal-size paper printed on both sides. Gold colored professional laminated paper was used. This sheet was expected to be a permanent fixture of the programmer's desktop.

The lecture included an explanation of the theory and demonstration with examples. Delegates were not given the opportunity to apply techniques; however, they did get a chance to see examples worked through in their familiar technology stacks.

Although the course was well-received, there was no feedback mechanism put in place to see if delegates had retained important aspects of unit test implementation. Questions raised seemed to focus on the time efficiency of unit testing. Developers suggested that designing unit tests would add a step and slow down programming, contradicting management directives to speed up programming. Several developers raised questions which suggested that independent testers did not seem to use systematic test design approaches. There were also concerns that unit testing would be redundant to testing done by others.

The developers also expressed an interest in the mechanics of technology stack specific testing, including asserts and mocking.

3. On-Site Small Group Class

Robert Sabourin developed and delivered a course entitled "Task-Oriented Unit Testing." It was delivered as a two-day on-site programmer training course.

"Task-Oriented Unit Testing" emphasized that programmers' testing has to do with ensuring they have completed the task at hand. Programmers often manipulate and create several objects, methods, classes, procedures, functions, algorithms, and data schemas. This course teaches programmers the type of testing activities that naturally fit into their assigned tasks and are used to ensure programmers have achieved "done."

Table 1. Two Day Course Content

Topic	Class Time	Exercise
Test Theory, History and Philosophy	30 minutes	Group discussion
Testing in SDLC	30 minutes	Group discussion
Test Economics	30 minutes	Group discussion
Unit Test After	60 minutes	Programming example and exercise
Unit Test-Driven	90 minutes	Programming example and exercise
Mocking & Stubs	30 minutes	Walkthrough
Unit Test Ideas	90 minutes	Exercise
Variables	30 minutes	Exercise
Domain	30 minutes	Exercise
Scenarios	30 minutes	Exercise
Story Tests	30 minutes	Exercise
Control Flow	40 minutes	Exercise
Business Logic	40 minutes	Exercise
Combinations	40 minutes	Exercise
Failure Modes	30 minutes	Walkthrough
Code Coverage	30 minutes	Walkthrough
Other Coverage	30 minutes	Walkthrough
Risks and rewards	30 minutes	Group Discussion
Total	720 minutes	12 hours

"Task-Oriented Unit Testing" has been offered over twenty years in either an on-site or public form. In the public form, programming activities are simulated by constructing flow charts using Velcro and laminated index cards. In the on-site form, programming activities are implemented using specially constructed examples using the developer's IDE and programming language. Class engagement is higher when developers are allowed to complete programming exercises in their IDE. Although for public courses, we also see the same level of engagement in the Velcro and index card exercises.

On-site groups are often competitive and tend to compete to come up with the cleanest solution in the least amount of effort.

A common question delegates raise is, "when should each test design approach be used?"

Although there have been systematic attempts to collect feedback about which practices have continued to be used after the training, the evidence collected is anecdotal.

One customer used the concept of Unit Test Ideas as the first step in programming for over ten years. This customer was a group of software developers that implemented transactional software for a major life insurance company. Projects were similar, and the group used agile methods like Scrum.

Several customers identified the continued use of heuristic models to support domain analysis.

Many programmers have adapted pairwise testing to their unit testing workflow. Pairwise approaches are popular for creating different configurations of AWS images and then launching them as part of test environments during continuous integration.

Development teams in regulated environments find failure mode test design as being especially useful.

Delegates have highlighted that this course does not teach specifics of Unit Test Tools, Assert Libraries, or Technology Stack Specific tools. Even though the course was developed as tool-agnostic, programmers express a strong desire to have training specific to their IDE and associated tools.

4. Agile Team Course with Coaching

A major American Corporation, the client, engaged Robert Sabourin to adapt and deliver a customized version of "Task-Oriented Unit Testing".

The client had a small number of Scrum teams interested in improving the quality of deliverables by reducing bug escapes to production. The teams were comprised of 5 to 7 programmers, a Scrum Master, and between 1 and 3 domain experts supporting requirement analysis, software testing, and end user documentation tasks.

The client wanted to reduce rework required after the software was deployed. The client had a support system and gathered detailed metrics about the cost of operational downtime impacted by field-discovered defects. Agile teams also collected metrics summarizing the cost of repairing field-discovered defects during a subsequent sprint.

Executive management at the client was also interested in the "Shift-Left Testing" (Smith 2001, 62) movement and felt encouraged to move testing activities as close as possible to development activities.

Since the course "Task-Oriented Unit Testing" was primarily designed to teach testing skills to programmers, it was considered a natural fit for some of the client's training needs.

The client required a custom version of the course with the following characteristics.

- Delivery would be to one Scrum team at a time.
- All examples and exercises would need to be done in the technology stack of the Scrum team.
- The entire team, including the Product Owner and the Scrum Master, would attend the training.
- The basic course would be delivered in two days on-site.
- For two weeks after the course was delivered, two instructors would remain on-site and available to meet with delegates privately or in small groups to offer coaching and guidance in the implementation of the skills taught in the class.
- Each group would share examples from their product and sprint backlogs with the instructor to support the preparation of customer examples and exercises.
- Terminology and concepts should match corporate programming policies and practice standards as much as possible.

It should be noted that all preparation work for the course and post-course coaching were charged to the client at agreed-upon consulting rates. This amount was budgeted into the training costs before the course. Negotiation was with a group focused on improving development practice at the client. Stakeholders were savvy regarding software engineering, testing, and agile development practices. At all other on-site examples, the negotiation was with training stakeholders who generally balked at developing custom examples and exercises in favor of generic examples.

Scrum masters and product owners actively participated in the training and paired with other team members during programming exercises.

In each team, programmers were experts in their technology stacks but were not familiar with software test design approaches. The programmers were familiar with the unit test tools available with their Integrated Development Environment (IDE) and the use of Mocking Tools at their disposal.

The flow of the course is illustrated in the following table.

Table 2. Agile Team Course with Coaching

Topic	Class Time	Exercise
Test Theory, History and Philosophy	30 minutes	Group discussion
Unit Test-Driven	*90 minutes*	*Programming example and exercise*
Mocking & Stubs	60 minutes	Programming example and exercise
Grooming Stories	*30 minutes*	*Walkthrough*
Story Tests	*30 minutes*	*Exercise*
Agile Planning	*30 minutes*	*Walkthrough*
Unit Test Ideas	90 minutes	Exercise
Variables	30 minutes	Exercise
Domain	30 minutes	Exercise
Scenarios	30 minutes	Exercise
Control Flow	40 minutes	Exercise
Business Logic	40 minutes	Exercise
Combinations	40 minutes	Exercise
Failure Modes	30 minutes	Walkthrough
Code Coverage	30 minutes	Walkthrough
Other Coverage	30 minutes	Walkthrough
Retrospective	*60 minutes*	*Group Discussion*
Total	720 minutes	12 hours

Note text in italics refers to elements of the training specific to the customer's agile lifecycle model. The generic course described above in Table 2 applied to many different lifecycles.

After each exercise, the Scrum Master facilitated a miniature lesson learned team session and took detailed notes of elements directly applicable to the team's self-organized workflow.

At the end of the course, Robert was invited to attend the team's 60-minute course retrospective meeting. During the retrospective, they agreed on how to implement some of the lessons learned in the next sprint. For the first sprint, they decided to have a unit test brainstorming session as part of sprint planning. The team also decided on how scenario-based and combinations-based test design could be implemented immediately. Other test design approaches would be introduced if they were relevant to the technical work being implemented.

Robert was able to follow up with each team participating in the training. He found that several ideas were sticking but that the specific ideas depended on the team. Because they build retrospectives into the training and decided to change their self-organized process, and because the team and Scrum Master followed up, no ideas were dropped prematurely.

During coaching sessions, most team members chose to share large legacy code segments that they wanted to retrofit with well-designed tests. The topic of retrofitting unit tests into existing legacy code was not in any of the course outlines, but it came up in almost 100% of the coaching sessions. This may be biased since Robert asked delegates to bring code samples to the coaching sessions, and thus the legacy code samples arrived in abundance.

5. Agile Team – Example-Driven Development - Coupled with Generic Test Design

Robert Sabourin prepared and delivered the second half of a custom four-day course as two back-to-back two-day courses. Days one and two cover test design topics. Days three and four go over how test design fits into example-driven development. This includes test-driven, acceptance test-driven, and behavior-driven approaches.

The test design section of the course shares a series of exercises with the example-driven development section.

The exercises are based on a fictitious Lego® Parts Warehouse Management System.

> *Lego® Part Warehouse Manager*
>
> *Overview*
>
> *As gracefully described by Wikipedia: "...Lego, consists of colorful interlocking plastic bricks accompanying an array of gears, figurines called minifigures, and various other parts. Lego pieces can be assembled and connected in many ways to construct objects including vehicles, buildings, and working robots. Anything constructed can then be taken apart again, and the pieces used to make other objects..." (Lego, 2020)*
>
> *The Lego® Part Warehouse Manager is a software system used to coordinate storage and retrieval of Lego® components.*
>
> *The Lego® Part Warehouse Manager allows customers to acquire a wide variety of Lego® components for use in constructing Lego® models.*

The Lego® Part Warehouse Manager is operated by independent resellers of used Lego® components. The Lego® Part Warehouse Manager is not affiliated with The Lego Group. The Lego® Part Warehouse Manager software system is implemented as a series of processes which manage receiving parts, shipping parts and inventory management. User Stories and Acceptance Tests describe the behavior of the Lego® Part Warehouse Manager software system. Six user types are defined: Operator, Inventory Manager, System Administrator, Auditor, Warehouse Picker and Consumer. Over fifty user stories are defined to describe the Lego® Part Warehouse Manager.

During the test design section, each design approach is applied to elements of the Lego® Part Warehouse Manager.

During the example-driven development section, the test designs developed for the Lego® Part Warehouse Manager are implemented as Gherkin Scripts. (Wynne, 2012)

Different instructors were used for the two sections of the course.

Table 3. Agile Team Course with Coaching

Topic	Class Time	Exercise
Story Construction	60 minutes	Walkthrough example, small group exercise to define domain-specific user stories
Acceptance Criteria	60 minutes	Walkthrough example, small group exercise to define domain-specific acceptance tests
Gap Analysis	60 minutes	Perform gap analysis on domain-specific user story
Example Mapping	40 minutes	Perform example mapping on domain-specific user story
Complex Requirements	40 minutes	Define workflow for domain-specific user story
Path Analysis	40 minutes	Apply path analysis to domain-specific workflow
Personas	40 minutes	Define personas for domain-specific requirements
Continuous Integration	40 minutes	Walkthrough examples
Automating story tests	40 minutes	Walkthrough examples
Create Gherkin Scripts	60 minutes	Exercise based on acceptance tests defined earlier
Test Design Exercises with Lego® Part Warehouse Manager	120 minutes	Apply exercise results from Day one and Day two
Apply methods of choice to domain-specific problems	120 minutes	Apply any relevant test design approach to domain-specific problem
Total	720 minutes	12 hours

Developers pick up a lot of test design techniques in this course. Follow up was possible through on-site agile coaches hired to guide teams and help them apply methods covered in the test design training.

Feedback from on-site agile coaches, managers, and delegates suggested that the domain analysis, equivalence partitioning, and combinatoric test design techniques are used frequently. Gherkin is also used frequently. (Wynne 2001) Other test design techniques are used occasionally.

Developers requested that more programming exercises be added to the course material.

Developers requested more guidance around which testing problems are resolved by different test design techniques.

6. Undergraduate Case Study Single Semester Course

Since 1999, Robert Sabourin has been an adjunct professor of software engineering at McGill University. Robert developed the course "ECSE 429 – Software Validation," which is a mandatory undergraduate course. All Software Engineering Undergraduate students are required to pass Software Validation.

The following is a topical outline of "ECSE 429 – Software Validation".

Principles of Software Testing	Business Risks
History of Software Testing	Prioritization
Some Philosophies of Software Testing	Bug Advocacy
Quality	Test Workflow
Types of testing	Non-Functional Testing
Testing in different lifecycle models	Technology Specific Testing
Testing types based on when	Test automation
Testing types based on how	Test Design Black, White & Grey Box Techniques
Context factors	Taxonomies
Schools of Software Testing	Types of Test Ideas
Standards and Practices of Software Testing	Capabilities
Current Controversies of Software Testing	Failure Modes
Notions of test coverage and completeness	Quality factors
Notions of levels of testing	Usage Scenarios
Static testing techniques	Cross-Functional Testing
Walkthroughs	Environment Testing
Reviews	Unit Testing
Inspections	Integration Testing
Buddy checks	System Testing
Static analysis techniques	Live Testing
Test Planning	Model-Based Testing
Project Risks	Regulated Testing
Product Risks	Mutation Testing
Technical Risks	Fuzz Testing

Robert Sabourin and Ross Collard developed a System Performance Testing Study Guide for Undergraduate Software Testing Students based on the Commercial Case Study. The study guide was used in teaching System Performance Testing as part of the undergraduate Software Engineering course "ECSE 429 – Software Validation".

The "Performance Testing Case Study" (Collard, 2006) was originally designed to help mid-level professionals develop an understanding of a realistic performance-testing project relating to an Online Testing Book Club. The case study was designed to teach professionals about performance testing. The Performance Testing Case Study directs students to identify and analyze performance testing and develop a test strategy for the performance testing situation. Students learned how to predict whether the system under test is likely to perform in an acceptable manner when it eventually goes live.

The case study includes a structured series of questions that students use to guide the development of test strategy, focus of testing objectives, performance testing requirements, data collection, modeling, and testing approach. The first section of the case study focuses on the purpose of the testing. Students learn the relationship of business objectives to performance testing and how to identify which business objectives can be addressed in a performance-testing project. Students also learn to identify which data could be measured to evaluate the system performance to see if the objectives could be met.

An experienced professional is expected to take approximately 10 hours to complete the performance testing exercises. Mid-level professionals are expected to complete as many case study questions as they can as a homework assignment before the start of a tutorial about the subject. During the subsequent tutorial, the mid-level professional reviews tutorial sections and additional questions as part of small group exercises.

In a tutorial context, the case study was used not just to teach the concepts of performance testing but to encourage the type of critical thinking required to actively succeed in testing projects in general.

There is no way to determine which concepts stick like Velcro and which concepts slide off like Teflon. It was clear that students appreciated the value of learning through a realistic and comprehensive case study.

Case study-based instructor-led training presents an opportunity to teach many concepts realistically. Robert Sabourin has prepared several similar case studies, each of which teach different software testing concepts. The combinations case study teaches the value and practical implementation of pairwise combinations testing on a real high stakes project. The acceptance testing case study is a sanitized case study of acceptance tests done to accept critical security software on desktop systems in regulated environments.

7. Testing for Developers

Since 2009 Mónica Wodzislawski and her group from CES (Centro de Ensayos de Software - Center of Software Testing) have taught testing to developers, as reported in the Conference for the Association of Software Testers (CAST) 2010 light talks. This course becomes increasingly important with the imposition of agile methodologies.

As testing service providers, they detected two phenomena:

- Applications of poor quality prevent us from finding the most interesting, severe bugs.
- There is a lack of knowledge about the wide range of testing activities and possibilities.

CES decided to promote a shared commitment towards quality, teaching how to permeate the development process activities with testing, including its insights, strategies, techniques, and tools. It contains not only unit and integration testing but testing culture elements.

Table 4. Testing for Developers Course

Topic	Class Time	Exercise
Introduction to testing concepts and testability	180 minutes	Brainstorming about quality, bugs and errors, testing, stakeholders
Testing in development processes: Testing Pyramid and antipatterns	90 minutes	Define how they articulate testing activities through their process or methodology
Test case design techniques, variable identification	60 minutes	Define how they are used to test
Equivalence classes and limit values	60 minutes	Exercises
Decision Tables and Trees	90 minutes	Exercises
State Machines	90 minutes	Exercises
Test automation concepts	30 minutes	Brainstorming
Continuous Integration	30 minutes	Walkthrough examples
Unit tests automation (XUnit)	180 minutes	Exercises
Integration and Web Services tests (Soapui, Postman)	180 minutes	Exercises
GUI system tests automation (Selenium)	180 minutes	Exercises
Performance in Development	30 minutes	Identify common problems
Unit tests considering performance	60 minutes	Applying tools to real examples
Performance patterns and anti-patterns	90 minutes	Identify adequate and wrong practices
Evaluation and discussion	90 minutes	Improvements path
Total	1440 minutes	24 hours

Mónica has taught several instances (more than 12) of this course at different organizations and companies, sometimes to mixed groups, others on site, to a single development department.

It is worth noting several topics that have emerged from these instances.

Establishing quality objectives from the very beginning of an information technology (IT) project contributes to building better products and guiding the testing activities. As does discussing the risks throughout the project. We can see this topic as preventive testing or building quality software products, as a student once pointed out.

The errors made by the students when developing software are raised and discussed, trying to identify their causes. This is a useful foundation for building the structure of the course and elaborating on effective checklists for their work. In the last class, students sketch an improvement path for each person and/or organization.

Testability issues weave a tight web between programming and testing. Developers visualize which elements are worth monitoring, and testers detect incidents more efficiently. Both become aware of each other's concerns.

Developers realize how useful it could be to specify models for test case design before coding, preventing them from making many of the most common mistakes.

Part of this course - GUI system tests automation and Performance in Development - was also held at small and medium-sized companies in Uruguay and Mexico. At these companies, the performance patterns and anti-patterns examination was well-received. Clinic style walkthrough of many well-known problems and solutions designed to open and enrich attendees' participation. Automation patterns were also well-received. (Rasmussen, Jonathan, 2016)

Nowadays, CES has a new demand for this course to be online, with the main objective of guaranteeing a technically well-founded path towards DevOps. (Duvall, Paul, 2007)

8. Undergraduate Programming and Testing Courses

Mónica Wodzislawski also teaches testing at the CS Department within the School of Engineering at Universidad de la República, Uruguay.

The Computer Science Degree has several consecutive programming courses. She contributed to introduce testing starting on the second course. She promoted to dedicate one theoretical class to explain overall testing concepts and taxonomy, as well as to discuss the most common programmers´ mistakes. The course follows this outline:

- Balance between cost, time, scope, and quality when building a piece of software (Beck, Kent, 2000)
- Preventive testing, this concept is present in other disciplines (medicine, law) and is well suited for building software. (Hopkins, John, 2020)
- Edsger W. Dijkstra's quote: "Program testing can be used to show the presence of bugs, but never to show their absence!" (Dijkstra, Edsger, 1969)
    - Programming styles, simplicity, and elegance
- Preliminary classification
    - Unit tests using course examples
        - Homework includes two unit test cases on the course page
        - Coverage of sentences and complex conditions
        - Benefits and vulnerabilities
- Integration tests
    - The whole is not the sum of the parts (real-life analogies), so validate that the tested modules work together
- System tests
- Most common mistakes
    - Ask students what mistakes they make
    - Write some on the board
    - Present slide of common developer mistakes
- Introduction to test cases design
    - Variable identification, equivalence classes, limit values
    - Selection criteria: as many valid cases as possible, one test case every suspected invalid.

The practical exercise that accompanies the course´s mandatory task is to design and add test cases that verify and validate the students´ solutions.

- Cases that exercise at least what is assumed to work. (By assuming what is being done is facilitating the work, you must control less, but something always remains to be controlled)
- Cases that check error conditions

8.1. Post Your Test Case! Build Quality Collectively!

Students upload the test cases to a common repository. Code sharing is not allowed, but students have the great advantage of being able to share test cases, which will help them to find errors that others imagined or detected in their programs. They can perceive and enjoy that building software is a collaborative process.

Mónica is responsible for the 8th semester´s elective "Software Verification and Validation Workshop" that has been required since 2008.

The vast majority of students are already working as programmers and choose this workshop to complement their testing knowledge, to help them build better quality software.

The workshop topical outline includes Functional Testing, Testing Automation, and Performance testing, with a theoretical and practical approach.

- Introduction: workshop presentation and testing overall concepts
  - Software quality
  - Mistake, defect, fault
  - Software testing definition and types
  - Testing's coverage in extension and depth
- Testing Strategies and techniques: Study and apply the most used approaches:
  - Scripted testing
    - Equivalence classes and categories partitions
    - Limit values
    - Decision tables and trees
    - Pairs combination
    - State Machines
    - Test cases derived from User Stories, Use Cases or CRUD
  - Exploratory Testing
    - Session-based
    - Mind mapping
    - Charter
- Unit Testing: white box testing review, Xunit tools for automated unit testing
  - Static Verification
  - Dynamic verification
  - Black and White box testing review
  - Xunit, Junit
  - Code Coverage
  - Good practices
- Automated testing: Methodology and tools for other layers automation
  - Testing pyramid
  - Web services and API testing

- GUI and end-to-end automated testing
    - Selenium WebDriver
- Performance testing: Methodology and tools for planning and executing this type of test
  - Overall concepts
  - Apply methods from real-world case studies
  - Jmeter
- Testing management: Testing activities and processes, monitoring and evaluation
  - Testing in different software development models
  - Testing in agile methodologies

In addition to solving exercises related to each topic, the evaluation method includes mandatory tasks consisting of applying different types of manual and automated testing, preferably to real software products.

It is rewarding to mention that several workshop students become so interested in software testing that they have picked this subject for their graduation projects (grade thesis). Some examples:

- "Test School" a tool for teaching testing
- "TEGMA" - Exploratory testing and its management in agile methodologies
- Building a continuous integration and testing framework

9. Postgraduate and Professional Testing Courses

The Performance Testing Workshop is part of the Software Engineering Specialization offered by the Postgraduate and Professional Update Centre (CPAP) at the CS Department within the School of Engineering at Universidad de la República, Uruguay.

Its main objectives are that attendees might reflect on the need to perform performance tests, incorporate the related concepts and methodologies, delve into performance testing strategies and techniques, and take the knowledge and learn to apply different tools and manage performance testing projects.

The workshop's content outline includes:

- Course presentation and Introduction
- Performance testing overview
- Types of Performance Testing
- Architectures and Performance Testing
- Performance Test Stages
  - Requirements Analysis
  - Test Automation (tools)
  - Test environment setup
  - Test Execution and Results Analysis
- Performance Patterns and Anti-patterns
- Single user load testing
- The team
- Performance Clinic

The evaluation method consists of a final task based on a real case study.

The attendee's groups are heterogeneous because there are postgraduate young students and professionals with different expectations. As such, the final task evolved from planning and executing a performance test to identifying performance test needs, explaining the corresponding performance testing plan, and defending it with solid arguments.

10. Testing in Agile Methodologies

There are many courses and coaching about Agile methodologies, but very few cover the importance of software testing to succeed. Mónica Wodzislawski prepared and dictated this online course to help Uruguayan testers and companies overcome this deficiency.

She describes the essential concepts of Agile methodologies and testing activities in the context of integration, testing, delivery, and continuous installation of quality software products.

- Introduction
  - Brief history and essence of Agile methodologies
  - Scrum, EXtreme Programming, Kanban, Lean
  - Continuous integration
  - Continuous testing
  - Continuous delivery and deploy, DevOps

- Testing in agile context
  - Agile testing quadrant in different versions
  - Automation pyramid
  - Agile requirements and testing
    - User Stories and acceptance criteria
    - BDD, TDD, ATDD
  - Exploratory testing

- Agile Testing, Team, Roles
  - Agile testing activities
  - Collaboration between developers and testers
  - Presentation and discussion of real experiences

- Agile Testing Management
  - Planning and estimation
  - Deal with
    - An iteration (sprint)
    - Multiple iterations (sprints) (Agile Project)
    - Multiple teams and products (Agile Project Portfolio)
  - Agile fluency model

The evaluation method consists of exercises related to each topic, and a final work about students' experiences and testing improvement proposals for their teams and companies.

The exercise related to topic "Testing in agile context", for example, is to install Cucumber and apply BDD to several user stories. Another interesting exercise, according to Mónica, is to elaborate a comparative study about values, principles, and practices of different agile methodologies, for the students to perceive similarities and differences. It is not easy to map them in a meaningful way without understanding the intrinsic value.

11. Concluding Remarks

The authors have identified ten risk factors, in which concepts do not stick, like Teflon, which may be helpful if avoided when teaching test design techniques to programmers.

1. Avoid the exclusive use of paper and pencil exercises. Although some paper and pencil exercises are effective, especially in test idea generation, programmers prefer to have exercises that involve some degree of programming work.
2. Avoid heterogeneous groups from the point of view of the technology used in software development. Diverse programming tools, development environments, programming languages, unit tests and mocking frameworks and solution architectures direct a lot of questions to discussions of how different things are implemented in different technology stacks rather than how test design should be implemented.
3. Avoid heterogeneous groups from the point of view of the life cycle model used in software development (SDLC). Diverse SDLCs direct a lot of questions to discussions of how different things are implemented in different SDLCs rather than how test design fits in the development process. Debates often break out about the pros and cons of Agile versus Planned SDLCs.
4. Avoid having programmers wait for exercises to complete. Include many additional optional steps to keep the faster programmers engaged while waiting for the slower programmers to catch up.
5. Avoid exclusive use of trivial examples. Developers want to see how complicated testing problems are solved with one or more techniques. Build on examples as new techniques are taught.
6. Avoid code coverage models that distract programmers from risk-focused testing. Code coverage models help developers identify what they did not test but do not tell developers that the code they did test works. Many bugs fixed by programmers require adding code that was missing and therefore, could not be reflected in any code coverage models. Code coverage-based testing exercises the existing code
7. Avoid "how to use a specific tool" centric courses.
8. Avoid teaching with template filling approaches.
9. Avoid exclusively teaching how to test "code," consider non-functional testing such as Usability, Accessibility, Security, Power Consumption, and many others.
10. Avoid overemphasis on regression test automation. Some programmers feel this is the only type of developer testing needed.

The authors have identified ten success factors that stick like Velcro, which may be helpful in teaching test design techniques to programmers.

1. Include plenty of test-related programming exercises. Programmers like to program.
2. Teach developers to brainstorm a large list of relevant test ideas before they start coding a story. They should learn to identify the most important ideas.
3. Teach fundamental testing techniques but share examples of how they apply to complex problems. Ensure the examples are real.
4. Since testing is intractable, teach programmers to use models of risk to help decide the scope and depth of testing. They must learn to decide what to test, how deep to test, and what not to test.
5. Show examples to the developers of the bugs detected in production, which could have been avoided with an automated unit test case. This helps them to appreciate their value.

6. Encourage developers to discuss and set quality goals for the software product they will build and to pursue the most appropriate standards or guides in the context (e.g. OWASP, if security is the goal). The awareness of quality objectives helps risk identification and mitigation.
7. Teach how to use the different tools but with a conceptual approach to the topics. If the tools are there today and not tomorrow, the knowledge that supports them remains.
8. Patterns and antipatterns are important topics for developers to learn good practices, especially for automatization and performance problems recognition.
9. Share with programmers the most common faults, problems, and their solutions you met in your professional life, in a Clinic style presentation: symptoms, diagnosis, treatment. They will appreciate it and learn to identify these risks in their own context.
10. Expose programmers to detailed case studies emphasizing how project context, business, technical, organizational, and cultural factors influence testing techniques.

12. Acknowledgments

The authors wish to thank the thousands of students who have participated in their test training courses over the past several decades.

References

1. Myers, et al. The Art of Software Testing. John Wiley & Sons, 2012.
2. Kaner, Cem, and James Bach. Lessons Learned in Software Testing. Wiley, 2001
3. Pólya, George. How to Solve It: A New Aspect of Mathematical Method. Doubleday, 1957.
4. Tarlinder, Alexander. Developer Testing Building Quality into Software. Addison-Wesley, 2017.
5. Sommerville, Ian. Engineering Software Products. Pearson Education, Inc., 2020.
6. Wellington, C., and G. Wellington. A Developer's Approach to Learning Java. CreateSpace, 2017.
7. Miller, E., and W. Howden. Tutorial, Software Testing & Validation Techniques. IEEE Computer, 1981.
8. Copeland, Lee. A Practitioner's Guide to Software Test Design. Artech House, 2008.
9. Smith, Larry (September 2001). "Shift-Left Testing". Dr. Dobb's Journal. 26 (9): 56, 62.
10. Koskela, Lasse. Effective Unit Testing: A Guide for Java Developers. Manning, 2013.
11. Feathers, Michael C. Working Effectively with Legacy Code. Prentice Hall PTR, 2013.
12. Collard, R. Performance Testing Case Study. Collard and Company, 2006.
13. Sabourin, R. Charting the Course Coming Up with Great Test Ideas Just in Time. AmiBug, 2020.
14. Beck, Kent. Test Driven Development. Pearson Education (US), 2002.
15. Beck, Kent. Test-Driven Development by Example. Addison-Wesley, 2014.
16. Bowman, Sharon L. Training from the Back of the Room. Wiley, 2009.
17. Kernighan, Brian W., and Dennis M. Ritchie. The C Programming Language. Pearson, 2015.
18. Hendrickson, Elisabeth. “Do Testers Have to Write Code?” Test Obsessed, 20 Oct. 2010, www.testobsessed.com/2010/10/testers-code/ (accessed 2020-06-27)
19. van Delft, Nathalie. “The End of the Testing World as We Know It.” Capgemini Worldwide, Capgemini, 30 Oct. 2017, www.capgemini.com/2017/06/the-end-of-the-testing-world-as-we-know-it/ (accessed 2020-06-27)
20. Hamming, Richard R. Art of Doing Science and Engineering Learning to Learn. CRC Press, 2014.
21. Rungta, Krishna. “Model Based Testing Tutorial: What Is, Tools & Example.” Guru99, www.guru99.com/model-based-testing-tutorial.html#2 (accessed 2020-06-27)
22. Rasmussen, Jonathan, The way of the Web Tester, Susanah Pfalzer, 2016.
23. Duvall, Paul, Steve Matyas, Andrew Glover, Continuous integration, Addison-Wesley, 2007.
24. Beck, Kent, Martin Fowler, Planning Extreme Programming, Addison-Wesley Professional, 2000.
25. Mike Cohn, Succeeding with Agile: Software Development Using Scrum, Addison-Wesley, 2009.
26. Lego, Wikipedia entry, https://en.wikipedia.org/wiki/Lego (accessed 2020-06-27)
27. Wynne, Matt 2012. Aslak Hellesoy, The Cucumber Book, Pragmatic.

28. Hopkins, John, “Screening Tests for Common Diseases.”, https://www.hopkinsmedicine.org/health/treatment-tests-and-therapies/screening-tests-for-common-diseases (accessed 2020-07-14)
29. Dijkstra, Edsger, “Programming methodologies, their objectives and their nature.” 1969

Quality-Focused Software Testing in Critical Infrastructure

Zoë Oens, Schweitzer Engineering Laboratories, Inc.

zoe_oens@selinc.com

Abstract

When testing software, it is typical to hear that 100 percent coverage is unachievable. What happens, then, when we are asked to provide 100 percent? If the software being tested is used in critical infrastructure (e.g., power systems, water, medical, or banking), then an escaped bug is not a trivial thing. The quality of critical infrastructure software needs to have as close to 100 percent coverage as possible. This is not easy to achieve. It is even more difficult to achieve in a time-effective manner. This paper tackles the dilemma of building quality without exceeding a schedule and budget when it comes to critical infrastructure.

Biography

Zoë Oens graduated from Eastern Washington University in 2014 where she studied electrical engineering. She joined Schweitzer Engineering Laboratories, Inc. (SEL) that same year as a manufacturing test engineer. After a year and a half, she transferred to the research and development division as a firmware test engineer, where she has applied her knowledge of quality-focused testing into SEL's software development cycle. She has given many presentations and trainings on automation and quality throughout the company.

1. Introduction

Software produced for critical infrastructure is held to standards that ensure the safety of not only those who use the software but also those who are directly affected by the software being used. Software protecting the power system does not only affect the power company that uses it but also all people who receive electricity from that company. Development of such software requires the use of the best quality practices to avoid major malfunctions while continuing to deliver new features in a cost-effective and time-efficient manner. The iron triangle (or project management triangle) shown in Fig. 1 is a good way to visualize this problem. The triangle represents the tradeoffs made between scope, time, and cost and the effect they have on the quality of a product. Scope represents the work assigned to complete the project, time represents the timeline allotted to complete the project, and cost represents the project's budget (Schenkelberg n.d., 11–12).

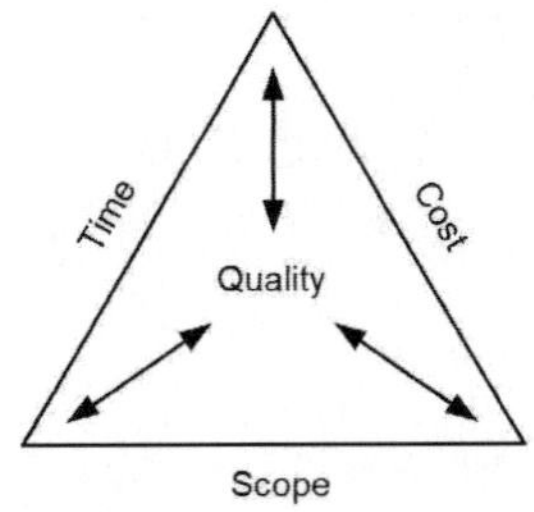

Figure 1. The Iron Triangle

If quality is set as a static value, a set point that is to be achieved, then increasing one of the variables can decrease the others if needed. However, if the goal is to increase the overall test quality, separating the process into each area allows for a more focused approach to improvement. When focusing on the scope of testing, objective methods for determining test coverage can be put in place on a feature-by-feature basis. Reducing the amount of time spent not only running tests but also writing and reviewing test results can allow more time for exploratory testing. Building trust in testing and providing proof of its value helps to convince others that investing in testing is worthwhile. Focused incremental improvements in each area can improve the quality of the test process and, as a result, improve the quality of the software.

2. Scope: Ranking Functions by Criticality

For products used in critical infrastructure, removing the wrong tests or limiting testing on the wrong feature could result in a bug escape, which could lead to serious damage, injury, or even death. Therefore, it is important to determine the proper amount of testing needed to ensure a quality product without over testing. To determine this, there should be an objective way to analyze the testing investment for each feature released. For example, in network security, there is a method used to rank the amount of protection needed for a new device on the network. Predetermined inputs such as information value, device value, and vulnerability are used to determine how much effort is put into an asset's protection. This same method can be applied to determining the proper amount of testing that should be done on a new feature.

A common method for calculating such ranking is called the Kim and Kang method (Kellett 2016, 5). Using this method, a list of decision factors is created to encompass the important possible shortcomings of testing. This list is used across all features to make comparisons of test importance between features possible. Each decision factor is given a weighted value. The higher the weight, the more important the decision factor is to the software process. Features are evaluated one decision factor at a time, ranked according to each factor. The weighted values are multiplied by each rank and summed into a deterministic ranking that reflects the importance that should be considered when testing each feature.

For example, some decision factors for testing might be:

- Safety: “If this fails, what is the safety risk?”
- Reach: “If this fails, how many devices fail?”
- Usability: “How much would a bug from this feature affect the end user?”
- Complexity: “How complex is this feature?”

The decision factors are then assigned a weight:

- Safety: 1.0
- Reach: 0.8
- Usability: 0.7
- Complexity: 0.7

With all the setup done, a feature can now be evaluated. As a group, the ranking that is most appropriate for each decision factor is assigned. A weighted rank is calculated for each additional decision factor by multiplying the weight by the assigned rank, and then the weighted ranks are summed together, resulting in the feature risk (see Table I).

Table 1. Calculating Feature Risk

Decision Factor	**Weight**	**Assigned Rank (0–5)**	**Weighted Rank (Weight • assigned rank)**
Safety	1.0	5	5
Reach	0.8	3	2.4
Usability	0.7	3	2.1
Complexity	0.7	1	0.7
Feature Risk			10.2

Feature risk is an objective value that is used to determine the amount of testing that needs to take place. There are a couple of ways this number can be used. A simple implementation involves predetermined tiered decisions (Wikoff 2006, 9). Test engineers must preset a testing intensity based on a threshold system. When a score is above a threshold, they can test to the stringency of that threshold. Another option is to use this number to objectively define the coverage that is needed to meet the test plan for this feature, using a percent of coverage as the final target.

Using this method or another objective ranking method helps to evaluate the priority of a feature. Having a consistent way to determine test scope ensures that the same decision-making process is used for all features. If issues with the calculation method itself occur, the weights or decision factors can be fine-tuned until they meet the needs of those using them. Since everyone on the testing team was involved in ranking the feature risk, there should be no uncertainty regarding the amount of testing required. For these reasons, the Kim and Kang method is a valuable tool for evaluating and properly limiting the scope of testing.

3. Time: Reducing Time of Critical Tests

A key component of being able to expand test coverage is reducing the amount of time spent developing, executing, and recording tests. The faster each test is completed, the more tests can be run. The problems faced in a manufacturing environment are similar. Therefore, there are a lot of lessons that can be learned from examining how extremely complex manufacturing processes are simplified and automated. Those lessons can then be applied in any aspect of software development to understand how best to improve processes. Using that knowledge, along with analyzing where in the process to focus efforts and knowing when it is best to implement automation, will ensure that the best improvement is made.

In manufacturing, a key part of any time-saving project is to properly understand the flow of the product through all parts of the factory. The assembly line receives parts, assembles them, and sends a product down the line to their customer. In the same way, software testing can be thought of as a single station on the assembly line. Code and specifications are received from suppliers upstream, and then test results are produced and shipped downstream to customers. Even in a rapid development environment where specifications, coding, and test writing are happening at the same time, it is helpful to understand which part of the process might cause a slowdown or stoppage in testing. Within the station itself, there are multiple tasks that can be improved individually to help the overall process.

Examining the test process from an external perspective can be very helpful in finding places for improvement (see Fig. 2). Creating good relationships with those who supply code and specifications can eliminate a lot of miscommunication and vague expectations. A design-for-test document can be created to communicate the coding practices to be followed that benefit testers and make automation easier. Creating consistent test results that are easy to evaluate is a good way to eliminate rework. In summary, when looking at testing from an external perspective, focus on communicating, trusting, and understanding group members to make huge strides in reducing test times.

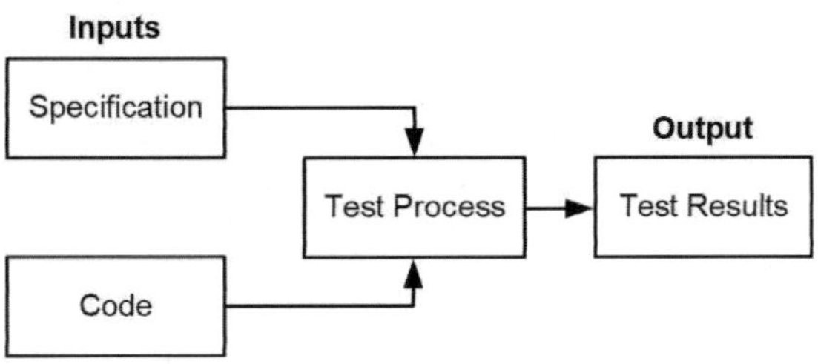

Figure 2. External Test Process

First, the expectation of what a station on the line will receive from the supplier upstream and deliver to the customer downstream should be well-documented. This documentation should not cover the content of what is being delivered, but rather how the delivery should happen. Doing so allows for clear understanding of how best to approach reducing the time it takes to accomplish the task at the station. This can be accomplished for test suppliers by using a design-for-test document that outlines consistent software design and documentation practices. Similarly, creating template results that can be easily filled out and used consistently reduces the number of errors in test result creation, making the job of the reviewers easier.

When there is a problem at the station, it is important to document what caused the problem, how long it stopped work, and what the solution was (Schonberger 1986, 18–20). This allows the station to reduce downtime and keep work stoppages to a minimum. A frequently used term to describe this process is root cause analysis. It is important to share this analysis with both suppliers and customers. Sharing this information frequently allows others working on the project to eliminate work stoppages and avoid the same issues in the future. Using a whiteboard visible by the whole team to collect issues is a good way to share information with everyone in real time. Teams should discuss these issues together to come up with solutions to the most pressing matters.

When an issue arises that could put a stop to all work on the project, it is important for all parts of the assembly line to know, so that all who are affected can work to fix the issue to get everyone back up and running. Helping other stations on the assembly line continue to run smoothly helps keep the assembly line running as a seamless unit. Communicating directly with someone using a real-time communication method (e.g., face to face, via instant messenger, or over the phone) is a much faster resolution than logging a bug or sending an email (Schonberger 1986, 40).

Once there is consistent communication between stations, work can be done to reduce the time it takes to execute a test. Testing can be broken into four categories: test write, test setup, test execution, and results creation (see Fig. 3). Each area has unique challenges that provide opportunities for improvements. Clearly defining these different sections can be helpful when planning to improve the test execution overall. This paper uses the following definitions:

- **Write** is the act of taking a specification and defining repeatable test steps. This could be in the form of a test case specification, writing test code, or a manual test write.
- **Setup** is any required action that needs to occur before a test is executed. This could range from hardware changes to software installations.
- **Execution** is any action that results in the test passing or failing. When focusing on improvements in speed, this is usually where most of the work takes place, and it is the section most likely to be automated.
- **Results creation** is the documentation of the execution results.

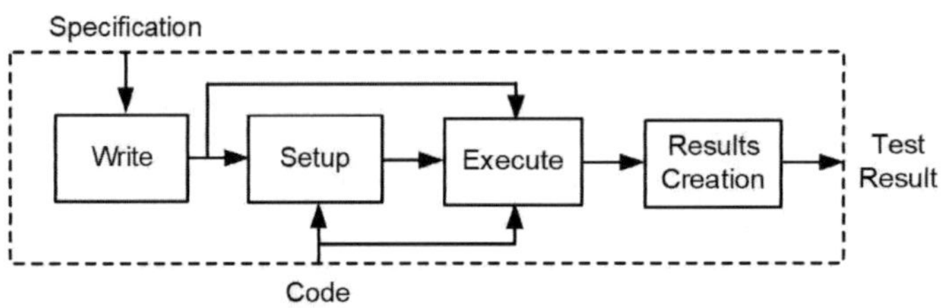

Figure 3. Internal Test Process

3.1. Test Write

Test write can be thought of as a data conversion. Using the specification as input, the raw data outlining the operation of a feature can be transformed into a sequence of steps for testing that feature. Thinking this way makes it easier to find features that are similar and makes it possible to devise a way of automatically converting the specification into tests. Consider the following example. A testing team receives specifications for buttons on different webpages. There are hundreds of buttons and all of them must be tested the same way. The specifications read something like this: "Button 4 should be placed in the top left of the page. Its size should be 100x200 pixels. It should read 'Okay,' and when pressed, it should navigate to webpage.com."

In this case, someone would be required to write a unique test for each button that is specified in this way. If the specification is machine-readable and consistent, though, then the conversion from specification to test could be automated, saving time in test write and allowing more time for execution. The test code needs to be implemented in a way that will handle all possible behaviors displayed by a button, regardless of its location, size, or function. The specification can then be passed to the test code directly. In this case of button testing, a test engineer could start by defining the required testing the button needs to undergo. Based on the previous specification, they could run tests on the location of the button, its size, the text on the button, and its function. If the specification is written in a data storage language like XML or JSON, then no conversion is needed. Otherwise, if all button specifications are structured and worded consistently, then a parser could be used to interpret existing specifications into such a language.

Either way, the goal is to have a file that can easily be converted to a structure in a given testing language. The test code then oversees interpreting the specification and executing the proper battery of predefined tests. Automating the data transfer requires open communication and cooperation with partners upstream who supply the specification. Once the test writes are automated, it is equally important to have the testing infrastructure ready so that the test can be started quickly.

3.2. Test Setup

Preparing a test environment capable of handling tests can be a daunting task. It can be thought of as similar to setting up an assembly line station, where having all the tools needed to complete the job of the station is crucial. Tools that are used most are positioned closer to the assembler, whereas tools that are used less often are positioned farther away. The positioning of tools is the same between stations. Similarly, if software testing requires hardware, it is helpful to follow the same rule and organize the equipment so that the most commonly used equipment is easily accessible. Program installation locations between machines may seem trivial, but when there is a problem, removing even the smallest variable can reduce complexity. If the same set of testing is run consistently enough, it may warrant a separate station to only run that one test. A well-developed setup creates a smooth transition into test execution.

3.3. Test Execution

Most of the focus of reducing test time goes into the test execution stage. Implementing automation for test execution is important in reducing test time. However, it is important to consider all the factors before investing time into automating a test. The most important factors to consider are the time it takes to run a test manually, the frequency of test runs, the frequency of test changes, and the time it takes to automate the test. It is also important to be consistent. The more people who work on automation, the more important it is to create consistency in how the scripts look and execute, the functions they use, and the layout of the results they may create. Creating this consistency will make maintenance of automation easier as time goes on and the amount of automation grows.

3.4. Test Results Creation

Results creation is often overlooked when it comes to reducing the time it takes to run a test. Receiving a request to make changes or discuss a test result and its formatting consumes time that could be used doing more testing. Having consistent test results and formatting the results in a way that the reviewers can easily understand are two main ways to reduce rework for results. When a test is automated, results creation can often be automated as well to help ensure the consistency. The automated results should still be formatted in a human-readable manner. The results should be easy to evaluate when all steps pass and easy to debug when a step fails.

As a final note, automation is extremely important when reducing the amount of time spent on testing. It is also an effective way to increase the consistency of testing across similar features and ensure coverage. However, in any step of the test execution that uses automation, it is important to be prepared for two of the many automation pitfalls. First, no automation system is perfect. It is always necessary to spend time keeping the system running. There will always be a new feature or a change that breaks the test automation. Second, it is important to train others to use and maintain any automation created. It is best to train everyone who is willing to learn. The more people who know how the automation works, the faster any future problems within the system can be fixed.

With all the focus on reducing time, it is important to not lose sight of the end goal of improving test coverage. The faster a test can be run, the more tests can be run in the time given. Finally, the more quality testing is done, the more confident a team can be that the product being released will be ready to be used, as if someone's life depended on it.

4. Cost: Selling Quality

A lot of work is put into deciding how much testing should be done to balance cost, time, and scope to ensure that critical infrastructure software has zero defects. This is clear to testers; however, it can be difficult to convey this to other team members. It is critical for the entirety of the team to understand the importance of zero defects when it comes to software in critical infrastructure. Sometimes, that means helping them understand the cost of a failure. Often, a good way to help others understand how critical a failure could be is by showing them the estimated cost of a potential failure. This includes the cost of running a bug fix project; the cost of retesting; the cost to the end user to update software for a new release; and often, in critical infrastructure, the cost of someone being injured. These are all effective ways of convincing a team to be more quality focused.

The next step is to measure quality in an objective way. Tracking quality metrics, specifically focused on tests to determine the effects of any test decision, is important when conveying the results of the decision. When focusing on quality, it is important to be able to measure quality as the team is making strides to improve. Every team is different, and there is no universal answer for what metrics should be used to measure a testing group. However, there are a few that are worth noting here:

- **Change failure rate** measures how many failures occur after release that require immediate attention (Duvall 2018, 17). Tracking this number will allow the team to make changes and, after the fact, determine whether the change has an effect. The downside to this is that it can only be measured after the issues have already happened. Within tests, this process can be used to track false failures and to identify weak points of automation.
- **Business value delivered** can be preemptive and used in a pitch when suggesting new testing techniques or suggesting expanding coverage (Phillipy 2014, 3). It can also be used to put a price on a specific bug that was found or missed to explain the necessity of testing.
- **Customer satisfaction** involves solid channels of communication and giving opportunity for internal customer feedback. Gaining the trust of other team members and internal customers helps to strengthen the drive toward quality. This metric can be tracked through surveys or one-on-one communication with customers to determine what are perceived to be the pain points in testing.

These are simple metrics that are easy to implement and maintain, but the value of any applied metric should be consistently scrutinized to find what works best for each organization. As there are no two people who are the same, no two organizations are the same, and so the focus of improvement for each should be individualized.

5. Conclusion

When testing software in critical infrastructure, it is important to analyze all parts of the testing process to improve the overall quality, so understanding what drives quality is essential. Testers who strive for quality have the responsibility to increase the quality of testing while simultaneously reducing the variables that drive quality. Improving the selection of test priorities ensures that coverage goals are met while avoiding excessive testing. Using an objective method for determining priorities increases traceability and understanding of the necessity of testing. Understanding the flow of the test process and breaking that process down into its individual parts improve the overall process. Finally, convincing all involved in the software process to make quality the highest priority ensures that everyone on the testing team is on the same page about quality expectations. Exploring each of these options to improve quality is the best way to ensure testing does not exceed a schedule and budget in critical infrastructure.

References

Duvall, Paul. 2018. “Measuring DevOps Success with Four Key Metrics.” Stelligent. Accessed May 26, 2020. http://stelligent.com/2018/12/21/measuring-devops-success-with-four-key-metrics/

Kellett, Matthew. 2016. “Kim and Kang’s Approach.” In “Ranking Assets Based on Criticality and Adversarial Interest,” 5–9. Defence Research and Development Canada 168.

Phillipy, Mark A. 2014. “Delivering Business Value: The Most Important Aspect of Project Management.” Proceedings of PMI Global Congress, Phoenix, AZ.

Schenkelberg, Fred. n.d. “Introduction to the Quality Triangle.” Accendo Reliability. Accessed May 21, 2020. http://accendoreliability.com/introduction-quality-triangle/

Schonberger, Richard J. 1986. World Class Manufacturing: The Lessons of Simplicity Applied. New York: Free Press.

Wikoff, Darrin. 2006. “Managing Assets by Criticality.” Plant Services. Accessed May 26, 2020. http://www.plantservices.com/articles/2006/125/?stage=Live

Testing Floating-Point Applications

Alan A. Jorgensen, Connie R. Masters
AAJ@TrueNorthFloatingPoint.com
CM@TrueNorthFloatingPoint.com

Abstract

Testing the results of floating-point in large, complex scientific and engineering applications is problematic. Though floating point is standardized by IEEE, there are serious deficiencies. IEEE standard floating point has no indication of whether representation of a real value is exact, much less anywhere near correct. The correctness of the real value represented is tainted by accuracy and completeness of source data, algorithmic error, and accumulated floating-point error. Available techniques for testing complex calculations are expensive and unreliable. This paper describes a new testing technology for complex floating-point calculations employing bounded floating point, which is a device and methodology for calculating and propagating the bounds on floating-point calculations and alarming when a calculation does not meet a specified precision. This paper presents a demonstration of a software model of bounded floating point detecting a failure in Muller's recursion, an algorithm known to fail undetectably using IEEE standard floating point.

Biography

Alan Jorgensen is a computer engineer and scientist with decades of hardware and software design experience, particularly test engineering. He has degrees in Electrical Engineering and Computer Science. He has spoken internationally on software testing as well as previously at PNSQC. In addition to teaching as Adjunct Faculty at various universities, his latest work has been obtaining patents for an "Apparatus for Calculating and Retaining a Bound on Error during Floating-Point Operations and Methods Thereof," a technology called "Bounded Floating Point" first presented at PNSQC 2018 as a poster.

1. Introduction

I have spent my career improving computer systems' quality. Hardware was usually easy, but software quality often proved problematic. One problem in particular has plagued me - enough that I have lost sleep over it. This is the longstanding problem of unknown inaccuracies when using floating point in computers to represent values and results.

The first shock to my psyche occurred after I developed a test to evaluate compatibility between software floating point and a hardware floating-point implementation. My test showed that they were not compatible. Management decided that was okay. That was okay? It was okay to get two different answers? This was vexing to me, so over time I began to study floating point and to deliberate on possible approaches to resolve the problem of inaccuracies in results due to floating point.

As an engineer I have learned good problem-solving techniques that I have applied, for instance, to system problems in live nuclear power plant computers. I endeavored to apply these problem-solving techniques to the unresolved floating-point problem, but it was not an easy problem to solve.

2. IEEE Standard Floating Point

Floating point was standardized in 2011 at the instigation of the "Father of Floating Point," William Kahn [IEEE 2011]. Standard floating point is a data structure emulating scientific notation with a sign, exponent, and fraction (known as the significand). Fig. 1 shows the generalized floating-point format.

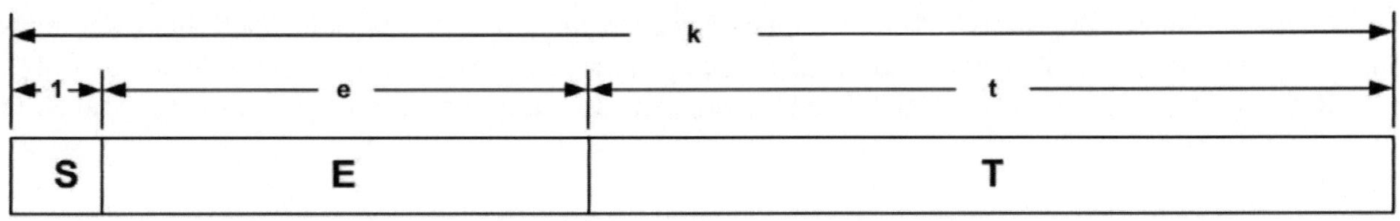

Figure 1 IEEE Standard Floating-Point Format

As I studied standard floating point, to my horror I discovered that floating-point error has killed dozens of soldiers due to a Patriot missile failure [GAO 1992], has destroyed a $370M rocket [Lions 1996], and has halved the value of a public stock trading business [Lilley 1983], [Kahan 2011]. I came to the realization that standard floating point is a significant computer system quality problem.

Sierra, the author of the first patent for floating point that I could find, said in his patent:

> "... under some conditions, the major portion of the significant data digits may lie beyond the capacity of the registers. Therefore, the result obtained may have little meaning if not totally erroneous." [Sierra 1962, p. 2]

Totally erroneous? How can we proceed with a calculation when we know the result obtained may be totally erroneous?

What to do? We know we can't "test-in" quality, but I realized it would help if we could at least KNOW if we HAD a problem.

3. Testing Floating-Point Applications

I investigated to see if others had proposed means to determine if a result was erroneous. Professor Emeritus William Kahan is very helpful in this matter. He identifies 3 testing methods as follows [Kahan 2011, pp. 39-48]:

- Recomputation with Redirected Rounding;
- Recomputation with Higher Precision; and
- Temporary Exception Handling.

The first two methods mentioned by Kahan are fault injection techniques, and the third is error trapping.

3.1. Recomputation with Redirected Rounding

The default rounding mode in standard floating point is "round to nearest," but other modes are available, such as round to zero, round to +infinity, and round to -infinity [IEEE 2011]. Recomputation with redirected rounding uses a comparison of the results when the calculation is performed using multiple modes of rounding.

Some language instantiations provide a means of setting the rounding mode. For instance, GNU's gcc library [GNU Rounding] provides:

*int **fesetround** (int round)*

where round = FE_TONEAREST, FE_UPWARD. FE_DOWNWARD, and FE_TOWARDZERO

The application can be run in more than one mode, and the results of running the application with each mode will differ, but the results should not differ radically. If they do, a branch and bound technique will be required to determine the source of significant error. This is an expensive, time-consuming, repetitious, and manual method.

In contrast, using bounded floating point with required intermediate precision will isolate the location where precision is lost. Bounded floating point presents a range where the lower bound is the standard floating-point result, rounded to zero, and the upper bound is computed based on D, the number of lost bits, which is the number of bits that are not significant.

3.2. Recomputation with Higher Precision

The second method to test the accuracy of a result is to compute the result using an original precision, and then test it by using a higher precision. Standard floating-point precisions are 32-bit (single precision) and 64-bit (double precision). Some environments allow 128-bit (quad precision). Though using higher precision is a means of testing the accuracy of a result, higher precision requires more time and space, which may make implementing and testing in this way problematic.

GNU gcc, which does not have a direct "quad" type declaration, attempted to provide an indirect means of defining a lengthened precision, which is only partially functional. In this indirect method, normal C language functions, like casting and automatic type casting are not available [GNU 2018]. The method compares the results of an application test with normal precision, and then the result of the same application test with lengthened precision, which should indicate only a small difference. If there is a greater difference, there is a hidden floating-point defect undetected by IEEE standard floating point. In contrast, this defect would be detected during the execution of the calculation by the use of bounded floating point.

3.3. Temporary Exception Handling

The third conventional testing method, temporary exception handling, uses error trapping. Standard floating point provides several different exceptions, such as overflow, underflow, divide by zero, and Not a Number, (NaN). An exception is a hardware generated interrupt (or trap) that provides program notification of an error that requires special handling by the software. Examples include, dividing by zero or taking the square root of a negative number. Exceptions are "handled" by servicing the interrupt. The "Try-Catch" pair of operators is a high-level language construct to provide a scope in which an exception interrupt may be recognized and serviced. The software "Throw" command creates a hardware exception interrupt and is used whenever the program discovers a failure from which it cannot gracefully recover. If any hardware exception is not serviced by the application generating the exception, then the operating system services the exception and fails the application catastrophically. A similar exception handling policy caused by floating point error lead to the failure of the Ariane 5 rocket launched by the European Space Agency [Lions 1996].

The Try-Throw-Catch exception generating/handling mechanism may catch something you were not fishing for [Kahan 2011, p. 55]. But it is best to keep exception handling in the test/diagnostic environment, and using it sparingly in production applications, particularly in mission critical systems where an improperly handled exception may cause a catastrophic system failure.

In gcc, Try-Throw-Catch, requires the use of the <setjmp.h> functions. I have included the exception code that I use for checking significance of floating-point values in Appendix A.

In contrast, bounded floating point provides the capability (under program control) of generating an exception when a result does not have sufficient precision.

4. Bounded Floating Point

I think my serious consideration of floating-point error started in the late 90's when I had some free time at work, and, being a life-long tester, began playing with the Microsoft Calculator available on my Windows desktop. It did not take long to discover anomalies, which I documented later in my Ph.D. dissertation [Jorgensen 1999, pp. 138-146]. Many of these anomalies were caused by incorrect floating point.

Some of this work led to my publication of "Why Software Fails." In summary, that work presents that the frequent cause of software failure is the failure of the programmer to constrain program operations, such as constraining input, calculations, storage, and output to reasonable values [Whittaker et al. 1999].

Floating-point error continued to be a burl in my brain. I would go to sleep thinking of a problem caused by floating point, but instead of waking up with an answer, I would wake up with a question to ask. I knew this problem had been around for a long time and bright minds had tackled it. So, why hadn't anyone solved it?

I began pouring information from leaders in the field into my brain [Kahan 2011], [Goldberg 1991], [Muller et al. 2010]. I examined the various attempts that others had made to solve floating-point problems, such as interval arithmetic [Hickey et al. 2001], error analysis [Higham 1996, pp. 74-78], and more.

While absorbing these various approaches and the current state of the art, I was seeking an insight that might lead me down a path to a solution. I went to sleep mulling over the problem and woke up with the realization that the current format did not provide sufficient information – more bits were needed for storing additional information (whether the standard format was shortened or more bits were added to the standard format). Based on this realization, I added information to the IEEE standard format by adding another field. This new field would be one that described the error in the value, limited that error, or provided a bound for that error. Thus, "Bounded Floating Point" (BFP) was born, creating a method of constraining floating-point operations.

After a few false starts, I came to realize that the problem was that there are two kinds of error: rounding and cancellation. To produce a solution, I must find a way to simultaneously retain information about both kinds of error.

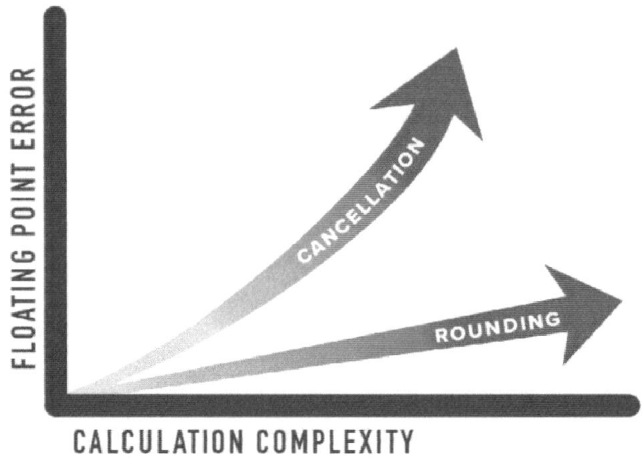

Rounding error occurs because it is necessary to truncate the representation of some numbers. An easy example in the decimal numbering system is Pi or 1/3; both of these require an infinite number of digits to express exactly. Correspondingly, standard binary floating point cannot accurately represent any number that is not the sum of a limited range of powers of two. For example, one tenth (0.1) is a repeating fraction in binary and must be truncated, with rounding. Rounding error accumulates in a linear fashion.

Cancellation error, which occurs when subtracting "similar" numbers, multiplies existing error – exponentially.

Adding error from both cancelation and rounding is like adding apples and oranges i.e. things that cannot be practically compared. Yet, I needed to do this. And, as apples and oranges can be added by using a common characteristic, such as fruit or weight, I found that the common characteristic of cancellation error and rounding error was logarithms.

Consequently, the error field of bounded floating point is composed of the summation of cancellation error (which is logarithmic) and the logarithm of the summation of rounding error.

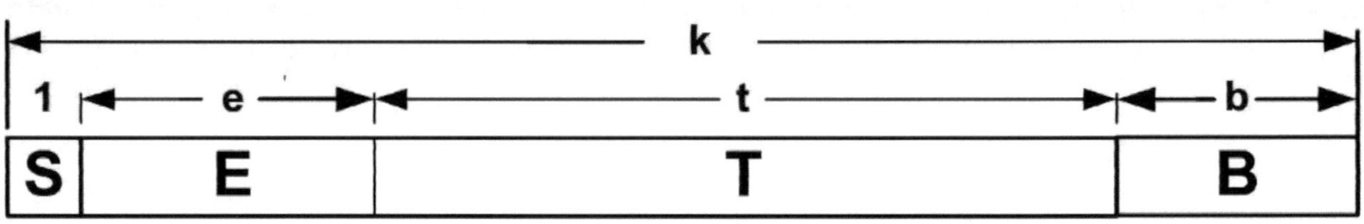

Figure 2 Bounded Floating-Point Format

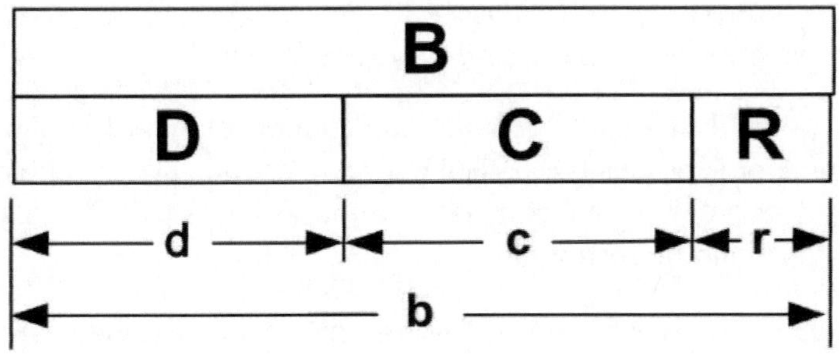

Figure 3 Format of Bound Field, B

The final revelation came from a visit with the Father of Floating Point, himself. This discovery was that operations on exact floating-point numbers yield exact results. "Exact" means that the numbers are accurate to + or – 1/2 unit in the last place (ulp), because this is as accurately as a number can be represented in the standard floating-point system [Jorgensen et al., 2020]. However, standard floating point has no way to inform you whether or not a result is exact. In contrast, bounded floating point can tell you if a number is exact because if the number is exact, the number of lost bits, D, would be zero.

5. Examples of Testing with Bounded Floating Point

I have developed a C language bounded floating-point model and have provided input, output, and debug capabilities. The model provides conditional display of specified system logic. It is this model, which uses 80-bit bounded floating-point format, that I have used in these testing examples.

Bounded floating point is modeled with k = 80 (FIG. 2); with the bound, B, having b = 16 bits; and with S, E, and T remaining identical to 64-bit IEEE standard floating point where e = 11 and t = 52. The bound field B is defined with D (FIG. 3, with width d=6), c = 6, and r = 4. The C and R fields contain the current sum of the rounding error.

Having an operational model of bounded floating point meant that I could perform testing with it. So, I applied the model to some problems that were known to be difficult. The first problem I attacked was finding the area of a thin triangle [Kahan 2014].

5.1. Kahan's Thin Triangle

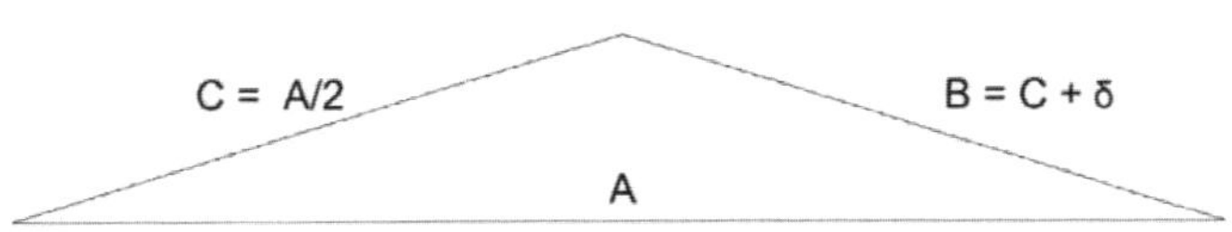

Figure 3 A Thin Triangle.

As the triangle becomes smaller and smaller (δ => 0), the area has fewer and fewer significant digits IEEE floating point will not tell you this, but bounded floating point will. Using the model, we are able to use a stress test (shown below in Table 1) in which we require greater and greater precision until we have a failure. This technique allows us to stress test significant scientific or engineering applications.

This thin triangle problem comes from Kahan's work [Kahan 2014], which extends the work of Pat H. Sterbenz [Sterbenz 1976 , pp. 152-153] who states:

"However, we can produce a good solution for the problem if we assume that A, B, and C are given ***exactly*** *as numbers in [floating point]." [Emphasis added]*

But what happens when A or B or C are NOT exact? Further, standard floating point does not even provide any indication that A or B or C is exact. But bounded floating point establishes exactness, where a representation is exact if and only if the dominate bound lost bits field, D, is zero; this indicates that there are no insignificant bits in the representation.

The Kahan formula [Kahan 2014] for determining the area of the thin triangle is shown in (1), where A ≥ B ≥ C. The Area =

$$SQRT(A+(B+C))(C-(A-B))(C+(A-B))(A+(B-C)))/4 \qquad (1)$$

Table 1 presents the data from stress testing the Kahan formula for 3 values of δ (delta), where the difference between the length of C and the length of B is δ. The results from standard double precision floating point (64-bit), standard quad precision floating point (128-bit) and bounded floating point (80-bit) compared. A one ulp error is injected into the "A" values by adding 1 to the significand field (T) of the 64-bit and 128-bit standard floating-point values and by adding 1 to the lost bits field (D) of the bounded floating-point value. Injecting a 1 ulp error into any one of the values, A, B, or C serves to inject an error into the Kahan equation subjecting it to cancellation error.

In the results from Triangle One, using B=0.8001 (where δ=0.0001), the first column of the first row shows that 10 significant digits are required. In the second column, double precision standard floating point indicates that there are seventeen significant digits. In the third column, using the recomputation with higher precision testing technique described above, quad precision identifies (by manually comparing the two results) that only eleven of those seventeen are actually significant. In the fourth column bounded floating point displays only the digits that are significant, which in this case is eleven. Thus, bounded floating point verifies the results of the recomputation with higher precision test and identifies the actual number of significant digits in the double precision result. In the second row, 11 significant digits are required, and we calculate with the same values and get the same result – there are 11 significant digits. In the third row of Triangle One, 12 significant digits are required, and we calculate with the same values. The double and quad precision results are the same, but bounded floating point displays a quiet Not-a-Number (qNaN.sig) indicating Equation 1 cannot be solved for Triangle One using double precision to achieve a result accurate to 12 significant digits.

Table 1
Stress tests of Kahan's thin triangle equation for various increasing required significant digits

Stress Tests			
δ is embedded within the B value			
Required Significant Digits	Area Using Double Precision	Area Using Quad Precision	Area Using Bounded Floating Point
For Triangle One, A= 1.6, B=0.8001, and C=0.8			
10	0.00715552931654077180000	0.00715552931654910837456	0.0071555293165
11	0.00715552931654077180000	0.00715552931654910837456	0.0071555293165
12	0.00715552931654077180000	0.00715552931654910837456	qNaN.sig
For Triangle Two, A=1.6, B=0.80000001, and C=0.8			
6	0.00007155417437995153200	0.00007155417539179666768	0.00007155417
7	0.00007155417437995153200	0.00007155417539179666768	0.00007155417
8	0.00007155417437995153200	0.00007155417539179666768	qNaN.sig
For Triangle Three, A=1.6, B=0.800000000001, and C=0.8			
2	0.000000071545439186697031	0.000000071554175280004451	0.000000715
3	0.000000071545439186697031	0.000000071554175280004451	0.000000715
4	0.000000071545439186697031	0.000000071554175280004451	qNaN.sig

5.2. Muller's Recursion

Another test I performed was on Muller's recursion. This is a nasty counter example that converges – but to a completely incorrect value [Kahan 2011, pp. 37-38].

Muller's (Counter) Example:

XN+1 := 111 – (1130 – 3000/XN–1)/XN for N = 1, 2, 3, …
(2) Where X0 := 2 and X1 := –4

Using bounded floating point's ability to generate an exception when insufficient digits are available for an intermediate result, I detected the precise point in the recursion where it fails.

Table 2
Muller's (Counter) Example - Bounded Floating Point vs. IEEE 64-Bit Floating Point

X[0] =	2.000000000000000	2.0000000000000000
X[1] =	-4.000000000000000	-4.0000000000000000
X[2] =	18.50000000000007	18.5000000000000000
X[3] =	9.37837837837878	9.3783783783783790
X[4] =	7.801152737756	7.8011527377521679
X[5] =	7.15441448103	7.1544144809753334
X[6] =	6.8067847377	6.8067847369248122
X[7] =	6.592632780	6.5926327687218027
X[8] =	6.44946611	6.4494659340540812
X[9] =	6.348454	6.3484520607489294
X[10] =	6.27448	6.2744386627644761
X[11] =	6.2193	6.2186967691620172
X[12] =	6.187	6.1758538651440409
X[13] =	sNaN.sig	6.1426273215848903
X[14] =		6.1202511650793756
X[15] =		6.1661267427176769
X[16] =		7.2356654170119432
X[17] =		22.0695591545310310
X[18] =		78.5848925812682500
X[19] =		98.3504165513462850
X[20] =		99.8986263421841020
X[21] =		99.9938744412531260
X[22] =		99.9996305954946080
X[23] =		99.9999777432241790
X[24] =		99.9999986599719650
X[25] =		99.9999999193672550

As seen in Table 2, Muller's recursion converges to 100.0 when the correct answer is 6.0, but bounded floating point signals a loss of precision at a midpoint in the calculation of the recursion. In recursions, loss of significance in an intermediate result propagates to the final result.

Interestingly, when using floating point, error in intermediate results may not propagate to the final result, because successive alignment of the binary point may eliminate previous error bits by shifting them out of range.

Nevertheless, bounded floating point will track the error in the calculation in real time.

6. Summary

Bounded floating point, implemented in hardware or software, is very useful for testing complex scientific and engineering calculations, as shown by the application to Kahan's thin triangle problem and to Muller's Recursion.

Instead of a designer of an application hoping that a result has the required number of significant digits, bounded floating point will assure that it does or notify if it does not.

Bounded floating point can also identify whether a number is exact.

No longer do we need to proceed with a calculation knowing that the result obtained may be totally erroneous.

7. Appendix A

```
// TRY-THROW-CATCH Defined
#include <setjmp.h>
#define Place jmp_buf
#define Mark ex_buf__
#define MarkPlace(place) setjmp(place)
#define ReturnToMark(ReturnValue) longjmp(Mark,ReturnValue)
#define TRY do{ Place Mark; if( !MarkPlace(Mark) ){
#define CATCH } else {
#define TRY_End } }while(0)
#define THROW(Exception) ReturnToMark(Exception)
```

Application to bounded floating point sNaN.sig:

```
char Exception[25];
int BFPChk(bfp op1, int MaxLostBits)
{
   int Exception = (int) "sNaN.sig";

  TRY
  {
          if (D(op1.B) > MaxLostBits)
                    THROW(Exception);
          return 0;  // No Exception
```

```
    }
    CATCH
    {
            return (int) Exception;  // Returns integer pointer to "sNaN.sig"
    }
    TRY_End;

    return 0;
}
```

Where D(op1.B) is a macro to retrieve the lost bits of the bounded floating point operand, “op1”

8. References

Investigations and Oversight, Committee on Science, Space, and Technology. House of Representatives. Accessed 5 June 2020, https://www.gao.gov/assets/220/215614.pdf

GNU; 2018. “The GCC Quad-Precision Math Library.” Accessed 3 June 2020, https://gcc.gnu.org/onlinedocs/gcc-8.4.0/libquadmath.pdf

GNU; “C Library 20.6 Rounding Modes.” Accessed 6/4/2020, https://www.gnu.org/software/libc/manual/html_node/Rounding.html

Goldberg, D. “What Every Computer Scientist Should Know About Floating-Point Arithmetic.” ACM Computing Surveys, vol. 23, no. 1, pp. 5-47, 1991.

Hickey, T., Q. Ju, M.H. van Emden. 1999. “Interval Arithmetic: from Principles to Implementation.” Journal of the ACM (JACM). Accessed 6 June 2020, http://fab.cba.mit.edu/classes/S62.12/docs/Hickey_interval.pdf

Higham, N. J. “Accuracy and Stability of Numerical Algorithms.” Philadelphia, PA: SIAM., 1996, pp. vii-xxviii,1-688.

ISO/IEC/IEEE 60559. “Information technology - Microprocessor Systems – Floating-Point Arithmetic.” Piscataway, NJ. Institute of Electrical and Electronics Engineers, 2011.

Jorgensen, Alan A. “Software Design Based on Operational Modes”, A dissertation submitted to the Graduate School of Florida Institute of Technology in partial fulfillment of the requirements for the degree of Doctor of Philosophy in Computer Science, Melbourne, Florida. 1999. Accessed 11 June 2020, https://repository.lib.fit.edu/handle/11141/103

Jorgensen, A. A., A. Masters. 2020. “Exact Floating Point.” To be published. Springer Nature - Book Series: Transactions on Computational Science & Computational Intelligence.

Jorgensen, A. A., A. Masters and R. Guha. 2019. “Assurance of Accuracy in Floating-Point Calculations - A Software Model Study,” in 2019 International Conference on Computational Science and Computational Intelligence (CSCI), Las Vegas, NV, USA.

Kahan, W. M. “Desperately needed remedies for the undebuggability of large floating-point computations in science and engineering.” IFIP/SIAM/NIST Working Conference on Uncertainty Quantification in Scientific Computing. Boulder, Colorado. 2011. Accessed 6/5/2020, https://people.eecs.berkeley.edu/~wkahan/Boulder.pdf

–. “Miscalculating Area and Angles of a Needle-like Triangle.” 4 September 2014.. Accessed 13 January 2020, https://people.eecs.berkeley.edu/~wkahan/Triangle.pdf

Lilley, Wayne. "Vancouver stock index has right number at last." The Toronto Star. November 29, 1983.

Lions, J. L. "Flight 501 Failure, Report by the Inquiry Board." Chairman of the Board. Accessed 5 June 2020, http://sunnyday.mit.edu/nasa-class/Ariane5-report.html

Muller, Jean-Michael, Nicolas Brisebarre, Florent de Dinechin, Claude-Pierre Jeannerod, Vincent Lefevre, Guillaume Melquiond, Nathalie Revol, Damien Stehle, and Serge Torres. 2010. "Handbook of Floating-Point Arithmetic." Boston: Birkhauser.

Sierra, H. M. "Floating Decimal Point Arithmetic Control Means for Calculator." 5 June 1962. US Patent No. Patent 3,037,701.

Sterbenz, P. H. "Floating-Point Computation." 1976. Prentice-Hall, Inc. Englewood Cliffs, N.J.

United States General Accounting Office. February 1992. "PATRIOT MISSILE DEFENSE Software Problem Led to System Failure at Dhahran, Saudi Arabia." Report to the Chairman, Subcommittee on Investigations and Oversight, Committee on Science, Space, and Technology, House of Representatives. Accessed 5 June 2020, https://www.gao.gov/assets/220/215614.pdf

J. Whittaker and A. A. Jorgensen. "Why software fails." ACM SIGSOFT Software Engineering Notes, vol. 24, no. 4, p. 81–83, 1999.

Staying the Course: How Rigid Processes Create Flexibility

Leona Parent Grzymkowski
Leona.Grzymkowski@gmail.com

Abstract

Processes – a developer's worst nightmare. So why did we work to add more of them?! The answer is that processes give developers a structure to rely on. The processes are the common bond of all development tasks. If done well, processes give tasks a roadmap to completion, eliminating the need to decode and decipher them. In her current role, Leona Grzymkowski has taken on implementing structured quality assurance processes into an already established software development lifecycle (SDLC).

This presentation will outline the path First National Bank of America took to change the perspective on how development work is accomplished, who is involved in the process, and how to open the lines of communication between internal groups.

Processes are hard work, but by providing guideposts along the path to a formalized and rigid SDLC process, this presentation will help to reveal the benefits. Throughout this presentation, examples of what First National Bank of America has done on their journey to become as streamlined and productive as possible and how they handle unprecedented disruption in their day-to-day work will be highlighted.

Biography

Leona Parent Grzymkowski is a Quality Assurance Leader at First National Bank of America. Her interests include opening communication and fostering connections between developers and users, process documentation, and building clear and actionable processes. Her work experience has given her experience in roles like QA Tester, Development Support Help Desk, Process Analyst, and Data Analyst. She has a Bachelor's of Science in Management Information Systems from Michigan Technological University.

1. Introduction

This paper will walk through the past few years of process implementation and formalization for the software development group at my employer, First National Bank of America. It will discuss the state of the development department each year, methods and tools that we tried, and descriptions of our team format. The goal is to provide information on how to implement processes to allow flexibility when it is most needed and explore the benefits of flexibility and rigidity.

2. The State of Things: 2018

2.1. Software Development Lifecycle

At the beginning of 2018, First National was utilizing Phabricator (a web-based suite of development tools) for development task management. There were very loose guidelines on what a task should look like and the sizing of the task. Business Units were typically calling on 'their' developer to complete work for them. We did not have any broad view of how much work we were actually doing, and the recurring issues were masked by a lack of tracking and problem definition. Users had no clear definition of their role in the development process. Much of the business logic was owned by developers, as they had been tasked with designing the systems that supported all business operations.

2.1.1. Roadmap to Change

2.1.1.1. The Phoenix Project

In March 2018, as part of our commitment to staff education and advancement, our department read The Phoenix Project by Gene Kim, Kevin Behr, and George Spafford. It is a novel that discusses the relatable problems of an IT department and their relationship to the business.Reading this book inspired big changes to the way that we handled our development tasks.

2.1.1.1.1. The Kanban Board

As a department, we created a physical Kanban Board, which gave us a way to visualize the work we were doing. Every request that came in got its own card on the board. We divided the board into seven sections: Specify, Implement, Review, Validate, Staging, Done, and Track. Each section has a maximum number of tasks allowed in that status at a time, called a WIP (work in progress) limit. Tracking task progress in this manner allows us to identify bottlenecks in the process, and once we learn about a bottleneck, we can take direct action to reduce the blockage. In many cases, the bottleneck can come from the WIP limit being too low. For example, if code reviewers can only work on one task at a time, a bottleneck will occur for tasks in Implement Done status. To combat this, we would adjust the WIP limit to allow for three tasks to be in Review WIP at one time. We would use that WIP limit and determine if it needs to be adjusted again based on workflow. Over time, we have adjusted and found WIP limits that meet our workflow needs, but are always monitoring the limits and are able to make adjustments as needed. We utilize the WIP limits like smoke detectors – if there is a status that is over the WIP limit, we investigate the root cause of the problem. If there is a fire (a true problem with the WIP limit), we will make the appropriate adjustments to prevent the problem in the future. More likely though, it will be a false alarm, like a smoke detector going off because it is too close to the stove. In this case, the root cause may be that there are outside circumstance to the bottleneck, like someone being out on vacation or waiting for approvals from the business units.

The benefits of adding the Kanban board to our process include aggregation of the work being done across our team, finding the bottlenecks in our workflow, and creating a clear picture about where tasks are in the process for anyone to reference, including business users.

2.1.1.1.2. Categorizing Work

We also took on categorizing our work in four ways: internal improvements, unplanned work, change work, and business work. Understanding where developers were spending their time in these four categories gave us a way to control our technical debt (internal improvements), and to ensure that we were working on the right tasks at the right time to add business value.

2.1.1.1.3. Three Ways

A big focus of The Phoenix Project was understanding the Three Ways as defined by Gene Kim and Mike Orzen. They say "We assert that the Three Ways describe the values and philosophies that frame the processes, procedures, practices of DevOps, as well as the prescriptive steps." (Kim)

The first way is understanding the performance of your entire system – understanding the whole puzzle and how it goes together versus just understanding the value of the piece in your hand. By implementing the Kanban board, we finally got a big picture view of what our department was dealing with as a whole.

The second way involves understanding where feedback comes from and how to act on it. The goal is to have short feedback loops, which is known as 'shifting left'. Shifting left means that the feedback happens earlier in the SDLC, or, if you were looking at it written, closer to the left side of the cycle. The sooner a problem is identified, the less disruptive and expensive it is to fix. We worked to honor the second way by keeping a watchful eye on the Kanban board. If a task appears to be stuck, we worked to address it as soon as possible. Each day, we had stand up meetings to give a big picture view of how the department was doing. It also gave everyone a chance to understand the tasks in motion, and provide or ask for help from peers to complete a task.

The third way is a call to create a culture where it is okay to ask for help and also to experiment and take risks. In our team, there is a big emphasis to work with others and take on learning. For our department, learning new and better ways to do the work is an important part of the process. By always thinking forward, we are able to better serve our customers with safe, dynamic, and maintainable solutions.

2.1.1.2. Jira

In May 2018, our teams began using Jira to track our tasks. After operating with a physical Kanban board for a few months and working to get the hang of the workflow, we decided it was time to refresh the way we tracked tasks. Jira worked well for us because we were able to create a digital Kanban board that reflected all the rules and WIP limits we set up on the physical board. Utilizing digital technology meant that the information was now available to everyone without having to leave their desk to make updates or changes. It also gave us a flexible platform to document task details and do reporting. As we got comfortable with Jira, it expedited the feedback loops from one time per day to any time a person noticed an issue. This faster feedback led to fewer large changes, and more fine-tuning of the process.

2.1.1.2.1. Minimum Viable Product

Around this time, we also started to work towards making our tasks as small as possible. The industry term for this is minimum viable product, or MVP. By working towards the smallest change that delivers the functionality requested by the business, we create the fastest feedback loop for informing the next piece. Instead of tackling a task that could take weeks, we started breaking down large tasks into smaller pieces using epics. In Jira, we would create a task as an 'epic', which is a large task that can be broken down in to smaller pieces, called 'child' tasks. The child tasks are worked each an individually developed a piece of the epic request. This allowed a few things to happen: multiple developers could work on child tasks at the same time, feedback from the first tasks informed requirements for the later tasks, and in many cases, we found that the change was not as large or complex as first thought. All these benefits sped up the process by providing faster feedback loops and sparking more conversation between developers and the business units. Before introducing this concept, we would have tasks that would be hung up on non-crucial details, which could have easily been split into a new task. We also had larger and more risky code deployments, which resulted in large and risky code rollbacks if the change failed.

2.1.1.2.2. Workflow

While we got our Kanban board up and running with Jira, we needed to set up a workflow for how tasks moved across the board. One principle of Kanban is that the work cannot flow backwards. Another is that the work should not be pushed forward, but pulled ahead when the developer is ready to work on it. With these principles in mind, we set up a workflow that allowed work to be put into the next status by simply clicking a button. We also made it difficult to move a task backwards on the board. In setting up the workflow this way, we allowed it to become trackable – we can see how much time a task spends in each status, and how quickly it moved through the SDLC. One of the benefits of implementing this workflow is being able to track the average time for a task in each step of the process. Doing this allows us to focus on making small improvements to areas of the workflow that are significantly higher than others or that begin to take longer than they had in the past.

2.2. Team Structure

Our team of developers and support totaled 14 people in 2018. All developers worked under one manager, and there were no formalized teams for a system or business unit. Each developer, worked on 'their' systems, and supported others who were pulled in to work on tasks in that specialty. Once we implemented Kanban, we knew we would need to reframe our team structure to focus on providing value to our business users. Our department leadership began planning how we could do this, but in the meantime, work carried on as usual.

2.2.1. Red Time

Developers had a rotation of on-call during business days. Each developer was on the schedule to be red-time. For us, red-time was the point person fielding production issues throughout the day. Any emails or phone calls directed to the development group by IT escalation or direct contact were handled by the on-call person for that day. If the problem was a bug fix, the developer would work on that task throughout the day. If the task was deemed to be a long-term problem, a Phabricator ticket would be created to address it in the future. Red-time work sometimes carried over into the next day for developers, since there was less communication with business users, and often times, the process to get a task user tested and scheduled for release was not achievable in one day.

2.2.2. Yellow Time

Similar to red-time, yellow-time would spend their day in the rotation as developer operations. This could involve code-reviewing their peers work, assisting with questions or techniques that other developers wanted input on, or researching new methods, training opportunities, and process improvements for the department. The developer on yellow-time would also work as the red-time backup, in the case that the red-timer was overwhelmed with help requests.

2.2.3. Green Time

For developers, green-time was when they were working on the tasks that they had picked up. Ideally, this time would have few to no interruptions, allowing for continuous focus. Any interruptions or requests received by a developer on green-time would be redirected to the red- or yellow-time developer.

2.3. Roadblocks and Complications

2.3.1. Defining Measurable Goals

The first challenge our team faced in changing our workflow was gaining buy-in from each team member and management. Because software development is not a tangible good, it was important to show what a real, physical impact a perspective shift could have on quality and productivity. We set out to find ways to show the cost of the way we were working, which included time tracking with Toggl, and also worked to quantify the number of hours we spent on tasks and rework. This gave a measurable number: the cost of each task (time spent in hours * developer rate).

2.3.2. Leadership Buy-In

An important part of making these changes to how our department accomplished work was gaining approval from department leadership and company leadership. In our case, we were fortunate to have IT leadership on board, but still needed to create our case for company leadership. As with any new process, there was a learning curve that we needed to account for, but were able to show the efficiencies that would be gained by tracking our work and identifying patterns to solve large problems.

2.4. Benefits Gained

Overall, 2018 was the start of major changes for our team. The benefits we gained included a large scale picture of the type of work that we were doing, a way to measure how long the work took, and the ability to identify bottlenecks in the process. All these things laid the foundation for moving forward into 2019, and for us to identify places where we could improve our processes to be more efficient and to provide clarity to our business users.

3. The State of Things: 2019

3.1. Software Development Lifecycle

In 2019, we pressed forward with our Kanban method of completing tasks. As we became more comfortable, we worked towards our target conditions of small tasks (MVP) and one week maximum in the software development lifecycle. We added a new Jira workflow for Code Review in the last quarter of 2018, and also added two new formal development support teams in 2019: quality assurance and release management.

3.1.1. Release Cadence

In 2019, our development team released an average of 7.44 tasks per week. This number is slightly lower than our 2018 results[1] of 8.03 tasks released per week on average. However, we found that more tasks were making it through the entire process. This means we were selecting more viable and important tasks to complete.

Our department found that it is important to be able to release new code to production throughout the workday. We have no set date or time for weekly releases. Rather, our Release Management team works to deploy code on demand. We are able to release changes during business hours for all repositories except one. We chose to exclude this one repository due to its size – it would take the production system offline for almost every user for around 5 minutes. We deploy this repository off business hours only.

[1] 2018 results only include June 2018 – December 2018. We began using Jira as a service at the end of May 2018.

3.2. Team Structure

Our teams went through some big changes in 2019. We split our release management role out from the DBA role, added our first glimpse of a development operations team, created a quality assurance role, revamped and grew our code review team, and defined our development teams as distinct business unit support groups.

3.2.1. Business Unit Teams

Business unit teams are comprised of developers who support one designated discipline of the organization. Each business unit team has a team leader, who guides a daily stand up for the group. These teams are responsible for working tasks on the Kanban board, and for communicating and collaborating with the business users who are stakeholders of each task.

3.2.2. Developer Support Teams

3.2.2.1. Code Review Team

The code review process has existed in our department for a while, but in the past, there was no dedicated team. Each developer would be assigned a day to review code for tasks that their peers were working on. The schedule was a rotation and included all developers. Now, with a formal code review team, we have a dedicated team of developers who support the three business unit teams. The developers on the code review team also work as part of a business unit team. Each business unit has dedicated reviewers, and there is a Kanban board lane dedicated to Code Review. Tasks in the Code Review lane can only be set to done by a member of the Code Review team.

3.2.2.2. Quality Assurance Team

The quality assurance team is considered a development support team. This team formed in July 2019 with one person working to implement some quality control processes in the existing SDLC. The first order of business was to implement standards around writing specifications for tasks. To do this, the team provided written guidelines and tips for writing strong requirements. In doing so, we created clearer paths to success, and worked with the business units to make sure they were framing their requests as desired outcomes. We also worked with developers to change the way that they wrote specifications to exclude technical terms that would not be easily interpreted by the business users. By creating specifications that both parties could easily understand, we built trust and rapport between the two groups.

3.2.2.3. Release Management Team

The release management team was, for a long time, one person's responsibility. In 2019, the department leadership divided this role from the database administrator role. At this time, our team worked to make the largely manual and undocumented process more transparent and easy to understand. In just under a month, we created written documents outlining the process of taking a task from Validate Done status through staging and release to production. The next piece of creating a transparent release process was to create a way to digitally track where tasks were, not only in the larger SDLC, but also where they were in the release management process. Once again, utilizing Jira, we worked to create a release management board, which allows developers and users to check where their task is in the process, who is working on it, and when the task is scheduled to be released to production. This board also gives the release manager flexibility for when they are out of the office or pulled into another issue; the backup can easily review the board and pick up where the schedule left off.

3.2.2.4. Business Analysts

In 2019, one business user group has provided a business analyst. We worked to train them on the Kanban board, SDLC, and new process teams. This person has been an excellent advocate for their business unit group. They have worked to create methods of ranking and prioritizing the group requests, which, hopefully in the near future, will help other business units prioritize their work requests to maximize the value of tasks that are accomplished for them. We have a long way to go with the business analyst role, but are hoping to quantify the benefit and provide an example for how a business analyst can streamline the business units' communication with the development team.

3.2.2.5. Additional Support Teams

You may have noticed that none of these new groups directly address production issues (red-time, as it was called before). In April 2019, our team made the decision to have one person triage user requests from help desk, phone calls, and emails. This way, we are able to organize and group similar problems and work toward solving the root causes rather than just putting a temporary fix on them. This also reduces the interruptions developers experience throughout the day. It also helps us understand the cost of unplanned work within our group. Understanding these costs drives efforts to improve initial code that make it to production.

3.3. Roadblocks and Complications

3.3.1. Peer Buy-In

Over the course of the year, we added many new pieces to the development support team. It was important to build trust with both developers and business users that these new processes, although a little more work, would be worth it. The new support teams needed to show that the process changes could provide more accurate task descriptions, better quality code, and constructive feedback for both developers and business users. We worked to open the lines of communication with all task stakeholders, and offered guidance and coaching for the new processes. These measures helped develop the necessary and important buy-in of our peers.

3.3.2. User Buy-In

Another big test of the new processes and methods we implemented was the users. Because the majority of the changes we made in 2018 were internal to the development group, there was little change to the user experience. However, in 2019, we worked to empower the business units to own their domains and to take more ownership in development tasks by collaborating to write the specification for each task. We also looked to business users for explicit approval on testing plans. As we rolled specification requirements out, we worked to guide and teach business users what we were looking for. As with the development team, it was important to build trust and provide open communication. We are still working on providing documentation so that the software development process is as transparent and defined as possible.

3.4. Benefits Gained

In 2019, we continued to improve the software development process. By utilizing the Kanban board, we were able to identify some ways to improve our process. We chose to break the release manager role out as a defined role, which lead to improvements around the clarity and communication of the release process. We also chose to define a code review team – previously, developers were asking any peer on the team to review their changes. Now, there is a small team, still made up of peers, but each dedicated to a particular business unit. This brings a more focused review by someone who is familiar with the existing code base. One last improvement was the addition of Toggl. Toggl is a time tracking tool, and by creating categories for each department, we are able to show more accurately how much time the development team spends working on tasks for each business unit. We are also able to show how much time we spend during each Kanban phase by utilizing labels for the Toggl entries.

4. The State of Things: 2020

4.1. Software Development Lifecycle

In 2020, our SDLC remains largely the same as it was in 2019. We continue to intake tasks after the business unit has prioritized them, and work through each stage on the Kanban board. We have stabilized throughput of tasks quite a bit, and have settled into Kanban WIP limits that allow an optimized workflow. At this time, it is not likely that we will make large changes, but we will continue to utilize feedback and metrics to make small changes and tweaks. The next change that will be implemented is a formalized test plan requirement for all tasks, and a review and approval method for testing plans. Our team also has a goal of creating a robust regression testing suite to further ensure the success of new code entering production.

4.2. Team Structure

4.2.1. Development Operations (DevOps) Team

In 2020, we have begun to work toward the formalization of a development operations (DevOps) team. This team will include many of the teams and functions that already exist, including quality assurance, release management, production support, and even some other groups like database administration. The DevOps team is still a work in process at this time, but combining the efforts of these groups should really drive change and increase our ability to support developers and business users. We are also looking into how we can apply these efforts to make improvements for our system administrators, help desk, and backend support teams. Unifying the whole Information Technology department will allow us to provide a better service and experience for our business users overall.

4.3. Roadblocks and Complications

4.3.1. COVID-19

In March 2020, COVID-19 tore across the headlines. Gradually at first, and then all of a sudden, it was knocking on our door. Michigan public universities switched to online instruction, public schools closed down, and soon a shelter in place order was issued for our state. In all of this, our helpdesk and IT teams worked aggressively to outfit our many in-office workers to become remote. Overall, they achieved preparing 92% of our workforce to work remotely. Of course, everyone being remote all at once could be a big problem – how could our development group prepare? Fortunately, because of the effort and investment we have been putting in for the past two years on improving processes, creating development support, and creating a reliable and predictable SDLC, we have been able to continue serving our business users without much interruption at all. In the first week of remote work for all employees of the bank, 14 tasks rolled out to production with no rollbacks. We continue to follow our processes, collaborate with business users, and provide clear and consistent support for developers and business users alike.

4.4. Benefits Gained

By implementing a DevOps team, we have offloaded much of the work involved with Jira and Confluence maintenance, process improvement, and environment maintenance from the development team. The DevOps team is focused on providing the development team with consistent, optimal performance so they can focus on developing code. In the first half of 2020, the DevOps team was able to implement consistent retrospective meetings, update the priority scheme across the organization, pay down tech debt by implementing software upgrades for developers, create a clear and concise definition of each step in the SDLC, and much more. The DevOps team is actively working on engaging developers, IT, and business users to continuously improve our processes for all who are involved in them.

5. Flexibility in Process

Having invested the time and energy into making rigid processes, we are now seeing the benefit of flexibility where it really matters. Now, with the majority of our company working remotely, we are truly putting our processes to the test. We are not flailing, not taking shortcuts, but rather, finding it possible to maintain the same accuracy and communication as when we were all available in the office. Our specifications, code, and test plans continue to be reviewed, business users continue to participate as the drivers of getting tasks to development, and testing continues to be completed. We are able to lean on these processes as a guide, and now, more than ever, we are relying on the communication and trust that we built up to complete necessary work to bring the most value to our teams and customers. If a developer or user has questions about the process there are resources available and clearly documented. If there are questions about the status of a task, they can easily be addressed by looking up the virtual Kanban board on Jira.

In the end, by creating and enforcing rigid processes, we have created a stronger team who works well together and produces high quality software consistently for our business users. By continuing to fortify our processes, we will be able to continue providing exceptional value for our business users and customers.

References

Books:

Kim G, Behr K, Spafford G. The Phoenix Project: a Novel about IT, DevOps, and Helping Your Business Win. Portland, OR: IT Revolution; 2018.

Websites:

Kim, Gene. “The Three Ways: The Principles Underpinning DevOps.” IT Revolution, 22 Aug. 2012, www.itrevolution.com/the-three-ways-principles-underpinning-devops/

Let's Focus More on Quality Engineering and Less on Testing the Software

Joel Montvelisky
joel@practitest.com

Abstract

What value do we provide as testers?
The short answer is that Testing has no value in itself. The testing team provides a service to our organizations, so we (the whole organizations) can deliver value-adding products and services to our customers.

Today, due in part to the evolution of development practices and in part due to the adoption of new technologies, engineers who used to "only" test can expand their value-adding activities towards Quality Engineering in the broader sense of the word.

In this paper we will briefly review the forces pushing forward the changes in the way we create and deliver products today.

We will map the way a traditional tester might fit into this new reality and expand her activities, roles and responsibilities.

Then we will explore the value these additional responsibilities can provide to our organizations as we actively take on the role of Quality Engineers.

Biography

Joel Montvelisky is a Co-Founder and Chief Solution Architect at PractiTest.

He has been in testing and QA since 1997, working as a tester, QA Manager and Director, and a Consultant for companies in Israel, the US and the EU. Joel is also a blogger with the QA Intelligence Blog and is constantly imparting webinars on a number of testing and Quality Related topics.

Joel is also the founder and Chair of the OnlineTestConf, and he is the co-founder of the State of Testing survey and report. His latest project is the Testing 1on1 podcast with Rob Lambert, released earlier this year - https://qablog.practitest.com/podcast/

Joel is also a conference speaker, presenting in various conferences and forums worldwide, among them the Star Conferences, STPCon, JaSST, TestLeadership Conf, CAST, QA&Test, and more.

1. Introduction - Evolution

Every profession or practice finds itself in constant evolution as the experience of its practitioners, the knowledge in the field of practice, and the technology used to perform it improve and expand constantly.

This evolution is usually the result of a number of factors converging in the same place and at the same time, interacting to push towards a more efficient and effective place overall.

An interesting finding is that, in many cases, the most important of these converging factors for evolution is "need". If there is a strong desire to become better, faster or more efficient then we will look for ways to fulfill this need - and hopefully find them.

As has been apparently mis-attributed to Plato countless times:

"Necessity is the mother of invention."

The origins of this quote may be unknown, but its accuracy is still very real.

Software Development is a profession in constant evolution. It evolves because we continue generating more advanced tools and technology. It is pushed forward as we find better languages and processes to do our work. And yet, the most important contributing factor to its evolution is the business need to constantly come up with newer and better solutions to the everyday needs of humans in their daily lives.

If that wasn't enough, market and competitive forces constantly challenge organizations to deliver products faster, and we respond by evolving the way we work in order to answer their needs.

This means that we are on a constant path of forced improvement. We are far from reaching a final goal, a goal that is destined to move constantly away from us.

2. From Waterfall to Agile and then to DevOps

2.1. Waterfall

Back in the 90's the predominant development practices were based on Waterfall processes. The most common representations of them being the V and W development models.

These development models were used in tens of thousands of projects (or more), with very good results and delivering many of the most complex products and projects of the time.

There are many details and processes that form "waterfall" based practices. But here we want to focus on only a number of these characteristics of teams working under this approach, the ones that are most relevant to our topic.

These points are the following:

1. The assumption is that customers know from the very beginning of the project exactly what they want to get from the finished product and are able to articulate it on a Requirements Specification document.
2. During the actual process, each step is separated into encapsulated phases for requirements, design, programming, and testing; followed by the delivery of the product and its ongoing maintenance phase.
3. In order to advance to the next phase in the process, the previous one needs to be completed.
4. If an issue is detected on any of the previous phases (e.g. if testing finds an issue with requirements), then the team will need to repeat (at least partially) all the phases from the one where the issue was detected and corrected.
5. Internal teams (product, programming, testing, etc.) work independently. There is no collaboration between the teams other than to provide feedback from one to the other.
6. Products, once finished, are shipped to external customers and end-users. Any feedback to the team is provided back via indirect channels such as Support or Customer Services.

Looking specifically at the QA teams, most of the time the objective testing on Waterfall projects was something along the lines of:

Find all the bugs before releasing the product.

Ensuring the final product has reached the desired levels of quality and stability.

Without going into too much detail, it is obvious that both these points are problematic.

Focusing on the first part, it is impractical and highly cost ineffective to run the number of tests necessary in order to ensure "all the bugs" are found before the release of any product. This is why this is done only in products where the cost of a defect released to the field is extremely high and/or can cause the loss of human life (such as the aviation, safety and healthcare industries).

And looking at the second part of this objective, as much as we can provide our inputs (the ones of the testing team) with regards to what we expect to see in the product, it is very hard to come up with the exact criteria of what the end user actually expects to see. This is the case, because in most cases there are hundreds or thousands (or more) of them, and each user will have her or his individual expectations and ideas regarding the product. And even in those cases when we are able to come up with such a list, it will still be second guessed by the additional members of the development and product teams who have other thoughts or interests in the matter.

2.2. Agile (Iterative processes)

Iterative processes started popping up in the late 90's but they took off only in the early 2000's with the spread of Agile approaches and Scrum methodologies.

For the sake of simplicity and pragmatism, in this paper I will encapsulate all the iterative approaches under the name Agile or Agile approach given that it is the current industry practice.

Depending on who you ask there are a number of different reasons why Agile processes caught on.

The one I find most appealing is the need to include customers in the development process to provide their constant feedback on the product as it was being created.

When Agile was first introduced, we understood that it was unrealistic to assume the customer could know exactly what he wants from the beginning of the project. It is also unreasonable to believe changes in their needs can be avoided (or even fought), and here Agile processes come to factor in change and flexibility into our operating approach, and to adopt it (their need for change) as a reality.

Again here, there are many characteristics we can mention about Agile approaches that are relevant to our analysis, but the most important ones are the following:

1. Only users know what they want, and sometimes it is hard to understand their needs up-front. That is why it is best to constantly show them what we are creating for them and get their feedback on the evolving product.
2. The reason for working in small chunks or User Stories, is to get this feedback and make the necessary changes and corrections to our product as quickly as possible.
3. Our process should be simple, and be ready to fix bugs and solve issues quickly as they appear.
4. The most effective way for a team to work is integrated and focusing on constant communication, with all its members interacting and collaborating with each other in order to achieve the goals of the team faster.

5. Our products are still being "shipped" to external customers. This means that once the product is released we get feedback from indirect proxies such as Customer Support, Professional Services, and sometimes from our Product Teams.

Following a similar exercise as we did before, we can define the intrinsic objective of the testing team as:

Work together with Developers to test and deliver products quickly, receive feedback from users, and continue the iterative development process.

There are a number of changes here from what we saw in the waterfall approach, but some of the most important are:

- The realization that bugs are not the responsibility of the tester, they belong to the team as a whole.
- The focus has been shifted (maybe too much?) from ensuring quality to delivering quickly.
- The aim is to get feedback from users in order to validate and continue moving forward

Due in part to this shift from quality to speed, when some organizations started adopting Agile methodologies such as Scrum one of the first actions they did was to get rid of all their testers. The idea was that if testing was the responsibility of the developers, then they could work without testers in the team.

In most cases, after one or two terrible release cycles, most of these teams went back to hiring testers and including them as part of their Agile teams.

2.3. DevOps

The transition to DevOps is a typical example of evolution being caused by the convergence of two separate major factors that are apparently unrelated (plus a big business push for speed running in parallel to them).

Factor 1 - Web Technologies, that allowed organizations to stop shipping products to customers using media they would need to install in their servers or even clients. The solution being to host these applications as Services in their own cloud infrastructures (e.g. AWS or Azure).

Factor 2 - Widespread adoption of Agile and the reduction of the time it took to release updated versions to customers. Or in other words, the increasing number of releases a team had to do in a specific time span.

As companies started running their own products on their web infrastructure instead of shipping CDs to customers to install them in their own environments, it became easier to encapsulate features into a number of smaller user stories and just release them at an increased rate.

This forced the development teams to create products ready to be deployed faster and easier. Meaning that the development had to understand a lot more about the deployment process and environment better.

In parallel this also forced the operations teams to learn how to cope with issues in the products being deployed faster, bringing them closer to the work of development.

With time the lines dividing the development and the operating teams blurred more and more, until we started seeing integrated teams that were in charge of both developing and operating their products - Hence DevOps teams.

At first glance there is not a big difference between teams working based on good Agile processes and those working on DevOps approaches. But once you look closer there are some important differences to mention:

1. We have the same integrated teams defining and creating the features, and then deploying and running them in production. This means we can monitor the usage of our products and features directly from production, and understand if customers are happy with our products.
2. We can now detect, understand and fix problems as they happen in Production environments faster and better than ever before. This means that the cost of releasing a bug (and fixing it once it has been detected in the field) has been greatly reduced. So much so, that sometimes it makes more sense to skip parts of the internal testing process, if the potential bugs we would find in them are cheaper to fix only if they materialize in the production environment - or as it is known Testing in Production.

What is the objective of Testing in DevOps teams? In a sense it is similar to that of Agile but with some important variations:

Work with "Dev" to release quickly, enabling stability on the deployment process, engineering fast feedback from production.

Notice that the focus here, similar to Agile, is to release quickly by working with Dev, but a lot more emphasis is placed on stability of the process (not only of the product), and maybe the most important change is the focus on providing fast feedback from production.

This is the feedback that will be used in order to either fix issues quickly in production or to continue improving the product in its future iterations.

3. An "incomplete" but important introduction to Modern Testing

Evolution of processes happens when people start thinking, and many times talking, about how to make something better.

In the case of Testing and Quality Assurance, and specifically around the context of Agile & DevOps approaches, one of the best examples we can see is in the emergence of "Modern Testing" and its growing community.

Modern Testing (or MT for short) is a concept initially developed and still currently led by Alan Page and Brent Jensen as part of their AB Testing podcast.

The ideas behind MT have also spread, and are being constantly reviewed and commented on by a significant and increasing number of testers from around the world that have come together to form a community around this new approach to Quality in general.

You can read a lot more about this approach on the official MT website - http://www.moderntesting.org/, where you can also find links to the AB Testing podcast mentioned above (highly recommended) as well as to the community itself.

I am not going to do a deep review of MT in this paper but I still want to mention two very important aspects of it, its mission statement and its seven principles.

The Modern Testing Mission Statement is the following:

Accelerate the Achievement of Shippable Quality.

The statement is both pragmatic and vague at the same time.

The focus is on accelerating the process. The goal is Quality (in the context of the process around releasing or “shipping”). Finally, the word “testing” is totally absent.

MT has seven guiding principles to help practitioners understand the most important aspects of this approach. These principles are the following:

1. Our priority is improving the business.
2. We accelerate the team, and use models like Lean Thinking and the Theory of Constraints to help identify, prioritize and mitigate bottlenecks from the system.
3. We are a force for continuous improvement, helping the team adapt and optimize in order to succeed, rather than providing a safety net to catch failures.
4. We care deeply about the quality culture of our team, and we coach, lead, and nurture the team towards a more mature quality culture.
5. We believe that the customer is the only one capable to judge and evaluate the quality of our product.
6. We use data extensively to deeply understand customer usage and then close the gaps between product hypotheses and business impact.
7. We expand testing abilities and knowhow across the team; understanding that this may reduce (or eliminate) the need for a dedicated testing specialist.

One of the most important aspects we can take away as Test Engineers from MT, is that we are not in charge solely of testing. The only way to improve the process is to change the way we approach quality, understanding that (a) testing needs to be done by every member of the team, and (b) there are many more additional quality-related operations and actions that require our urgent focus and attention.

Testing being the responsibility of every member of the development team is a point that has been reviewed by many people and papers, and so we will only review this “in passing” on some of the coming sections.

We will go more in-depth on additional quality related tasks requiring our attention and focus within the work of our development teams.

4. Focusing on Quality at the beginning of the process

There is a cliché that we need to “Shift Left”, meaning to take part in processes that occur before the traditional (at least on Waterfall terms) testing phase. I prefer to call this focusing on Quality at the beginning of the development process.

There are a number of actions we can do, or actually need to do, as Quality Professionals that fall under this category.

4.1. Bring customers into the Process

As mentioned above, one of the most pragmatic business motivations for introducing Agile practices was to bring the customer's feedback earlier into the process, resulting in a better and more accurate product without delaying the release schedule.

The problem with this is that, when you bring customers into the process they tend to make a lot of "noise" that disrupts the developers during their work, and so for most organizations this is more of a "theoretical idea" than an actual practice.

We know that one of the traditional tasks of testers has always been to represent the customer within the development process. We can expand this charter into the more concrete and pragmatic task of bringing as much of the voice of our customers into our team's development process - without actually bringing the customer on-site.

Here are a couple of examples of things we can do, as Quality Engineers, to bring more of our "customer's voice" into the development process.

4.1.1. Visit customers to get their feedback first hand

This allows us to understand our users better, see how they work with our products in their environments, get more realistic inputs, and ask questions that we find relevant.

An additional bi-product of this activity is that it allows us to follow up with these same customers we visited later on, in case we have additional questions during our work on the development stages of the product.

I have been doing this for over 15 years, with great results for all my teams.

4.1.2. Bring real data / applications / configurations / etc.

Many times, if we cannot get real users to come to us, we can bring real data to help us understand more about how people are working with our products, and also allow us to test them closer to the way they will be used once we release them "into the wild".

If you are visiting customers in person, as mentioned in the point above, then it is relatively simple to ask for configuration files, or copies of environments, etc. But even if you do not visit them, there are ways to get this information.

Just as an example, some 15 years ago I was working for a company where we had a large Enterprise Product. A big issue with the release of this product was the upgrade of the database backend with every new version. The system was very complex and the upgrade would break if customers did any modifications or customizations to the database (DB) schema - and many customers did a lot of customizations to their DB schemas...

Each time a customer had an issue with the upgrade, they would contact our Customer Support team for help. Support would take their DB and try to upgrade it. When this failed they solved the issue, and if needed they would contact our Dev team for assistance. At the end, they would return the migrated DB to the customer.

After a while, we came up with an idea. We would ask our support team to request permission to keep a copy of the DB in store, so that we could test our upgrade process on it during the next development cycle. This would assure the users that their project would be successfully upgraded and it would give us real data for our testing.

About half the customers agreed, and within some months we had an automatic system running once a week, migrating tens of real databases from real customers and fixing bugs in the upgrade process as they were discovered.

Within two releases we cut DB migration issues by close to 80%.

4.1.3. Create "Personas" for your team

Persona or customer profiles are a great tool both for the design process, as well as for the testing or development operations of our teams.

If we have a descriptive and complete profile of our users, that includes things such as Age, Experience, Constraints, etc. this will guide us while designing our solutions and in case we need to make decisions regardless of things such as bug severities, prioritization of features, etc.

Personas are also a great tool when you need to create test scenarios, as they help you to envision the way users will interact with our solutions based on their personal characteristics and even constraints.

4.2. User story validation

Are we creating the right product? Focusing on the right feature? Moving forward while including the feedback needed for the process?

There are many points we can review in order to ensure our team's efforts are focused on the right path, and it all boils down to ensuring our user stories are correct.

4.2.1. Capture inputs from other departments

We have to make sure to get as much information to define the user story from places such as Customer Support, Professional Services, Customer Success, Documentation, etc. This will ensure the story is complete and also that it will not be delayed later on because we forgot to cover an important aspect. It will also help us to detect conflicts and inconsistencies with other areas of the product

As testers we are already used to looking at the big picture, encompassing all the application and not only the narrow area we are currently working on. This gives us an added perspective and the ability to find places where the user story may be in conflict with functionality already available in the product.

4.2.2. Generate an MVP - Minimum Viable Product

It is very easy to get carried away, and try and solve the whole problem in "one step". But the idea of an iterative process is to start small, validate, and then continue developing once we know we are on the right path.

One of the tasks we have as Quality Professionals is to ensure we follow this rule and limit the scope of our user stories to the minimum set of features (and value to our users) to get this validation.

4.2.3. Define success criteria and the instrumentation to measure it

We are looking to get validation on the functionality we are creating, but how do we actually know if the users liked it or not? When you are working on products with tens or hundreds of thousands of users it is not a matter of asking them for their individual feedback.

Instrumentation will help us to understand what is happening to the functionality in production when working on larger scale applications.

Are people using the feature? What parts are they using and/or not using?

If there is an error or an exception, do we have enough information in order to understand it and fix it quickly?

We need to think about everything we will want and need to know once the feature is released, and ensure we have the ability (within the code!) to know this.

If we do not have requirements for instrumentation as part of our user stories then we will be blinded once the feature is pushed out to production.

5. Quality Engineering towards the end of the process

There are also a number of actions we can take that fall either around the traditional (again, based on Waterfall terms) testing phase or in the phases that follow it within the DevOps process.

5.1. Coaching and Training on how to test

Even if your company “decided” that everyone in the development team will test, this does not mean that tomorrow all your Devs will be able to test (even if they want to). It is imperative that you, as the Quality and Testing Specialist come up with a plan that will train and coach your developers on how to test correctly.

There are a number of ideas that will help you to do this in a pragmatic and effective way.

5.1.1. New Dev Training program

Most organizations have an on-boarding process already defined, you need to make sure that the onboarding process for developers includes at least a couple of sections on testing.

Look for things such as testing techniques and heuristics, as well as how to set up environments, interview relevant people, come up with testing ideas, document tests and bugs, etc.

5.1.2. Pair testing sessions with developers and testers

I find this is the most efficient way to teach developers what testing is all about.

Most times developers are not even aware about the process of testing or how we, the testers, go about reviewing the system and thinking about additional scenarios to run.

A good and proven approach to pair testing is to start by pairing a Dev with an experienced Tester. Give the tester the lead during the first session, then on the second or third paired session the team can switch places, so that the tester can mainly provide feedback to the dev while she does most of the actual testing work.

It is also good to change pairs, so that both Devs and Testers can get the perspective and knowledge of others within their teams.

5.1.3. Test Process Definition

Having a defined process helps people to know what is expected of them, and what steps they need to follow. On the other hand, if your process is too heavy and exhausting, then most people will simply choose to ignore it.

Having a testing process that is specifically defined for Agile Teams is important, make sure it is based on communication between individuals, on documenting ONLY what is needed, and in having open collaboration between the team members.

5.1.4. Testing Briefings and Debriefings

These practices are important to all testing operations, and they are critical when doing development testing.

You want to make sure Developers have all the information they need before planning and especially before they run their tests. Most times the information on the User Story is only a small part of what we need, so it makes sense to take 5 - 10 minutes before the actual testing operations to ensure we have everything we need (knowledge, plans, tools, data, etc.)

Once we are done with our testing, it is important to take 5 minutes to review our work and findings, with the objective of verifying that all the important parts of the functionality were covered by our tests. This is done based on the previous knowledge or data, and also in light of the findings of the test itself.

5.2. Test enablement for Developers

In addition to training and coaching, we can operate in a way that will enable developers, testers and other non-testers to test more efficiently.

5.2.1. Create "Testing Cookbooks"

Cookbooks are informal step by step guides that help people who are not familiar or experienced in testing techniques to perform their testing operations.

They should include all the steps to plan, run and document their testing. They can also be created for different types of testing or areas of the product - with the idea of making them short, focused and easy to follow.

5.2.2. Develop Different Testing Artifacts

Different people will approach testing differently, and for this they may prefer different testing artifacts to guide their manual testing operations.

Some people will like detailed testing scripts, others will prefer Exploratory Charters, while some may even prefer checklists and heuristics, etc.

In the case of Developers my experience is that they are good at working with checklists and heuristics, and less good with Exploratory Charters.

In any case it is good to have artifacts to suit the needs of the different testers in your team.

5.2.3. Test Environments

How many times have you heard the phrase "it works on my machine"?

We all know that the environment and data have a lot to do with the results of your tests. The more realistic and "less clean" the testing environment, the higher the chances you will run into the kind of bugs that our users run into "in production".

It is unrealistic to think developers will take the time to create their own testing environments that include good data, realistic set ups, etc.

It is better to have a number of these environments ready, and to allow anyone in the team to use them whenever they need to.

With the use of containers such as Docker, Kubernetes, etc, this is even simpler and easier to achieve.

5.3. Deployment and Release process

Many think that deployment and releases should be the task of the Ops team and not the testing team, but they are missing a big point here - Deployment process, releases, and specially rollbacks need to be planned, developed and tested carefully and thoroughly, just like any other aspect of the product.

5.3.1. Release risk management

Every release is different, and they do not have the same level and type of risks. In many organizations the Test Manager doubles as the team Risk Manager, and in this case the Testing Specialist can also work as the Risk specialist of your deployments.

Do we truly understand what could go wrong? Do we have contingencies? Is this the only way or the best way to do this? Someone needs to ask these questions and get proper answers.

5.3.2. Staged processes

Does your team have different environments where to test the system? Is at least one of these environments realistic enough in hardware and software?

It is important to ensure all testing has been done, and enough of it in an environment that resembles the production system. It is not enough to have realistic data (as was covered in a previous section) if the machinery is radically different from the one we will work in production.

5.3.3. Deployment & rollback testing

We test how to work with the system, but many times we also need to test how we are going to deploy the system and what our behavior will be if we find something is wrong.

Rollback testing is something that is usually done in theory. "Yes, if needed then we will rollback the DB, bring a backup, and redeploy the production code to the previous version..." But what about the dependencies? Are there any other "surprises" that will only show themselves when we actually start running this rollback process in the real environment.

These are usually the times when you will need to work fast, and avoid thinking as much as possible, and so it makes sense to try and document all the steps needed, as well as rehearse constantly to ensure you know what to expect and how to behave in every step of the process.

5.3.4. Scheduling and notifications

Every hosted system undergoes maintenance and has scheduled downtime. When this happens, we need to make sure our users are aware of this, and can prepare accordingly.

Ensure the defined notification procedures are followed and that scheduling has been done according to the best available windows.

Especially when you are working on Software as a Service, we need to remember that a big part of this service is around communication with our users.

5.4. Production analytics

We talked about the need to monitor our products in order to ensure they are fulfilling the demands of our customers. In addition to that, we also want to have monitoring in place for the more menial objective of making sure our service is operating at the correct level and avoiding any outages.

5.4.1. Instrumentation planning and testing

Most of the time a system "falls" only after a steady process of deterioration. Resource availability decreases over time, response time starts to increase, one of the subsystems gets stuck, then another and another until the whole service falls.

Correct instrumentation will ensure timely notifications are given when there are still actions to be done and time to react.

What instrumentation to develop into the product? What deterioration levels should trigger alerts? All these are aspects to be analyzed, planned, reviewed, refined and constantly improved.

Instrumentation and alerts also need to be tested, especially since we will only notice their absence when it is already too late to do something about it.

5.4.2. Feature validation analytics

As previously mentioned, analytics and instrumentation need to grow as our product does. Every important new feature should include instrumentation, both for product health as well as for user adoption.

5.4.3. Dashboards and alerts

If you want people to improve something then it helps to measure this, and to share these metrics with as many people in the team as possible.

This is true about product monitoring and performance analytics as well.

Make sure the information is not buried in a dark and forgotten log, but displayed in bright colors and simple letters so that everyone can see it and understand what is going on with the system.

6. Conclusion – Quality Assurance work that generates value

I mentioned "in passing" that one of the initial by-products of the implementation of Agile in some organizations was the dismissal of their whole testing teams. This was followed by an almost Universal reverse process of re-hiring testers to be part of the Agile teams and either perform or lead the testing process internally.

When talking with a number of people who worked in these teams, many of them mentioned that one of the reasons for these actions was that the value of the QA team was perceived to be limited only to the actual testing.

This concept of "perceived value" is an important one, since it will guide not only the way others see the work of the tester, but also the opportunities he or she has to take an active role in additional tasks of the team.

Perceived value is very hard to measure or pin-point, and so we all just disregard it as something that is not really important to our everyday work. This could not be further from the truth.

We need to expand our perceived value, as this will be one of the tools we will use in order to expand our charters. Still, how can we get a better understanding of it, given that it is hard to define?

I have been working on this question with a number of colleagues in the field, and I was able to come up with a set of questions that will help you and your team understand what is the concrete value you provide to your organization.

These questions are the following:

- What decisions do you help to make in your team and process? How?
- How do you change and improve the process by which your company delivers products?
- If you and your team were not there, what would be different?

By answering these questions together with the non-testing members of your organization, you will be able to get a better understanding of your perceived value. Then you can use this information in order to plan how to expand your work into the additional areas you see fit.

References

AB Testing Podcast - https://www.angryweasel.com/ABTesting/

Modern Testing - http://www.moderntesting.org/

State of Testing Survey & Report program - https://qablog.practitest.com/state-of-testing/

Are You Ready for AI to Take Over Your Automation Testing?

Lisette ZOUNON, CSP- CSM, CALI, DTM
zzlisette@gmail.com

Abstract

We all know that Artificial Intelligence is here and here to stay. Every industry leader has been waiting for how and when AI will disrupt their work. Most teams are wondering how to leverage AI for their quality automation. Indeed, Artificial intelligence has made some major strides in recognizing patterns in software testing and the opportunity for QA engineers to leverage some features that can benefit testing activities and software delivery teams. Although there are several QA automations tools out there, there is a clear advantage in the modern software automation tool leveraging AI.

Attendees in this session will take away:

- Determine if your automation strategy can leverage the benefits of AI tools
- Discuss success case study of using AI tools as part of automation testing
- Leverage AI tools in your CI/CD environment
- Discuss the ROI for your project and your team happiness factor.

Biography

Lisette Zounon is a passionate quality engineering leader with over 16 years of experiences helping people and companies improve the quality of their applications, with solid tools, a simple process, and a smart team.

Lisette was responsible for leading and managing high-performing quality-testing teams throughout all phases of the software development testing cycle. This includes establishing and maintaining the QA strategy, processes, platforms, and resources needed to deliver 24x7 operationally critical solutions for many of the world's largest companies.

Lisette is a proven leader who thrives in a highly technical software development environment. She is a constant champion of employing best practices for QA, agile methodologies, and Scrum implementation to achieve high quality delivery and increase your team's and customers' happiness.

1. Introduction

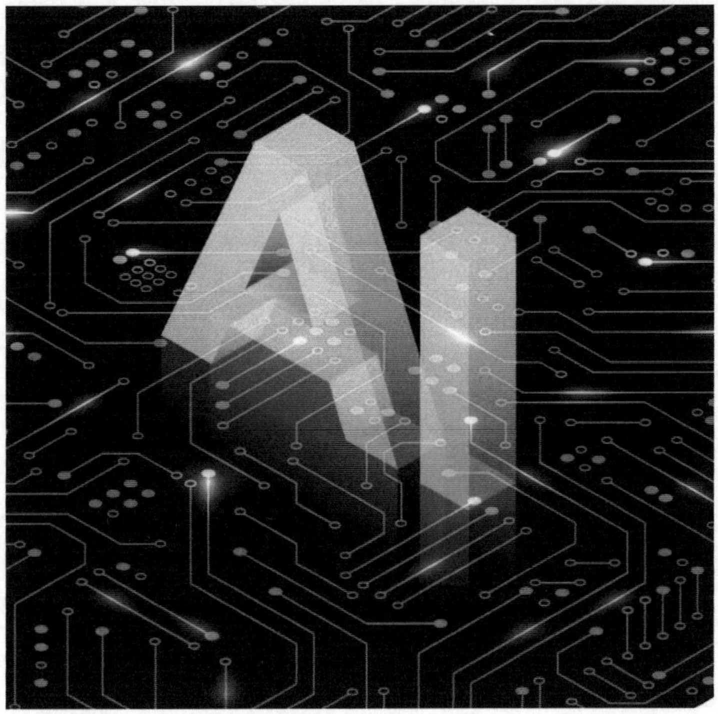

In the past ten years, most QA automation tools provide QA engineers opportunities to create test automation, but we still lack in some areas such as efficiency in execution, reusability of the test cases, and test maintenance update. Manual testing may take a long time whenever a break in the script occurs. QA automation has room for improvement to enable fast error detection. At its core, Machine Learning is a pattern-recognition technology—it uses patterns identified by your machine learning algorithms to predict future trends.

Artificial intelligence is becoming very crucial in information technology. In the last few years, software automation has been experimenting with AI and machine learning. Below I am going to detail some of the benefits of AI-based tools. My personal approach to this paper is really to be tool agnostic in terms of considering what benefits you can drive from Artificial intelligence. I am not going to provide you with a specific tool but focus on the functionality that AI-based tools can provide software testers and automation engineers.

2. Determine the benefits of using an AI-based tool

2.1. Visual validation testing

Because of the accuracy of AI-powered automated visual testing, they can be deployed in more than just functional and visual testing. Visual testing is about verifying if the visual aspects of an application seem appropriate to the end-users. Visual and functional testing complement each other to help you take a holistic approach to test the user interface (UI) of your application. Visual validation automation testing also refers to automated validation UI testing, uses Machine Learning to make sure that UI appears correctly to the users. From our naked eye, it is very difficult to spot very simple errors on the front UI of an application. Machine Learning tools can find differences that human testers miss. Visual validation testing comes as a technique to help supplement testers' role in finding annoying visual errors. Most visual bugs are usually rendering issues.

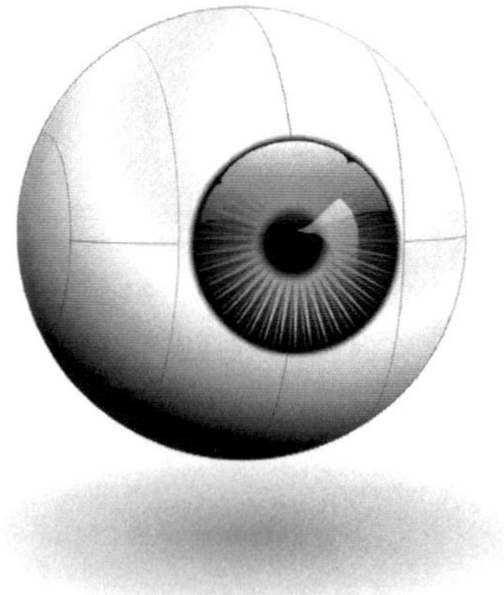

The software engineer creates a script that drives your app, your app creates web pages with static visual elements. Functional testing changes visual elements, so each step of a functional test creates a new UI state you can visually test. Automated visual testing evolved from functional testing. Instead of the unnecessary need to write multiple assertions to check the properties of each visual element, automated visual testing tools visually check the visual appearance of an entire screen with just one assertion statement. This leads to test scripts that are simpler and easier to maintain. Visual smoke tests can be created to automatically check important web apps and site pages for correct loading, visual changes, broken links, JavaScript errors, and network activity issues across browsers. AI-powered visual testing tools are crucial to validating any application that requires a constant change in content and format. Visual testing and monitoring capabilities include:

- Review captured screenshots of the app state during test runs
- Get notified about insights for detected visual changes
- See a side-by-side comparison with the visual diffs highlighted
- Update the visual baseline to adjust for intended changes
- Create a fixed visual baseline to identify all visual diffs, including dynamic content

2.2. Test APIs

Artificial intelligence-enabled API testing provides a leap forward in productivity and efficiency. You can capture all the steps in one set. In addition to functional testing, you can work with web requests and automate testing of your application programming interfaces (APIs). Unlike visual tests that need to interact with a browser, API tests are performed at the message layer (e.g. http protocol) and therefore, run much faster than browser tests, completing in seconds, not minutes. With an AI-enabled API, you can define something once and lock it in in a smart test template and share that template across a large body of testers. It helps to manage and understand the full API inventory. This lowers the threshold of the skills needed for API testing; therefore, businesses can build a sustainable API testing strategy.

2.3. Self-healing of automated tests

You are probably testing software that changes on a regular basis. Some changes are major and require old tests to be rewritten. But many changes, such as relabeling a button or layout adjustments, are minor. A person might not even notice these changes, but they can easily break automated tests. Automated tests require a lot of maintenance when you have an application that changes frequently. Self-healing or auto-healing is used to help adapt to any minor changes, so the tests keep working. Every time tests are run; it interacts with an element; it collects element attributes that it uses to find the element next time and track change overtime.

The test could track many attributes such as text, CSS Classes, data, and other information like location and size on the page. Any test step that interacts with an element on the page can be auto healed. Sometimes the best way to find an element is to look for related elements that have particular text or other attributes. In these cases, a collection of information about the element's ancestor elements is used to help find the specific element. The general process of identifying and potentially healing an element starts with looking for element candidates by matches to the tracked attributes and then choosing the best match based on which combination of attributes matches for each candidate and the history of finds for that element and similar elements. If an ancestor is recorded for the element, this process happens first for the ancestor, then it identifies candidates for the target element within the ancestor and again chooses the best match.

At the beginning, it is usually a challenge for testers to trust and rely on auto healing. For most testers, auto-healing has been a time saver and successfully helps in test cases maintenance. After some time and with some tangible results of auto healing, QA engineers easily embrace the self-healing of automated tests.

AI-enabled automation can provide some more intangible value to QA testers. AI allows your tests to be reliable because your tests can now adapt to developer changes. AI is not here to take over quality assurance, but it is more to allow the quality engineer to become more productive and focus on what QA does best. Below are some of the advantages, as an unintentional consequence of AI has proven.

3. Improve test cases creation

One of the unintentional consequences of using AI-based tools for automation is really improving test creation. AI/ML algorithms can “read” your application and learn about it. These algorithms build a data set that contains observations about your application, including how its various features should behave given certain conditions. This helps them to automatically create test cases where they record the expected results. Given that these tools “learn” using their algorithms, their ability to create test cases is far superior to what rule-based automation can achieve. AI/ML helps learn application, hence creating test cases where they show expected results. This provides the ability to create superior test cases.

4. Spot duplicate errors and new errors in code changes

Another advantage of AI-based tools is the ability to track patterns, spot derivations, and flag it as a potential issue. As a testing professional, it is a daunting task to analyze failures and test flow. This means that dedicated professionals need to continuously monitor the process and the order in which things need to be executed.

With an advanced AI-based test procedure, one can expect the system to analyze failures and decide how to fix the errors based on its previous actions.

6. Create more reliable automated tests

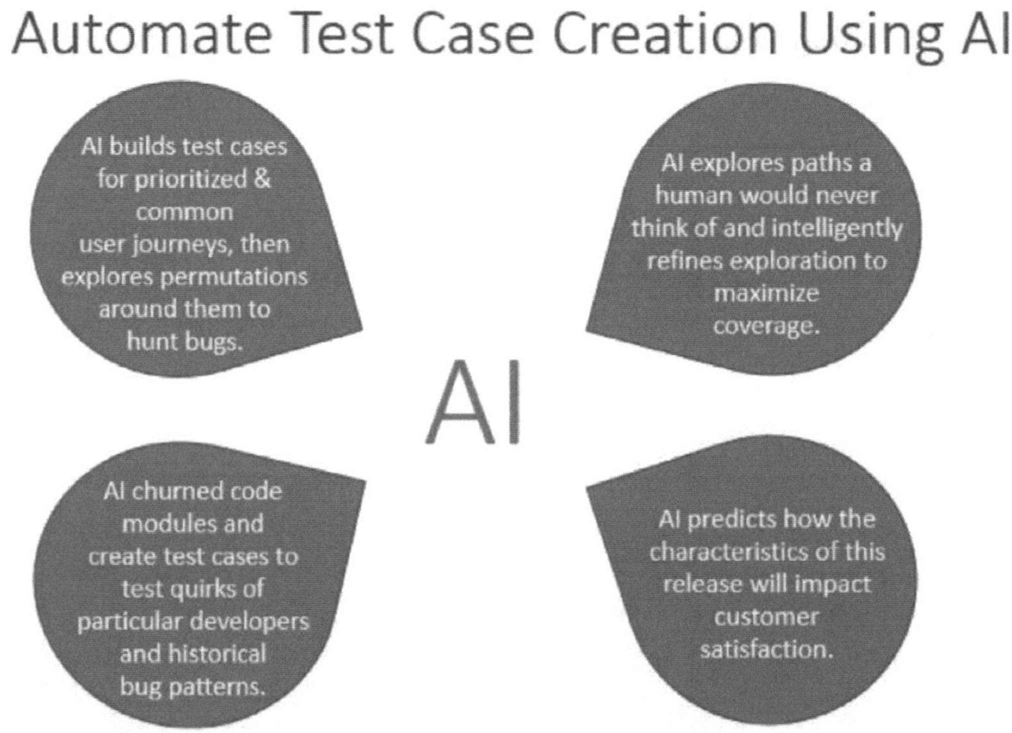

AI can open new possibilities in streamlining automation testing procedures for enhanced results. With AI, one can expect automation testing without coding. There are a lot of ways automation testing can be useful in lowering the efforts and reducing the time required to execute scripts multiple times. Reoccurring tests can be monitored without a test engineer with a machine learning approach. By enhancing the conventional testing procedure with machine learning, you can achieve results that surpass expectations.

7. Summary of successful case study of using AI-based tool

I have the opportunity to experience and use testing tools with functional testing and load testing, both leveraging artificial intelligence. In this paper, I would like to focus on one successful case study that leverages an AI-based tool for a QA automation transformation. Below is a summary of one case study among many using AI based automation tools.

7.1. Problem

For the last ten months, this high performing agile team has been working together on building a new site with various services for the customers. They had met the initial deadline after all the hard work to make the customers happy. But now they have a huge backlog of features that the customer expects them to deliver in the next six months. The team's concern is mostly around ensuring the new features; new code release does not break existing functionalities that the customers have come accustomed to enjoying. The only QA engineer in this agile team has created over 1100 test cases to successfully test all the features of this application. These test cases consisted of smoke tests, sanity tests, and functional test cases that are now part of regression test cases suites. QA engineer firmly believes that these test cases are a necessary part of testing for any new release. This QA member usually takes 2-4 days, three days on average to manually execute all the regression test cases after each code release in one environment. The goal is to ensure fast delivery, fast error detection from one environment to another, and finally fast feedback from the happy customers.

7.2. Solution

QA Leadership took charge of this problem and went out to look for a tool that can help solve this challenge and ensure fast delivery, fast error detection, and fast feedback. It was not an easy challenge to look for a new toolset. I personally believe in solid tools, simple process that empower smart team. I also like to ensure that you understand as a team the features and benefits that each testing tool provides. The features of the testing tools should support your QA automation strategies. We began by defining our QA automation strategies to select the appropriate testing automation tool. We reviewed dozens of QA automation tools from open source tools to paid testing systems. In terms of QA automation tools, most of the tools fall into two categories either a code scripting tool or a codeless tool. But there are few tools that leverage AI for visual validation, auto-healing, and API testing. We are in the area of intelligent testing so we set out to look for a tool that can:

- Offer intuitive interface to quickly create and manage test cases
- Not require specialized scripting expertise and no overhead
- Expand test coverage and evolve test quickly as application evolved

Here are our tool requirements and options for selection:

- Automation testing
- DevOps
- CI/CD, CT, CM (integration, delivery, testing, and monitoring)
- AI and bot for testing

We review the following tools available on the market at that time:

- Selenium
- Test complete
- UFT/QTP
- Katalon Studio
- Mabl

The learning curve was also a crucial part in choosing a testing system. With a small team with no coding experience and prior QA automation experience, it was important to ensure training with a new tool was not time-consuming for the new QA engineer.

Interested Ecosystem

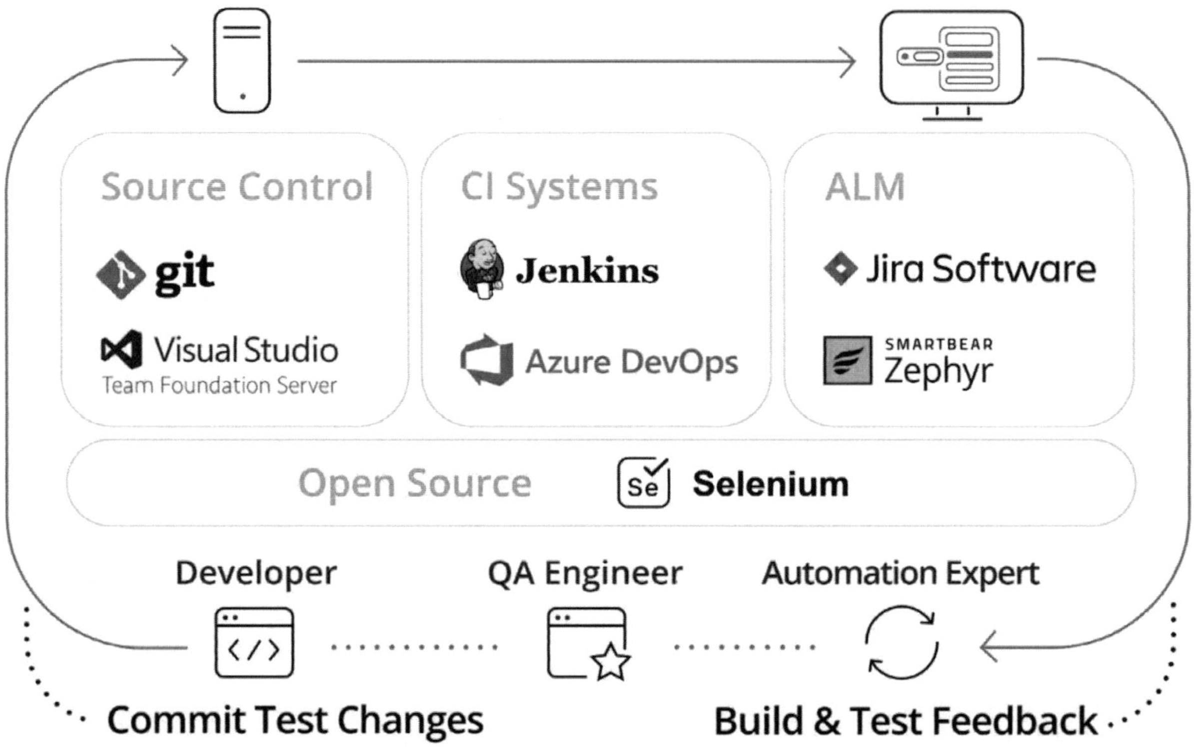

We choose an AI-based tool that the QA team member can leverage to solve this challenge. After sharing the tool with the agile team and demoing this tool for them, they all got excited and planned time in their sprint cycle for QA to automate the regression suite. The QA analyst with no prior coding experience starts creating test cases from smoke test, sanity test then regression test cases in the AI based tool in addition to training in parallel. We learn that the team can learn a new tool especially if they are focused with adequate documentation and support provided by a user community and support team. It took about 3-4 weeks for all these efforts in automating all the 1100 manual test cases. Every engineer's level of understanding and embracing a new tool is different. But in this case study, the total effort with training took about four weeks for this one QA engineer.

7.3. Result

With the implementation of test cases automated in the AI-based tool, the execution of the 1100 automated test cases take about 30 min to run successfully in one environment. Developers are able to leverage the smoke tests in the DEV environment. The sanity test cases were executed in the QA environment before the regression test cases were executed in the staging environment. These test cases are easily executed in another environment from QA to staging to production environments. The QA team is now focused on sprint work items testing and can leverage the regression suite testing to quickly execute test cases. QA team is able to leverage the test case automation in the CI/CD environment. This enables fast delivery of new features, fast error detection, and fast feedback to customers. The team now has a consistent execution of the same test cases in all environments. But the major ROI is the gain in time of execution of the test cases via the automated tool. Some of the advantages for the team is the quick error detection and the quick response from developers when a bug is found. QA is able to execute the regression suite for the entire application to provide a level of confidence to the stakeholders. We collect several quality KPI metrics for each test execution run and we realize that most of our success rate has increased. We also observed as a result that we have less than 5% of escape bugs found in production. This provides a high level of confidence to our stakeholders and customers were greatly satisfied with our collective efforts in investing in AI-based tools.

8. Return on Investment on the project and team happiness

The return on investment ROI on using AI-based tools in your QA automation is huge for your project and your team. Here are few that we know and have experienced:

1. Embrace lifelong learning mindset
2. Fast time to market
3. High-quality software
4. Fast feedback loop to customer
5. Fast response to the issue
6. Cross-functional team involvement
7. Increase team confidence
8. QA becomes a fun activity and no longer a bottleneck
9. Team happiness increase and better team engagement
10. Great teamwork and collaboration

9. The overall impact of AI on future of SDLC

Software development life cycle is definitely being impacted by artificial intelligence. With AI, the new approach will not only automate and facilitate the process but also result in models that are constantly trained and improved. Although agile development significantly accelerated the traditional software development life cycle, all components, including features, functionalities and integrations have to be manually managed and updated. Therefore, it leads to numerous bugs and inconsistencies due to the complexity of the system. With machine learning models, most of the features will be automated which means that human error will be eliminated. That is where the shift from agile to AI development is much more dramatic than that from waterfall to agile. One of the most important factors when it comes to software development is planning a budget and deadlines.

Unfortunately, artificial intelligence can be used to offer more precise estimates and predictions. It takes a lot of expertise and understanding of the nitty-gritty of every individual project, as well as being familiar with the implementation team for these estimates to be reliable. Machine learning can use the data from previous projects, including customer feedback, feature definitions, estimates, and final results to calculate how long it will take to build a new product and what its cost will be.

Although it has been quite a revolutionary change in software testing and quality automation, Artificial intelligence is still promising. Human interaction is still needed to create reliable, reusable test cases. And we know that there is still some bias embedded in AI-based tools.

10. Limitations of Artificial Intelligence

While AI presents an incredible amount of promise in software testing, there are some limitations that we must face, regarding current software testing efforts that involve AI. One of the first limitations is around the ability to create test cases. We don't currently have the ability to have test cases create automatically. We are still relying on engineer with subject matter knowledge to create test cases. Another limitation is around AI-related bias. Bias can creep in at many stages of the deep learning process, and the standard practices in computer science aren't designed to detect it.

11. Conclusion

Artificial intelligence has a profound impact on software development. No matter whether you opt for an approach entirely based on machine-learning models or stick to the traditional SDLC agile approach with a machine-learning facelift, you can expect to boost your productivity, cut costs, speed up the entire development process, and create a more successful, easily-scalable product. Over the next three years, executives expect automation to increase their workforce capacity by 27 percent: equivalent to 2.4 million extras full-time employees. In their embrace of more digitized ways of working, many have adopted robotics to automate repetitive rules-based processes. And the software testing industry has successfully embraced QA systems and QA tools are now seeking to scale these solutions and make them smarter by integrating AI capabilities.

Test automation is a key capability in the age of agile since it facilitates faster product iterations. Given their ability to "learn", AI-powered test automation tools bring a level of automation on the table that simple rule-based automation can't achieve. Whether you are an IT leader in an enterprise or a tester, you should be opened to embrace the innovation that AI has unleashed in the world of test automation.

References

https://support.smartbear.com/testcomplete/docs/testing-with/running/self-healing-tests.html

https://techwireasia.com/2019/07/what-is-self-healing-automation-and-why-is-it-important-to-devops/

https://applitools.com/blog/visual-testing/

https://www.parasoft.com/to-make-api-testing-easier-add-machine-learning-to-your-ai/

https://techbeacon.com/app-dev-testing/how-ai-changing-test-automation-5-examples

https://testsigma.com/blog/can-ai-driven-test-automation-enhance-test-automation/

https://www.technology.org/2019/12/15/how-artificial-intelligence-affects-software-development/

https://www.techfriend.in/pros-and-cons-of-ai-based-software-testing.html

TestCafe: grinding automation issues (End-to-End web testing approach)

Author: Juan Delgado
Co-Author: Erick Gutiérrez, Juan Carlos Patrón, Iván Medina

Juandedios.delgadobernal@gmail.com, erickd.gutierrez@up.edu.mx, 0194229@up.edu.mx, 0189863@up.edu.mx

Abstract

Testing is a crucial activity in the Software Development Process and effective testing produces high-quality software.

Software test automation is used widely to improve the quality and efficiency of the software, using techniques such as End-To-End (E2E) to test an entire flow such as the final user simulating their actions (clicks, inputs, etc.). This is quite useful since as the project grows the number of scenarios to test also increased but building a test automation framework handling E2E testing is not easy on the programming world and even more if so would like to be configured to run on a Continuous Integration (CI) system that can execute all the tests every X amount of time or after a deploy.

We'll be using TestCafe as our tool of choice, a free and open source node.js end-to-end automation tool used to test web applications able to run tests on different popular browsers to carry over multiple tasks and with the possibility to integrate our tests with CI pipelines.

In this paper we are going to dive into the world of this test automation framework and will show how to create a simple and efficient test automation framework project with TestCafe, making a demo with a script running across different web browsers configured with CI.

So, grab a cup of coffee, and let's try to finish our test before our coffee gets cold.

Biography

Juan de Dios Delgado has more than 15 years of experience as engineer. Currently as Test Manager, with Mobica. With strong project management skills, key areas of expertise include understanding complex business requirements & formulating robust test strategies; developing automated test solutions with the ability to interface between Development, Project, QA & Test Teams to ensure execution of test strategy; and extensive software engineering skills. Involved in the test management of Agile/Waterfall projects throughout Software Testing Life Cycle (STLC). Also creating structured processes & best practices to manage defects right through to resolution.

He has participated in several projects, in the last years. He has worked on site in the US and Europe; near shore from Mexico to the US, and offshore from Mexico and India to Europe; working strongly with Functional Testing focusing on Automated Testing and Business Analysis.

Also he is a Professor at Universidad Tecnológica de Aguascalientes and Universidad Panamericana in Aguascalientes, Mexico.

Creator of the "Enhanced Performance Engineering" program that aims to improve a career path of engineers to become them the high-performance professionals by way of improved learning through practice derived from participation in hands-on projects with close customer involvement, intensive teamwork, and the use of modern software development tools and processes. The program is acting as a support of learning experienced center (called Delber) inside of the Universities in Aguascalientes for the IT industry due to the current lack of engineers with experience in the latest trends in technology.

Co-authors:

Ing. Erick David Gutiérrez Hernández

Erick Gutiérrez is an Artificial Intelligence Engineer specialized in Engineering and Quality of Software Projects, also he is doing a Master in Sciences where is working in a project with Deep Learning in Computer Vision about Medical research. He has worked as a Machine Learning developer but also has experience with Software development, quality, and management.

Currently working as Lead Developer in a Company where he can combine his leadership, software skills, and quality assurance experience.

Also, has a passion for social projects were have been working in alliance with Teletón (the world's largest private child rehabilitation system) and Aguascalientes county with technological projects where it has been possible to continue helping people and developing himself a person.

Ing. Ivan Medina Dominguez

Ivan Medina is the co-creator, lead programmer and designer for two new startups in the sectors of 3D Printers and fashion accessories. Before that Ivan worked as an independent Automatic developer for testing webpages and mobile applications. When he's not working in the startups, you would find him learning German or researching about financial analysis, cryptocurrency and blockchain, because he thinks that those will be the next big thing for developers and the World.

Ing. Juan Carlos Patrón Ruano

Industrial Engineer with a specialization in Engineering and Quality of Software Projects. Primarily focused on Full-Stack Development with a passion for joining the Software and Business/Industrial worlds of a company.

1. Introduction

What is an e-commerce? You probably already know the answer to this question. One of the first e-commerce transactions dates back to 1982. Today, there is an estimated 12 to 24 million currently active e-commerce companies worldwide. However out of these millions of websites, only a significantly smaller percentage of these breakthrough $1000 in annual revenue.

The question arises as to why so many of these websites are not reaching this goal? "X", an e-commerce company that is currently in the development stages of their online sales platform, which is based on React, tasked our team with the responsibility of developing an automated testing framework that would test and guarantee their products end quality.

The following paper will discuss the technologies and methodologies that were implemented for the development of our automated testing framework and explain the reasoning as to why these choices were made. We will also analyze the structure of our framework as well as the results and benefits our end product yielded.

2. E-Commerce

2.1. Background information

E-commerce, or electronic commerce refers to transactions which are conducted via the internet. It can be either individuals or companies buying and selling products or services online, as well as online auctions, online banking, ticketing, etc. An e-commerce is a very attractive option for expanding a business's reach especially for small business owners or startups since it offers the possibility to sell your products 24/7, anywhere in the world, with extremely low operational costs. Due to the exponential growth of the internet and globalization it is projected that during this year retail commerce sales will reach an estimated $4.13 trillion. To put this projected growth into perspective, according to Nasdaq, it is estimated that 95% of all retail purchases will be conducted via e-commerce by the year 2040. However, with the ever-growing number of new e-commerce sites being deployed, new challenges begin to arise as well. Your e-commerce must stand out amongst the sea of websites and inspire confidence in the consumer, create customer loyalty, offer security and the best possible user experience.

A key metric to observe in an e-commerce is shopping cart abandonment rate. This is a term used to refer to visitors placing items in their shopping cart but leaving the site before completing a purchase. According to Baymard Institute the average shopping cart abandonment rate for e-commerce sites is approximately 70%. It is crucial to observe this metric since the customer displayed an obvious interest in a product, however something went wrong along the process and abandons the page before completing the transaction.

Of these reasons for abandonment 13% are caused by a website error, bugs, or crashes, 17% of the abandonments are due to the customer not trusting the platform with their credit card information. This lack of trust in the website can also be attributed to a website which is bugged or did not perform as intended. Lastly a staggering 21% is related to a long and complicated check out process. Baymard Institute also reports that with an optimal checkout process and design, a site can increase a second Key Performance Indicator which is conversion rate by 35.2%. This KPI refers to the percentage of your website visitors who conclude their visit with a purchase. The average conversion rate for an e-commerce worldwide is between 2.89% and 3.31%.

3. Business Case

"X" 's development process was stagnant, due to the lack of an adequate testing strategy. Manually testing their e-commerce was a long and tiresome process and validating that their platform upheld quality standards in a variety of browsers and versions was an extremely time-consuming task. This ultimately led their website to have an array of bugs and outstanding issues. Aware that the current situation would impact the quality of the final product "x" wanted to develop an automated testing framework based on Python utilizing Selenium Driver to test their platform. "X" contacted Juan De Dios to consult on the optimal way to approach this possible solution. Juan De Dios formed a team of his previous alumni, composed of a diverse group engineers to analyze this proposal.

After researching and understanding the ins and outs of the e-commerce market, it became apparent to our team that the framework would not only improve the development cycle of the e-commerce website, but it could potentially improve the KPI's previously mentioned. Since these indicators are so intricately related to the performance of the website in the final users' hands, the automated testing framework would directly increase the revenue in the stakeholders' pockets.

If an automated solution would standardize their checkout process, and test these thoroughly they would ultimately provide the customer with an easy bug free process to follow, building sense of confidence, and security inside their platform, thus the 70 % shopping cart abandonment rate can possibly be reduced by 51 % and the average conversion rate can be increased by over a third!

3.1. Mission Statement

As we know, in the e-commerce field, you can't afford any errors since it will directly lead to client and sale loses. The cost of opportunity is too high; thus, security is the key to have a better business and the best and most important way to get a secure site is though testing.

"X" company hired us to perform tests on their site, this was a simple e-commerce web app, however one in which we did not want to take any risk.

After the analysis, we realized that according to the needs of the client and our capabilities, it was best to make an automated test framework taking advantage of a simple tool in which we had some experience that is also easy to use, TestCafe which allows us to do E2E automation. After researching, we concluded that the best suited option for our framework was BrowserStack but to take advantage of the wonders of Continuous integration, we used Jenkins with GitHub for the control and management of versions.

3.2. Proposal

Before making the decision about what tools we were going to use to carry out our tests, we set out to analyze what would be most convenient for our clients. We observed that for the size of the project and the desired speed, we could choose TestCafe, a tool that is quite simple, very clean and incredibly simple for initial configuration.

Also, we combined the tests with BrowserStack and took advantage of its ability to test on different devices and in turn some browsers. Jenkins was employed for Continuous Integration to get an updated delivery project and for developing a simpler way to integrate the changes.

Thanks to the fact that both BrowserStack and TestCafe have had a lot of acceptance by the community, there is a way to integrate them together. When running our tests in TestCafe they will end up being reflected in the device and browser of our interest in BrowserStack with a log that will allow us to have control over our executions and their results.

We decided to use GitHub for version control of our code so that everyone could contribute to the project. The help of a software architect doing a code review for each code modification resulted in higher quality for each push. Continuous Integration let us create version of our project any time and detect errors in an easier way making our testing more secure, that as we said, is a key in this field.

3.3. Goal

Our intention is to build trust in our customers. To achieve this, it is necessary to have a complete flow of tests in which we can identify each type of error that may present itself to us so that, while in production, we can maintain and increase potential customers thanks to the created trust.

To achieve the objectives, the first thing to do is to acknowledge our strengths and weaknesses. We identified that our team has experience with an automated E2E test tool and that thanks to it we can take advantage of different options. Despite being simple tools, together they can be very powerful and we will be able to cover all the types of tests necessary for this project. Compared to other tools that need more set up time, we can take advantage of this by using this time for the development of our framework skipping the learning curve and taking better advantage of the time in an environment known to all members and be able to start contributing to the community.

This coupled with the wonder of continuous testing with the agile scrum methodology, we can have deliverables quite frequently and with version control and project quality monitoring with GitHub.

In conclusion, the goal of electronic commerce is to sell, but what if there is no trust? Exactly, there are no sales, and without sales, it ceases to be electronic commerce, so to maintain it is necessary to prevent all possible errors.

4. Methodology

4.1. Scrum

Working with Scrum methodology begins with identifying the problem and its core components. Nonetheless, one key identifier factor of this methodology is the subdivision of tasks to achieve, making the workflow more fluent. Knowing this we can work in a series of schedules, or sprints, to achieve our goal. We decided to work in sprints with a duration of one week, that way we tackle specific requirements and do not overwhelm ourselves with work that can be accommodated into another sprint. At the culmination of every sprint there must be a meeting held in order for the team to discuss the tasks assigned and their status of fulfillment.

The team was divided into three roles that ensure the workflow needed. First, we have the role of Scrum Master, this role is akin to a coach, who helps the team with its expertise. He focuses on improving the team effectiveness. In our project, the Scrum Master also serves as the link between the team and the e-commerce company, ensuring that the tests were fulfilling the e-commerce requirements.

The next role is the Development team, they work to deliver a potential releasable increment of finished tasks at the end of every sprint. Their task is to give structure to the project and determine the amount of tasks given to each member. The Scrum Master informs the developers what are the areas of interest for the e-commerce and propose a number of tests to evaluate the web page's performance. They also carry out the task of working on writing the paper.

Finally, we have the role of the Developer, this person writes the tests proposed by the Development team, using all the given tools, for identifying the possible flaws of the web platform. This person analyses the outcome of each test and documents their conclusions. Owing to the fact that this is an automated framework, the Developer also integrates the tools needed for the scalability and automation of the project.

4.2. Best practice testing

Working with Scrum methodology begins with identifying the problem and its core components. Nonetheless, one key identifier factor of this methodology is the subdivision of tasks to achieve, making the workflow more fluent. Knowing this we can work in a series of schedules, or sprints, to achieve our goal. We decided to work in sprints with a duration of one week, that way we tackle specific requirements and do not overwhelm ourselves with work that can be accommodated into another sprint. At the culmination of every sprint there must be a meeting held in order for the team to discuss the tasks assigned and their status of fulfillment.

4.2.1. Testing

During the development of this automated framework our team focused primarily on three main types of testing. Functional testing, black-box testing, and regression testing.

For functional testing we used a Business-process-based approach where we tested the scenarios involved in a day-to-day business use on an e-commerce. The four most important processes that were tested include the login and new user creation, password recovery, shopping cart, and the payment process. These four processes are the common denominator in every e-commerce platform and their optimal performance is crucial for the quality of the product and to inspire confidence in the end user. Black-box testing worked hand in hand with our functional testing approach, as the inputs used for our test suites where based on inputs any consumer could introduce, and we verified the output of the system, thus guaranteeing E2E testing. After corrections were made, by fixing bugs or defects regression testing was employed to ensure that modifications did not cause any unintended side effects.

4.2.2. Testing techniques

To improve the quality of the tests inside our automated framework we utilized various techniques during the design process of our test suites. Our design process was dynamic, a combination of specification based with experience-based techniques. The specification-based techniques are primarily based on black-box testing which included techniques of its own such as use case testing, “state transition testing”, boundary value analysis, equivalence partitioning, among others.

Using experience-based techniques, such as exploratory testing or error guessing was an important part of our test design process due to our team being composed of engineers with different skill sets and backgrounds. This allowed us to have a variety of perspectives and insights which led our framework to be more robust.

4.3. Best practice coding

There’s no standard process when it comes to coding. Therefore, industries have been working on creating rules or tools that ensure that all code has the same structure and have an organic flow throughout the code structure.

4.3.1. ESLint

ESLint is a Tool that Find and Fix structural and compilation problems in the JavaScript code. ESLint is a pluggable tool that help identify and report patterns found in JavaScript code, with the goal of making the code more consistent. You can make your own set of rules, or you use the rules that industries like Google or Airbnb employ.

4.3.2. Code reviews

Code Review is the process in which a programmer consciously and systematically checks the code for mistakes or structural mistakes. The code reviews have proven that it helps to accelerate the streamline of the development process for projects.

Code Reviews, when done right, can improve the programmer workflow, reducing the amount of time the Quality Assurance Team requires to check the code, therefore saving time in general.

Particularly in this project we employed the Over-the-Shoulder style of code review. We decided to use this technique because it's the easiest and more intuitive type of style to adopt. Once the code is ready, the supervisor of the code downloads the branch of the GitHub that has the new code that needs to be reviewed. Once the code is reviewed and the team agrees with the changes, the programmer makes a merge from the review branch to the main branch of GitHub.

5. Framework

Web Pages undergo rigorous functional tests that ensure the correct functionality of the page fulfill the expectations of the customers. Usually we have two types of testing; manual and Automation testing. Maintaining and Automating these tests help maintain the quality of the web page releases.

By implementing the appropriate framework for the automated testing, we can significantly increase the speed and accuracy of testing, providing a higher ROI from the project.

Following the standards for a good Framework would result in achieving: Relevant automated test, Concise Reporting, Team Consistency, Implement and Maximize Re-Usability.

5.1. Tool

After discussing about what the tools used together in our project do, we will now talk in a particular way:

5.1.1. BrowserStack

It is a fairly simple tool to use that was perfectly adapted to our project for its power and ease. It was created for Node so its installation is very simple, just run the following lines of code on our console (having Node v6 installed and npm):

npm install -g testcafe

It is developed in JavaScript, so it will be easy for you to understand and do your first tests. Below there is a link where you can find the official documentation for this incredible tool:

https://devexpress.github.io/testcafe/documentation/getting-started/

5.1.2. GitHub

A tool that as a programmer, the more you use the more you begin to depend on it due to its incredible ability for version control and management. It allows us to collaborate remotely with all team members, something that today has even more value due to the ongoing world situation. This makes it perfectly suited for our project. Thanks to our use of the agile Scrum methodology we will have a higher quality and security of deliverables for each sprint, which is combined with a software architect who will constantly help us have better code in our project.

5.1.3. Jenkins

Last but not least, after having talked about GitHub, it is the turn of continuous integration. This system allows us to have deliverables perform a certain action. For example, if we want to do some tests from the master branch and depending on the result being able to deploy to production. This is possible thanks to this great tool. Automatic tasks that allow us to have greater quality and security in our code, in addition to taking advantage of our software architect will allow our code to be better. Thanks to the fact that the community has adopted it quite well, it is easy to integrate it with our GitHub repository, which makes it fit perfectly into our project.

5.2. Core (code structure)

5.2.1. Page model

This section contains the Model JavaScript files. Each file gather the web elements that will be used by the tests. It is important to point out that each Model JavaScript file corresponds to a Suite JavaScript file.

The files contain the precise web elements (input, button, span or an element) that are needed for each particular test.

- **LogIn_model:** Contains the web elements required for the Log In process.
- **Purchase_model:** Contains the web elements required for the Purchase process.
- **Registration_model:** Contains the web elements required for the Registration process.
- **ShoppingCart_model:** Contains the web elements required for Shopping through the web page.

5.2.2. Suites

This section contains the Tests JavaScript files. Each file contains the tests that were identified as inherent for assessing the correct functionality of the web page. The range of the tests go from Login, all the way to the Purchase process.

- **LogIn_tests:** Contains the following tests: Login into an existing account, login to a non-existing account, login with a special character, login with a Facebook Account, login with a Google account, try to login with an incorrect password three times, try to login without an email and try the forgotten account option.
- **Purchase_tests:** Contains the following tests: Fill with information the registration form, create an account associated to the web page, create an account associated with an error in one of the password options, create an account associated with a special character and create an account with no information.
- **Registration_tests:** Contains the following tests: Add flowers to cart and check the availability of the flower, add to cart more than one type of flower, check if the web page has a limit of orders and modify the amount of flowers in the cart.
- **ShoppingCart_tests:** Contains the following tests: Pay with a Credit card, pay with a Debit Card, pay with PayPal, pay with the OXXO payment method, change the Payment method and add a Note.

5.3. Libs

5.3.1. TestCafe

TestCafe installs a series of packages locally, that permits the developer to test the code on the user's computer. In order for TestCafe to keep current with the updates made to the web applications it needs to constantly remain updated to guarantee functionality. The libraries that use TestCafe ensures the functionality and compatibility with the web application.

5.3.2. BrowserStack

BrowserStack installs libraries that ensure a connection between the developer's computer and BrowserStack cloud. BrowserStack runs the test in their own cloud, the libraries used requires the user to make a link with their account. Because of this, the developer not only downloads the necessary libraries but also needs to itemize its profile data and environment variables.

5.3.3. Package

This is a JavaScript Object Notation file; otherwise known as JSON file, that contains information of the project, such as: Author, name, version, dependencies, etc.

5.3.4. Package-lock

This JSON file contains all the dependencies that the pluggable tool ESLint may, or may not employ.

6. Benefits

6.1. Engineer career path

For this project, the team assembled constituted of a variety of engineers with different disciplines. Because of this not only the project got richer but we as professionals acquire new sets of skills.

As previously mentioned, in our team we have two Artificial Intelligence Engineers, one Industrial Engineer and ultimately one Mechatronic Engineer. It may seem that we vary in our career formation, and we do, but as we worked in this project, we developed skills given by our colleagues. It was very enriching to be able to work with people with different academic backgrounds and styles of working.

Furthermore, we have a different method of analyzing and problem solving. Being a motley group, we got the opportunity of discussing how each would undertake the problem and how to solve it, giving us the opportunity to appreciate the problem in different ways, being able to see the problem from multiple angles. This first encounter with our different mindset opened our mentality to be more open towards a given problem.

Since we wanted to challenge ourselves, we assigned unfamiliar roles to each other. By this we ensured we obtained skills and working methods that we were lacking or needed to enhance. Nonetheless we were assured that at any given moment, if any of us had a problem we would help each other, as the purpose of the project was not only to create an open source automation program for web testing, but also to aggrandize our expertise, proficiency and team working.

6.2. Project benefits

This project started as a challenge since despite having knowledge of the area, we tried to improve our weaknesses by selecting a different role than our expertise.

However, this not only benefited the team members, this goes further since being open source we intend to allow our framework to be followed by the entire community with the intention of adapting it to their different needs.

Knowing the great impact that e-commerce has but even more because of the situation of staying at home in which we find ourselves, today this type of commerce has benefited. We are very excited to be able to offer our work to continue growing together. We believe that we can become an effective and safe technological tool to face the challenges of this field and that it can also be used in different parts of the world.

6.3. Outcome (Conclusions)

This project initiated only to fulfil the initial request from the e-commerce but evolve throughout the process of creating the Automated Framework. At the last stages of the project it ended up being a wholesome project that can be used by the community for web automated testing. After finalizing the project, we realized that we had just made an open source project that anybody can use and help them with the first steps of making automated testing.

Therefore, we started to invest time to make the GitHub and the code more organic and intuitive for beginners, stating what we are using in the code and why. We also decided to include a set of explanatory notes in main files to ensure that whoever that uses this project can adapt it to the webpage they want to use.

Making this project open source, we think that we can give to the community code that has been tested and that has the information to start an automation project. By making the project open source we can also benefit from the community, because the project could grow and adapt to the new practices in coding.

References

La mejor GUÍA SCRUM 2020 Aprende todos los conceptos. (July 23, 2020). Be Agile My Friend. https://beagilemyfriend.com/scrum/

Kayser, D. (2020). Implementation of Scrum - 7 Steps. forecast. https://blog.forecast.it/implementation-of-scrum-7-steps

Learn Scrum in 6 Steps | Axosoft. (2020). Axosoft.com. https://www.axosoft.com/scrum-guide

Jenkins. (2020). Jenkins. https://www.jenkins.io/

TesCafé, el aliado perfecto para el desarrollo de tus tests E2E. (may 28, 2020). Paradigma. https://www.paradigmadigital.com/dev/testcafe-el-aliado-perfecto-para-el-desarrollo-de-tus-tests-e2e/

41 Cart Abandonment Rate Statistics. (June 15, 2020). https://baymard.com/lists/cart-abandonment-rate

Law, T. (2020, August 26). 6 Crucial Ecommerce Key Performance Indicators (KPIs) to Track. (June 18, 2020) https://www.oberlo.com/blog/key-performance-indicators-kpis

Columbus, L. (2020, April 28). How COVID-19 Is Transforming E-Commerce. (June 18, 2020) https://www.forbes.com/sites/louiscolumbus/2020/04/28/how-covid-19-is-transforming-e-commerce/

The New Role of the Agile Tester - The General Contractor

Melissa Tondi
melissa.tondi@gmail.com

Abstract

One of the most misunderstood testing activities within the SDLC (Software Development Lifecycle) has been Regression testing. Historically, we build in days—or sometimes weeks—to account for regression testing, usually at the end of a sprint or while preparing for a big release. Most of the time, it is considered solely QA's responsibility. In some cases, the delivery team may swarm the work and execute test cases at QA's direction to accelerate the duration of the cycle, but the team usually expects QA to "own" the effort.

Biography

Melissa Tondi has spent most of her career working within software testing teams. She is in Quality Engineering leadership at E*TRADE and a Principal Consultant at Disrupt Testing, where she assists companies to continuously improve the pursuit of quality software—from design to delivery and everything in between. In her software test and quality engineering careers, Melissa has focused on building and organizing teams around three major tenets—efficiency, innovation, and culture – and uses the Greatest Common Denominator (GCD) approach for determining ways in which team members can assess, implement and report on day to day activities so the gap between need and value is as small as possible.

1. An Outdated Idea

The tradition of QA being solely or primarily responsible for regression testing is outdated. Don't get me wrong - during this time, Developers are helping where they can -likely supporting QA's efforts by being available to assist in fixing bugs testers find and perhaps executing test cases at QA's request. However, unless or until there are bugs to be fixed, Developers are usually disengaged from the detailed Regression testing and the valuable information that is being gathered by QA during this time - arguably, the most important part of this activity.

Meanwhile, during the Regression testing cycle QA is able to gather new information that the rest of the team may be missing, but because Developers are working on new work during this time and QA is heads-down in Regression, we've removed QA from being involved in any of the valuable collaboration efforts that happen to kick off new work. QA then must play catch-up to work they should have been integrally involved with from the start. The more unique Regression cycles scheduled in this outdated way, the more we create a chasm between Developers and QAs. This results in lost time, inefficiencies and ultimately creates a crutch.

Regression testing can and should be owned by either the delivery team as a whole, or Developers. When there's no firm charter of QA's responsibilities, a gap is created within the delivery team and, more than likely, QA will fill that gap and assume the ownership for all Regression testing. That's bad for QA because this takes us away from other important activities – like testing and interacting with the software to advocate for the users. It's also bad for Developers because the crutch of QA creates a false sense of ownership where they may no longer be responsible for a deeper understanding of how code additions and/or changes may affect other areas of the software.

It's time for a new way of thinking on what QA's role is within a delivery team, address the Regression testing crutch and other outdated assumptions on QA's responsibility, and recognize when that assumption becomes a crutch.

2. The New Role of QA - The General Contractor, Not Inspector

As IT professionals, we often loosely compare software development to building construction. In the construction trade you have a general contractor (GC), skilled tradespeople, architects, project managers, inspectors, and general laborers.

For example, a skilled tradesperson, like the plumber, comes into a building and ensures that the seals are tight, the drains are free, that water flows in and out of the structure as expected, and that everything is up to code. The structure of the design is assumed to be sound. Plumbers are not expected to provide input into the design, color or features; they focus exclusively on the plumbing.

If you compare Developers to skilled tradespeople, there are many similarities. They are usually deep experts in their own areas, but rarely have that same expertise across other trades. Each trade has an inspector who are trade experts, and there are usually many inspectors involved in a project. The inspector role is the role that ensures that trade code has been followed and serves as an independent and separate entity that certifies that something has met code.

In IT, the long-held perception is that QA is the inspector – the role that checks and signs off that requirements are met. However, they are not experts in every area the way a team of construction inspectors are. I'd like to introduce another opinion when making the comparison – QA as a General Contractor (GC). Think about it: QA pros are familiar with multiple components of the software development cycle, QA, like the general contractor, works with the owner/user throughout the course of the project and helps vet out requirements and specific needs every bit as much as a general contractor does when working with a homeowner. In addition, the GC ensures that the desired level of quality has been met, including design and user experience and offers timely and valuable feedback back to the tradespeople that add to the overall success of the project.

When comparing QA with the inspector role, it instills a false sense of non-ownership with Development and perhaps assumes that they cannot be trusted to check their own work against requirements. If another team (QA) is in place to check that activities have been done correctly (or according to building code) by tradespeople, then we may remove accountability and create an "Us vs. them" mentality – and ultimately a crutch.

3. Start Acting Like the General Contractor

The role of an inspector is to ensure the code has been followed; QA, as General Contractor, ensures that the desired level of quality has been met, including design and user experience., and to provide recommendations on how to improve. QA's role is to not necessarily make sure the electrician is installing each outlet correctly (although, they're certainly capable of this), but to provide valuable feedback on the functionality, experience, and that the needs of the client and industry have been satisfied. QA as GC provides consultation through most milestones – refinement, acceptance criteria, retrospectives, etc. They are also able to examine the situation from a 10,000-foot view and see the entirety of the project, incorporating all aspects that affect it. As general contractor, QA depends on the expertise of each “trade,” in this case the owner of each component of the software cycle, and fosters relationships between each critical member of the team. In addition, the General Contractor also helps guide conversations within the team and consults with them to understand what they can be doing on their own to ensure quality, collaborate on other quality metrics, and strategically promotes these topics before work is begun.

That’s why QA, using the example above, should not be solely responsible for regression testing: QA is not an inspector to ensure our team counterparts did what they were supposed to do and that it’s up to code, but explores the experience from a broader, more user-based vantage point.

When you take QA out of the analysis and refinement of new work and have them focus solely on an activity like Regression testing, you silo them to the Inspector role only and place them in a situation where they cannot be consultative when new work is kicking off. By shifting QA’s role to that of a GC, you let the process and workflow naturally tap in to their general, and sometimes deep, expertise of the “tradespeople” but also let them flourish and advocate for not only the software’s functionality, but the overall experience as well.

Software Based Disruptive Change Initiatives Require a Culture of Quality

Jack McDowell, MA
Office of the State CIO
State of Oregon
jack.mcdowell@oregon.gov

Ying Ki Kwong, PhD, PMP
Office of the State CIO
State of Oregon
ying.k.kwong@oregon.gov

Abstract

The theme for this year's conference is 2020 vision. Like in optometry, software quality relies on standards and best practices to guide improvement. Frameworks such as Agile, Devops, CMMI, ITIL, ISO 12207, and the PMBOK act like corrective lenses to provide sound development life cycle processes and, in theory, enable better software solutions to be delivered. However, frameworks and rubrics that are designed a priori often are deficient in addressing the nuances of emergent phenomenon and constructivist meaning in complex human endeavors, especially in large enterprises. This deficiency may lead to failure of an enterprise project, with the root cause ultimately traceable to implicit bias of the participants involved.

This paper treats software development as an emergent phenomenon and explores how the meaning of quality is dependent on cultural constructs and communities of meaning. The authors believe software emerges in reflection of an organization's culture, engendering a meaning of quality that is contextually dependent on that organization.

As part of Oregon state government's effort to respond to the COVID-19 emergency, the authors have observed the interplay of cultural differences and diverging meanings of quality across the State's different agencies. We conclude that the meaning of quality exists in the context of a community of meanings, and so quality cannot be disassociated from its social environment and context. This conclusion has important ramifications for software quality management, including Agile, and the value of diversity and inclusion.

Biography

Jack McDowell is an Operations & Policy Analyst for the State of Oregon's Statewide QA and E-Government Program. Before this, he was a web developer and the chief editor of a community newspaper in Arlington, Virginia. He was born in Buenos Aires, Argentina where he lived before attending college in the US. He holds a Master's degree in political science from the University of Oregon and a certification in ITIL.

Ying Ki Kwong is the Statewide Quality Assurance Program Manager in the Office of the State CIO in Oregon state government. Prior to this role, he was IT Investment Oversight Coordinator in the same office and was Project Office Manager of the Medicaid Management Information System Project in the

Oregon Department of Human Services. In the private sector, Dr. Kwong was CEO of a Hong Kong-based internet B2B portal for trading commodities futures and metals. He was a program manager in the Video & Networking Division of Tektronix, responsible for worldwide applications & channels marketing for a line of video servers in broadcast television applications. In these roles, he has managed software based systems/applications, products, and business process improvements. He received the doctorate from the School of Applied & Engineering Physics at Cornell University and was adjunct faculty in the School of Business Administration at Portland State University. He holds the PMP certification since 2003.

1. Introduction

The meaning of software quality evolves through time, and many of the systems that were considered state of the art when they were released are now unable to meet business needs. This paper treats software development as an emerging phenomenon and explores how the meaning of quality is dependent on cultural constructs and communities of meaning (Cohen 1989). In a way, quality is existence driven, existing in a time and place, and therefore abstracted frameworks (e.g. Agile, Devops, ISO 12207, ITIL, etc.) or quality metrics (e.g. defect count) and the emerging quality assurance tools which rely upon them such as Test Driven Development and Artificial Intelligence, cannot succeed without first encountering the dimension of culture and the meaning of quality within stakeholder units.

This paper seeks to build on concepts of organizational dynamics and cross-cultural understanding by addressing how software can emerge in reflection of an organization's culture, providing a meaning of quality that is contextually dependent to that organization. While QA in general in the last decade has moved towards Test Driven Development (TDD) and Automation, most recently employing Artificial Intelligence, Quality Assurance in general determines the success of a software product based on whether it meets business needs and meets specifications (Verification and Validation). These criteria are traditionally pre-determined at the outset of a project, setting the specs to which a project must conform. These criteria are then used for estimating, budgeting, planning and ultimately accepting a system. This paper aims to disrupt our understanding of project success and the meaning of quality by expanding our understanding of success to include additional scope. The authors argue that a project cannot be understood independent of its cultural and linguistic environment and that quality is therefore intricately linked to these intangible variables. This paper uses an ontological frame to explain how communities of meaning affect quality, provides examples of situations where communities of meaning affected project outcomes, and provides suggestions for improving inclusivity and therefore project success.

As part of Oregon state government's effort to respond to the COVID-19 emergency, the authors have observed the interplay of cultural differences and diverging meanings of quality across the State's many agencies during the state's response. We conclude that the meaning of quality exists in the context of a community of meanings, and therefore quality cannot be disassociated from its social environment. This conclusion has important ramifications for quality management with respect to diversity and inclusion.

2. Creating meaning through language

The history of quality assurance treats quality as a measurable and objective thing. Errors and deviations can be measured, modeled, and removed increasing product quality. In effect, much of the quality assurance literature has focused on these types of defect erradication mechanisms, from six-sigma, the Demmings Cycle, to the Toyota Production System. By nature, these models assume that there is an ideal end state to strive towards. For example, the Demming Cycle (Plan, Do, Check, Act) which is at the core of many quality improvement frameworks requires an evaluation (Check) to verify whether a change resulted in an improvement.

The idea that there is something to strive towards, an idealized goal, has its roots in metaphysical concepts dating back to Plato's allegory of the cave, whereby the observable world is a mere reflection of their true and perfect forms. This metaphor, which sets the foundation of western philosophy and culture is the foundation of the western claim to reason. As Jaques Derrida explains, metaphysics is a "white mythology which assembles and reflects Western culture: the white man takes his own mythology (that is, Indo-European mythology), his logos-that is, the mythos of his idiom, for the universal form of that which it is still his inescapable desire to call Reason." (Derrida 1974).

This claim to reason by western thinkers permeates the world of philosophy to our everyday world, and necessarily influences our understanding of "Quality" and the related discipline of "Quality Assurance". For example, when we attempt to produce widgets to a six sigma process, meaning that 99.99966% of all widgets will conform to an expected outcome, we are presupposing that the expected outcome is an ideal and definable one.

Things to be produced, be they widgets or software, are necessarily described through language. Suppose that instead of widgets, we were attempting to produce chairs; the signifier (word) would be chair, which would be tied to an idealized type of "chair" (object) (Saussure 2011).

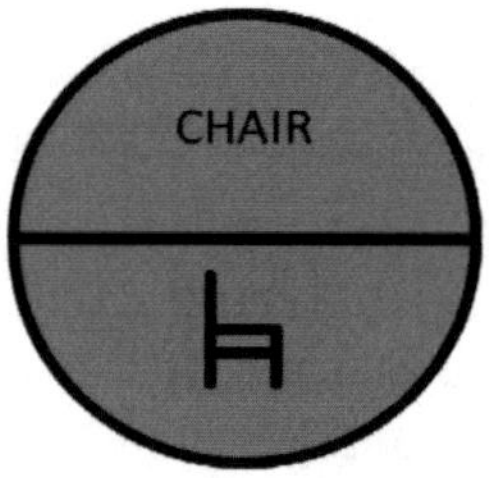

When we think of the quality of a "chair", we imagine something with four legs, a back, a seat rest, etc. If we were trying to improve the quality of a chair, we would make sure that our chairs were consistently produced in a manner that meets the ideal definition of "chair". Likewise, when we look at error QA frameworks, these are designed to measure deviation from the standard. In our chair example, if we used six-sigma, we would expect that 99.9999% of chairs produced would have four legs, a back and a seat rest, etc.

However, one can already start to gather that different people have ideal referents for chairs. Some may think that a simple wooden chair is an ideal, some may prefer a more padded office chair, and others may consider a three-legged stool to be the ideal type of chair. That is to say, even with a most basic example of a chair, it would be impossible to create a "quality checklist" that would create a universal chair. These differences may be cultural in a broad sense, or dependent on our experience, such that an office worker will think of an office chair while a waiter will think of a dining chair as their ideal type.

If we think of more abstract concepts such as quality, one finds it harder to even imagine a "thing" that the word quality refers to:

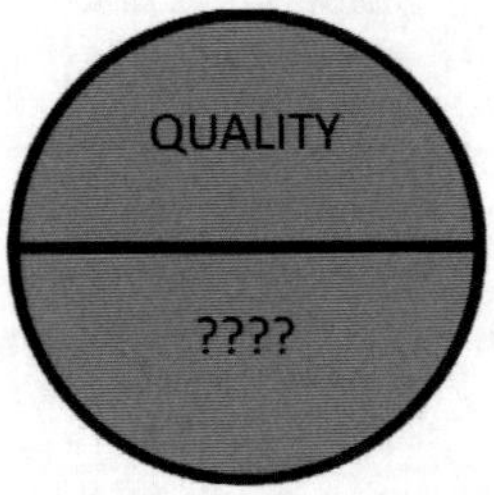

Quality is an abstract concept that can mean a multitude of things, and therefore can be better understood as a chain of signifiers, that is, referent words without a referent thing:

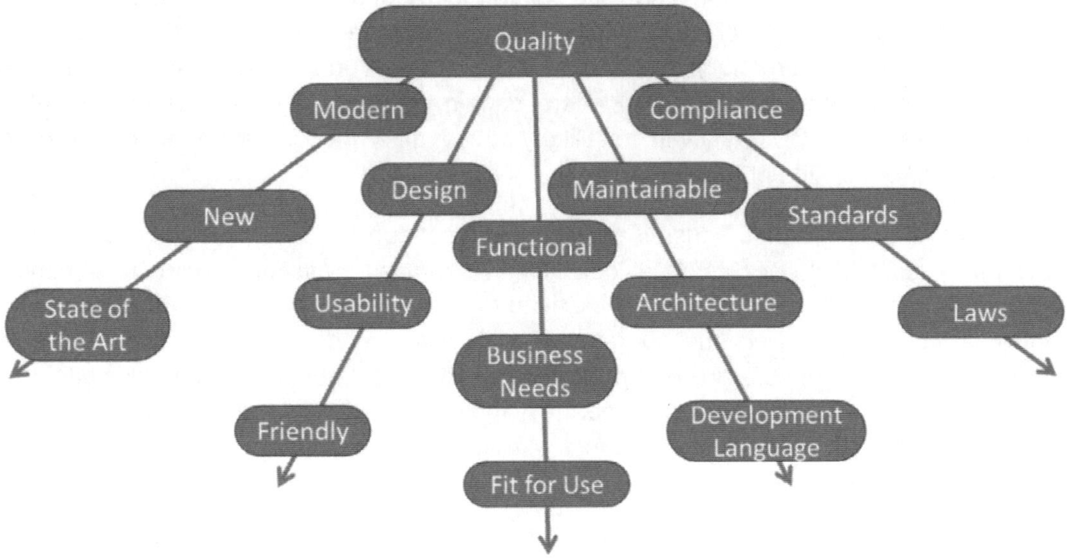

In the diagram above, we can see that each word is related to a different word, without necessary reference to a thing. These words in turn have different meanings depending on the observer. In the words of Derrida, "Speaking frightens me because, by never saying enough, I also say too much. And if the necessity of becoming breath or speech restricts meaning-and our responsibility for it-writing restricts and constrains speech further still" (Derrida 2017). Words are inherently imprecise not because their definitions may vary, but because language itself conjures a chain of related meanings. In speaking, this may be mitigated through conversation, but in written language, such as written requirements or standards, the original meaning is necessarily lost by the distancing between the author and the reader.

If we take the concept of "Accessibility", which the State of Oregon treats as a website that meets or exceeding WCAG AA standards. While this standard provides an actionable "ideal" set of prescriptions to strive towards, it does not account for diversity of culture and experience. One of the glaring issues with the standard is its Anglo centrism, which treats accessibility based on color contrast, font size, screen reader optimization, etc. Absent from these guidelines are inclusionary experiences and in particular language access. This in turn results in a myopic view of accessibility, which may result in websites that are considered accessible and yet are unreadable by different communities.

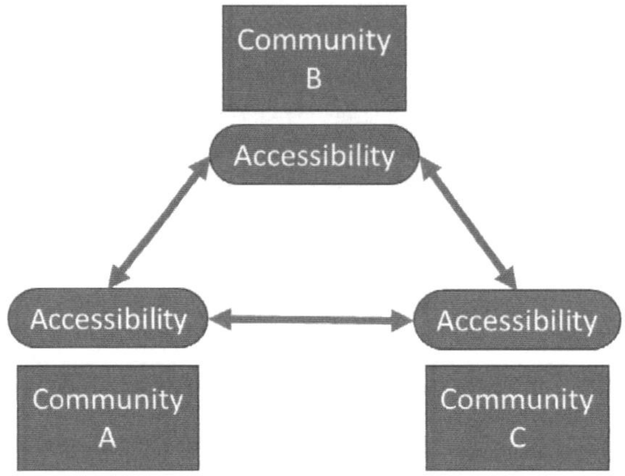

People understand their world through linguistic-cultural frames (Fish 2003). We call these frames "communities of meaning", as they can encompass groups that traverse or intersect national or regional boundaries. For instance, an international maritime lawyer in China and another in Argentina may share a community of meaning around maritime law, where certain concepts and understandings will be well defined. However, these two individuals will most likely have a different cultural understandings related to their specific communities outside of their shared world view.

The hybridized world in which we live adds an additional layer of complexity, in that to be Chinese or to be Argentine are rarely definable concepts. Consider Gloria Anzaldúa's description of the new mestiza, who learns to be an Indian in Mexican culture, to be Mexican from an Anglo point of view. She learns to juggle cultures. She has plural personality; she operates in a pluralistic mode" (Anzaldúa 2012). The result of these cultural interactions, of mestizaje, is the creation or elevation of communities of meaning. As we become more distant from our mono-cultures, be they Anglo-Saxon, mainland Chinese, etc., we instead form cultural hybrids through our lived experiences. As such, our being-in-the-world evolves, and so do our understandings and values.

While these concepts of thinking through the world through language may have appeared irrelevant to Software Quality, a discipline that strived for measurement and objectivity, we have already seen a striking number of instances where language has adapted to our changing cultural norms. In 2020, the Information Technology community has come to grip with the lack of inclusion in its discourse, in particular the use of the word "Master", such as Scrum Master (Agile), Master branch (git), or Master bedroom (NMLS). Traditionally these instances of the word Master have had a specific contextual meaning. The recent trend, as of mid-2020, to rename many of these instances of the word master to something more universal highlights the importance of this type of thinking in the modern era.

3. Applying the concept of communities of meaning to Software Quality

In their 2019 paper, "Software Based Disruptive Change Initiatives Require a Culture of Quality", Kwong and McDowell provided a framework which highlights the amplification of software risk as uncertainty increases. In this model, we identified three principal scenarios that present increasing uncertainty potential, from simple projects with a well-known to-be state (Scenario 1) to complex project with unknown and unstable to-be states (Scenario 3). While these models captured the perceived complexity of a project from a technical perspective, they do not account for cultural effects.

Software development has not evolved in a vacuum, but in response to the Zeitgeist through numerous paradigm shifts (Kuhn 2012). That is to say, an unemployment insurance system written in COBOL was possibly a huge success when released twenty years ago but is no longer able to adapt to the changing environment of Covid-19 and therefore fulfill its basic mission of providing unemployment assistance.

Expectations related to software development are the groundwork for defining requirements, and these definitions may mean different things to different communities, as with our example of a chair. In the authors' experience, they have observed that cultural understandings within communities of meaning can affect the meaning of quality and the success of a project to a greater degree than typical known risks.

There has been no greater recent coming together of "communities of meaning" in the State of Oregon than the COVID-19 pandemic. In the state of Oregon, the Office of Emergency Management (OEM) and the Oregon Health Authority (OHA) led the response to the crisis; two dissimilar organizations in almost every way. The Oregon Health Authority is led by a culture of providing benefits to the residents of Oregon and is led by experts in Public Health; it is a well-funded agency with broad autonomy within its scope that often leads change within the state. The Office of Emergency Management is a small agency that reports to the Oregon Military Department and is therefore used to working by following the chain of command; most of the crises that the OEM responds to are predictable and recurring emergencies, such as wildfires and floods.

COVID-19 upended the typical emergency response paradigm by placing two agencies in charge of the response, due to the health related nature of the response. With these two disparate agencies also came along disparate information technology challenges. OEM was used to thinking of information technology as a means to run its internal response, such as ensuring that wildfire fighters had access to communications and that the public could visualize fire progress. OHA on the other hand, in large part due to HIPPA regulations, was used to thinking of Information Technology as a means to assess disease as a way to create public policy.

COVID-19 presented a challenge in that the role of IT needed to satisfy both the traditional internal needs of these agencies and the needs of the public.

4. Websites, Masks, and the Meaning of Quality

The standard COVID-19 dashboard became the ARCGIS Dashboard created by Johns Hopkins University (COVID-19 Dashboard). As such, most states modeled their own websites based on this dashboard. However, the Johns Hopkins dashboard was never meant as a tool of public policy, nor as the standard COVID-19 reporting (Swenson 2020), it just happened to be the most reliable source at a time when data was sparse. From a quality standpoint, we can consider many possible issues with the Dashboard, such as the vast amounts of unqualified data that provide difficult interpretation to the layperson, a lack of mobile responsiveness, the alarmist color scheme, and the list could go on depending on one's perspective.

The State of Oregon rolled out a similar dashboard through the Office of Emergency Management for tracking COVID-19 cases and the distribution of masks, gowns, and other personal protective equipment.

The Oregon Health Authority on the other hand developed a strong social media campaign in order to communicate with the public on the public's terms. Their campaigns were multilingual and included plain language infographics to inform the public. However, where the Office of Emergency management attempted to put out as much information as possible, OHA was much more guarded in order to avoid running afoul of HIPPA or creating more public uncertainty.

Why would two agencies, responding to the same pandemic, have such different responses and understandings of quality? The answers lie in the organizational culture of each responding agency. OEM approached pandemic as a logistical problem, and evaluated its response based on their ability to execute logistically and provide this type of information to the public. OHA on the other hand approached the problem as a communications task and measured their success by analyzing customer engagement and social media feedback.

This paper does not aim to pass judgement or to indicate whether one type of response is better than the other, but to illustrate how "communities of meaning" can set a path and define the meaning of success based on the cultural context of an organization or group. In other words, from the perspective of OEM or OHA, both of their responses can be viewed as a success.

5. Diversity and Inclusion as a means to improve software quality

A "chair" becomes a "chair" when the observer believes it to be one, just as software is of quality when it is observed to meet certain requirements. The problem with quality in information technology is that the dominant paradigms have been created by a largely homogenous group of people, who approach quality from their own discursive "communities of meaning". When 17 white men created the Agile Manifesto in 2001, the idea that SCRUM as the practice of Agile would use terms such as "Master" to define what is a de facto project manager most likely did not raise any eyebrows.

Strategies for improving software quality include understanding the limitations and biases of the frameworks and SDLCs that are used, ensuring that all stakeholders are included in project planning and requirements gathering, and creating "intersubjective moments" where people from different backgrounds and with different roles can express their opinions regarding their understanding of quality. By creating "intersubjective moments", where people of from different "communities of meaning" come together to envision the best ways to solve problems across communities, a more inclusive meaning of quality can be achieved. Having people from different backgrounds and communities come together to help guide project requirements and the meaning of success, can reduce the quality challenges associated with divergent understandings of quality.

As the IT world reckons with its Anglo-Saxon roots, it is important to recognize that this is not just an opportunity to use politically correct language. It is crucially important to reflect on the assumptions and, thus, the regime of validity of the guiding frameworks that practitioners take for granted; paying close attention to implicit biases that tend to distort perception and judgment.

6. Implications for Software Development Lifecycles

The questions that we have raised so far regarding the meaning of quality have significant implications for SDLC. If we think of software as building a house, where a series of steps must be completed sequentially, such as planning, foundation work, general construction and finishing, it would be clear that a culturally unaware initial step would create a path dependency which would require significant rework in order to change.

Under the waterfall model, requirements set the foundation for design and implementation, and are then used to validate the quality of the work. Much like building a house, or a chair, if the requirements for developing software are defined for a specific community of meaning, they may be misinterpreted or reinterpreted by developers, testers, or users. For example, to require that a software have a "modern look and feel", or allow for "ease of login", are prima facie clear requirements. However, these requirements are clear to us as individuals in a community only because they work as a metaphor in our own understanding. A "modern look and feel" will quickly elicit vivid imagery in the mind of the reader, which upon reflection the reader will come to realize is based upon his or her understanding and experiences.

In order to minimize these miscommunications, the waterfall model has been largely supplanted by agile methodology, which seeks to place the developer in closer proximity to the product owner, and in SCRUM practice goes to pains in order to remove the appearance of formality by renaming the project manager role as a Scrum Master. Although these changes are meant to produce software that more closely approaches the desired understanding of quality, even agile falls short of this task on its own.

6.1. Implications for Agile

The authors of the Agile Manifesto assumed good software developers working in close proximity of well-meaning business users would lead to high quality software. This is true if and only if the following are true:

- developers are not more driven by the profit motive than quality;
- business users embrace change and are empowered to represent the business in bringing about change;
- stakeholders value the benefit of transformative change over potential loss of influence and power after such change.

The authors of the Agile Manifesto likely assumed good software developers would naturally work for good, thoughtful development managers. However, real organizations are imperfect with the effect of culture – organizational and national culture – constantly exerting its "invisible hand" of influence (Qiao 2018). Following our reasoning that meanings are socially dependent and that communities of meaning affect our understanding, the authors have observed the following consequences for Agile practitioners are:

- Organizations or cultures with high power distance between knowledge workers and their management may self-censor ideas. In Chinese and East Asian cultures, it may be unreasonable to expect knowledge workers to openly question their management in public forums, especially in front of contractors.
- Loyalty to the team or the collective and associated "group think" may drown out individual insight. In Chinese and East Asian cultures, knowledge workers may also be expected to make personal sacrifices to meet team objectives such as deadlines, potentially making it difficult for knowledge workers to question unrealistic timelines set by coworkers' consensus.
- Managers may exploit power distance and team loyalty to take advantage of knowledge workers by adding new scope without increasing development hours. This effectively imposes longer work hours for the same number of workdays.

7. Conclusion

Quality is inherently value(s) driven, in that our values, and the values of our communities of meaning define what Quality is and therefore how Quality Assurance is to be undertaken. It is not enough to tokenize diversity into our existing paradigms. The paradigms themselves may need to be disrupted in order to truly leverage diversity and inclusion. By recognizing inherent biases of our own communities and the frameworks that we preach, a more inclusive meaning of quality can emerge.

The tension between inclusive discourse and power dynamics is one which is difficult to resolve (Kelly 2010), and one that is beyond the scope of this paper. It may be tempting to describe the changes that we're observing in today's information technology world with the rise and diffusion of "politically correct" speech as a result of changing power dynamics in the world of IT. The idea of understanding these changes or tensions through power dynamics is not inherently new or western, but the idea of a zero sum outcome is.

In Chinese philosophy, Mengzi (or Mencius, 孟子) believes that human nature is inherently good in the absence of influence by upbringing or environmental factors (人之初, 性本善). Xunzi (荀子), on the other hand, believes that human nature is inherently bad or evil and requires moral cultivation to tend toward good (人之初, 性本惡). Both Mengzi and Xunzi would agree that human beings and human endeavors have the capacity or propensity for good. However, the path or process toward good (or away from evil) would be qualitatively different in the two worldviews (Xunzi 2004). Chinese culture understands the balance and limits of the tension created by a thesis and antithesis, and acknowledges the interplay and inseparability of both extremes as a dichotomy that constantly influences individuals or groups. Inherent to any paradigm shift, or moment of synthesis, is a linguistic interplay which necessarily causes a mestizaje of meaning.

As the hegemonic culture, American thought and value systems are proselytized across the world influencing information technology paradigms. In the American paradigm, the meaning of success is meant to be defined and measurable, with a single meaning of truth. As such, even the most cutting edge quality frameworks rely on known and expected outcomes which the software is tested against. In this paper, we have challenged this dominant paradigm, and demonstrated how even the most well-meaning frameworks are necessarily a reflection of dominant American thought. The drawbacks of these Anglo-centric frameworks are numerous, in particular since they do not translate well across cultures, and may produce suboptimal outcomes when software development or software products traverse different cultures and communities of meaning.

Through their practical experiences, the authors have observed how communities of meaning shape understandings of success, and how apparent clear requirements and missions inevitably cause mis-communications, in particular when homogeneous communities of meaning are driving projects. We believe the interplay of competing factors and their dynamic equilibrium and harmonization that we have described have important implications for software quality. Although mis-communication and divergent understandings can never be truly resolved, inclusion and diversity can act as “corrective lens” for the meaning of quality.

References

Anzaldúa, Gloria. Borderlands = La Frontera: the New Mestiza. San Francisco, CA: Aunt Lute Books, 2012.

Cohen, Anthony P. The Symbolic Construction of Community. Chichester: E. Horwood, 1989.

“COVID-19 Dashboard by the Center for Systems Science and Engineering (CSSE) at Johns Hopkins University (JHU).” ArcGIS Dashboards. Accessed August 31, 2020. https://gisanddata.maps.arcgis.com/apps/opsdashboard/index.html

Derrida, Jacques, and F. C. T. Moore. “White Mythology: Metaphor in the Text of Philosophy.” New Literary History 6, no. 1 (1974): 5. https://doi.org/10.2307/468341

Derrida, Jacques. Writing and Difference. Chicago, IL: University of Chicago Press, 2017.

Fish, Stanley Eugene. Is There a Text in This Class?: the Authority of Interpretive Communities. Cambridge, MA, MA: Harvard Univ. Press, 2003.

Kelly, Michael, Michel Foucault, and Habermas Jürgen. Critique and Power Recasting the Foucault/Habermas Debate. Cambridge, MA: MIT Press, 2010.

Kuhn, Thomas S., and Ian Hacking. The Structure of Scientific Revolutions. Chicago: University of Chicago Press, 2012.

Qiao, Xiuyu. “Analyzing the Impact of Chinese Cultural Factors on Agile Software Development,” 2018. https://dspace.library.uu.nl/bitstream/handle/1874/368072/5842107_Xiuyu Qiao_MBI Thesis.pdf

Saussure, Ferdinand de. Course in General Linguistics. New York: Columbia University Press, 2011.

Swenson, Kyle. “Millions Track the Pandemic on Johns Hopkins's Dashboard. Those Who Built It Say Some Miss the Real Story.” The Washington Post, June 29, 2020. https://www.washingtonpost.com/local/johns-hopkins-tracker/2020/06/29/daea7eea-a03f-11ea-9590-1858a893bd59_story.html

“Xunzi.” In Stanford Encyclopedia of Philosophy. Stanford, CT: Stanford University, Metaphysics Research Lab., 2004.

Recheck and the “Git for the GUI”

Dr. Jeremias Rößler
roessler@retest.de

Abstract

Ever had that: after a simple change, suddenly 50+ tests are failing! Brittle tests that hinge on GUI specifics and result in the dreaded NoSuchElementException are a main headache

when testing with Selenium. How about a tool that does not depend on HTML-IDs, CSS classes or XPath? Since they are invisible, they are essentially irrelevant from a user's perspective—yet they are crucial for the test to succeed.

The open source project recheck offers a simple and elegant solution. Not only is a virtual identifier unaffected by UI changes, you can define it for otherwise hard to specify elements, i.e. that would require complex XPath or CSS selector expressions. And on top of that, tests are easier to create and maintain and yet much more complete in what they check.

Biography

Dr. Jeremias Rößler (Roessler, @roesslerj, he) has a PhD in Computer Science from Saarland University and more than 10 years of experience as a software developer and tester. He is the founder and CEO of @retest_en (https://retest.de), a German-based startup that brings AI to test automation and one of the authors of the iSQI/GASQ "AI and Software Testing" certification syllabus.

His refreshingly unusual approach to test automation (difference testing) has many advantages over conventional test automation and he shows how to combine it with AI to overcome the oracle problem. He has been speaker at many international conferences, both in academia and industry, and attendees call his talks visionary and amusing. His talks are rated 4.28 out of five and ranked second best of the conference. He is a writer, blogger (https://dev.to/roesslerj/), developer & computer scientist.

He is very approachable and enjoys to be talked to, so don't be shy. You can contact him easiest on Twitter or LinkedIn (https://www.linkedin.com/in/roesslerj/).

1. The Problem

In software development and test automation, assertion-based testing is the classic JUnit approach, where manually created assertion statements serve as a test oracle (to distinguish between pass/fail) during test execution. Essentially, they check the result of a calculation—usually by comparing it with a manually defined expected value. For unit-based test automation (i.e. testing the system from within), this is very well suited. But applying it to testing an interface (specifically the user interface) has proven to be problematic, as this article will explain. Assertion-based Testing is a deny-list approach, i.e. only changes of the software that are explicitly checked by assertions are recognized and alerted (denied).

Selenium is a very good tool for web-based test automation. It doesn't promote assertion-based testing itself — however, most people use it in conjunction with an assertion-based checking library. To test a web application login, a typical Junit-style Selenium test could look something like the following. All examples in this article are available on GitHub

(https://github.com/retest/recheck-web-example).

```
class MySeleniumTest {

   WebDriver driver;

   @BeforeEach
   void setup() {
      driver = new ChromeDriver();
   }

   @Test
   void login() throws Exception {
      String file = "src/test/resources/demo-app.html";
      driver.get(Paths.get( file ).toUri().toURL().toString());

      driver.findElement(By.id("username")).sendKeys("Simon");
      driver.findElement(By.id("password")).sendKeys("secret");
      driver.findElement(By.id("sign-in")).click();

      assertEquals(driver.findElement(By.tagName("h4")).getText(),
            "Success!");
   }

   @AfterEach
   void tearDown() throws InterruptedException {
      driver.quit();
   }
}
```

As you can see, it opens a login page, fills username and password and clicks “sign-in”. Then it checks whether the text “Success!” is in the first h4 header.

Now you might want to change the HTML of the website under test. For example, you could change the CSS declaration `<link href="./files/main.css" rel="stylesheet">`. Changing a single character of the URL will cause the website to be displayed without formatting.

This change obviously is an error. However, when you run the test, it shows no problem and still executes without failure. This is clearly not what you expect from the test. Instead, try to change or remove the element IDs that are invisible to the user. Since these IDs are not visible, the change has no effect on the actual website from the user's point of view. But if you run the test now, you can see that it terminates with a NoSuchElementException. The change, which is irrelevant to the user, not only caused the test to fail, but also prevented its execution—in other words, "broke" it. Tests that ignore major changes but break when changes are invisible are the current standard in test automation. This is just the opposite of what you would want from a test.

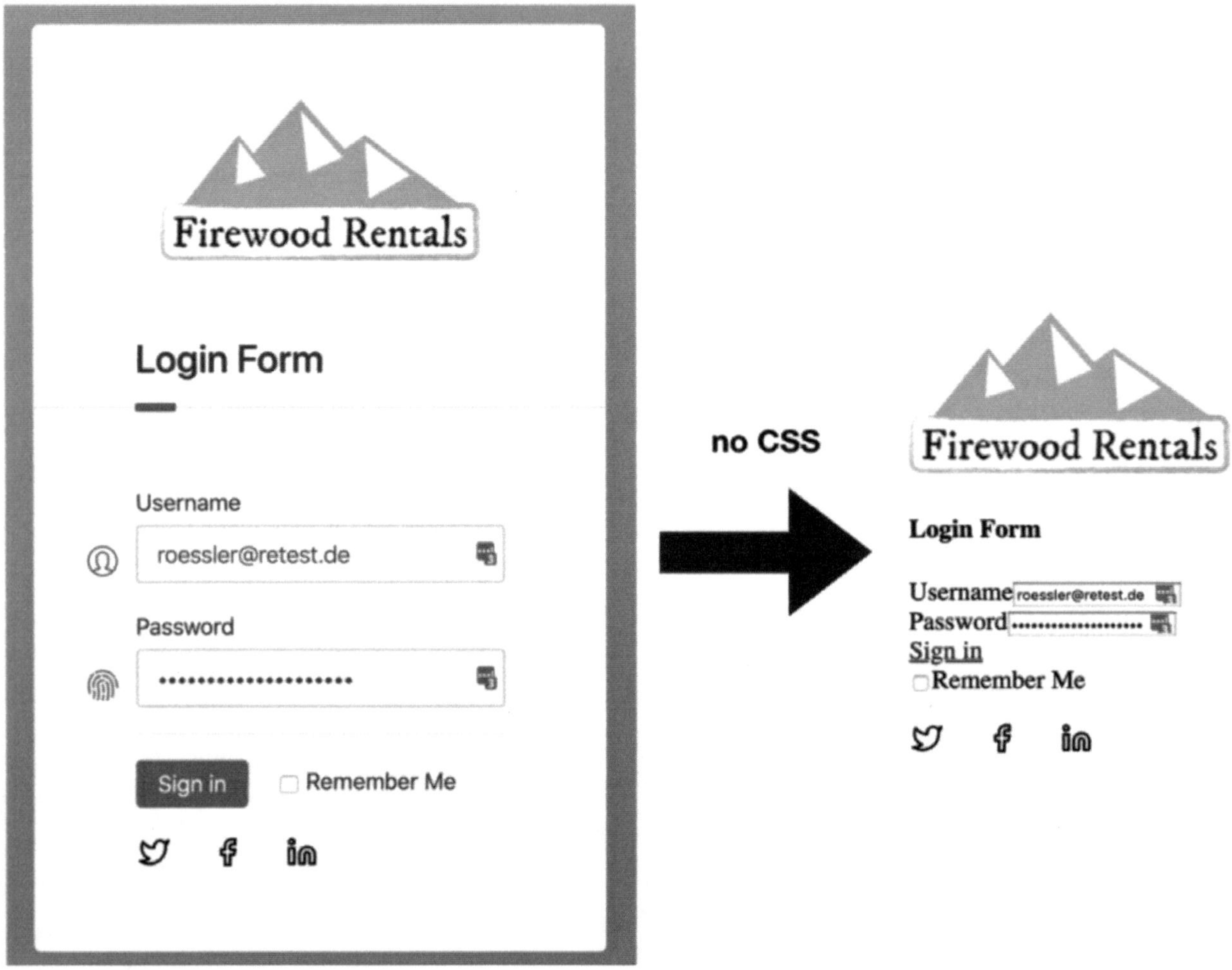

2. A different Approach

Difference Testing, in contrast, is a Golden Master-based testing approach (also called characterization testing and approval testing) that highlights the differences between different executions, such as between different versions of the software. With Difference Testing, all differences (including unexpected ones) are detected, and irrelevant ones can then be ignored. Hence Difference Testing is an allow-list approach, allowing certain changes to happen without alerting, while alerting for all changes that are not explicitly ignored. Again, this is essentially the opposite of an assertion-based testing approach, where you explicitly specify what should be checked — and all other changes are ignored.

The number of tools that apply an Golden Master-based approach to testing—such as Approval Tests, Jest, or recheck-web (retest)—seems to be constantly increasing. This approach promises tests with less effort (for both creation and maintenance) while testing more thoroughly. And in the case of recheck-web, the tests are even more robust (as will be shown below).

For our above example, all we need to change is wrapping the Selenium driver with a `RecheckDriver`:

```
driver = new RecheckDriver(new ChromeDriver());
```

With a correct project configuration, nothing else is necessary. You can now delete the assertion-based check. If you execute this test the first time, the Golden Master (the reference which to compare against) hasn't been created yet. So for safety, the first time you execute this test, it will fail and create said Golden Master. If you remove the CSS from the website with the above change after the Golden Master has been created, the test suddenly fails with many differences.

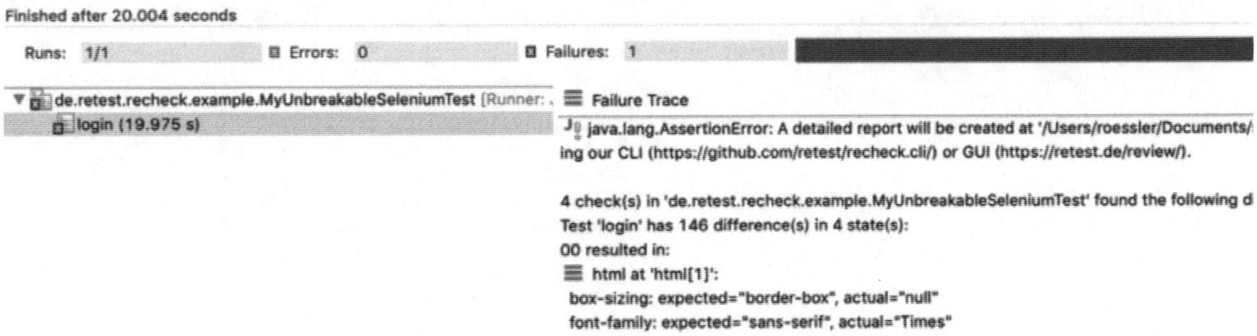

But what is much more interesting: If developers change or remove the HTML element IDs instead, the test is still executed successfully (works accordingly with name, CSS class, XPath etc.). Remember, these element IDs are being used to identify the element the test should interact with. Yet still without these IDs on the website, the test still doesn't brake—although it correctly reports these IDs as having changed. This is how a test should behave: It should detect changes that are important to the user and not break on changes that are irrelevant to the user.

3. An Open Source Implementation

Recheck-web is a free open source (https://github.com/retest/recheck-web) tool based on Selenium. It works according to the Golden Master principle, which essentially means that the first time the test is run, it creates a copy of the rendered website, and subsequent runs of the test compare the current state with this copy (the Golden Master). This allows the test to detect whether the website has changed in any undesirable way. After changing or deleting an HTML ID on the website to test, recheck-web can still identify the corresponding element by simply looking into the Golden Master (where the ID still exists) and find the element there. Using additional properties like HTML name, XPath and CSS classes, recheck-web can still correctly identify the element on the changed website and return it to Selenium. The change is reported and the test can then interact with the element as before.

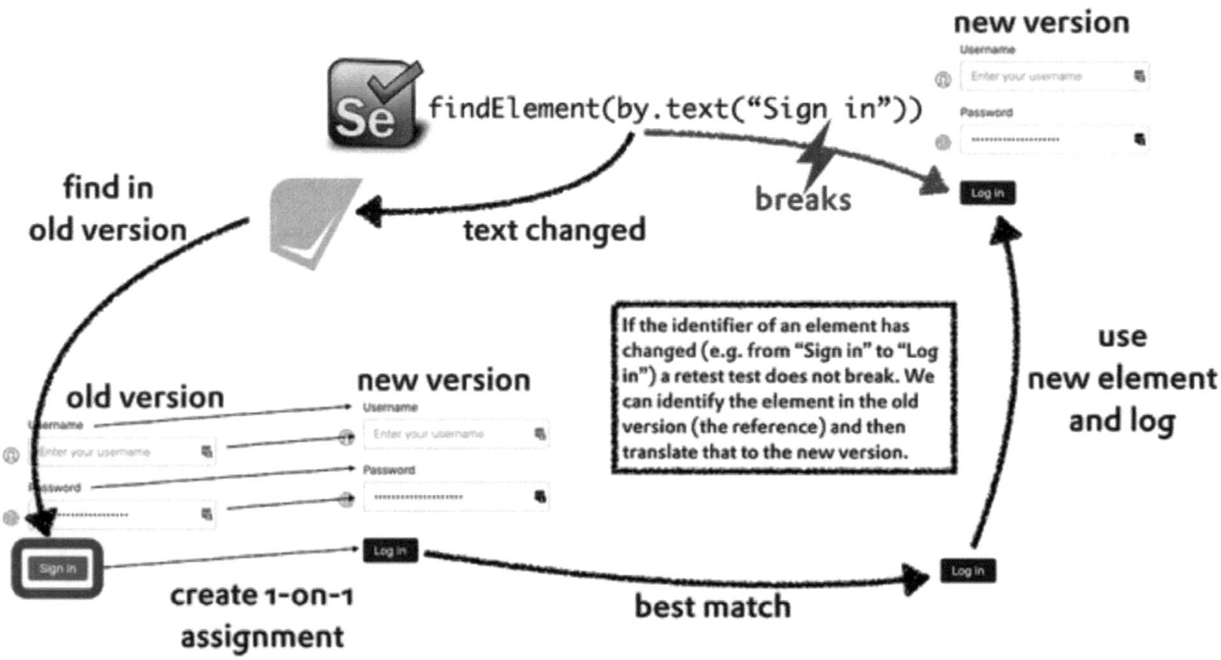

The idea to do testing Golden Master-based exists since probably the 80s. It has been made popular under the term "characterization testing" by Michael Feathers with his book "Working Effectively with Legacy Code". The reason for the approach to be not more widespread is probably based on two major disadvantages: noise and redundancies.

3.1. Noise and how to address it

Many changes are uninteresting and unproblematic (e.g. time and date changes and random IDs as well as many uninteresting style attributes). As was explained above, while assertion-based checking ignores *all* changes unless explicitly specified, Golden Master-based checking ignores no changes unless explicitly specified. Following that reasoning, one could argue that assertion-based checking is essentially creating and maintaining a deny-list of changes, while Golden Master-based testing is creating and maintaining an allow-list of changes.

Since this is a major cause of effort, recheck goes out of its way to make it easy to create and maintain that allow-list. For the same reason that Git uses the `.gitignore` file to ignore log files and other temporary and uninteresting files and artifacts, recheck-web uses the `recheck.ignore`-file. After executing a recheck-web test the first time, that file is automatically created in the correct (default) directory. As with everything, this can be configured if needed. With a Git-like syntax, it's easy to edit that file and add additional elements, attributes or changes to ignore. You can even create different such files for different purposes and scenarios (then called filter files like `positioning.filter`) and mix and combined them as needed.

Every line in a filter file constitutes to an ignore rule. It essentially boils down to

```
<element-matcher> <attribute(s)> <specifics>
```

An element matcher specifies which element and sub-elements the rule applies to. This can be done by type, HTML ID, CSS class, XPath, retestId or others. If there is no element matcher specified, it applies globally. Then is specified to which attribute(s) the rule applies, by name or regex. If no attributes are specified, the element and all of its child elements are ignored completely. At last, some specifics can be defined, making the rule apply only for certain values or differences. This allows e.g. to ignore a text, as long as it's a valid date, or a pixel-difference as long as it's less than 20 pixel. More details on that can be found online (https://docs.retest.de/recheck/usage/filter/).

The remarkable thing with the `recheck.ignore` file is, that it usually works project-wide. This means that you need to maintain just a single file for the whole project. And adding the next test usually means less effort in terms of the recheck.ignore file than the previous one was, until at one point, it becomes completely effort-less.

3.2. Redundancies and what to do with them

The second reason that Golden Master-tests can be cumbersome to maintain is redundancies. Several Golden Masters often have a certain, sometimes even a high overlap. Then the same change has to be checked and confirmed several times, which quickly nulls the efficiency achieved with the simpler test creation.

To counter that problem, recheck-web comes with its own CLI (https://github.com/retest/recheck.cli) that takes care of this tedious task. With it (or the commercial GUI) users can apply the same change for the same element to all Golden Masters or simply globally apply or ignore all changes with a single or very few commands, like

```
recheck commit --all test.report
```

If you want to apply a change so a subset of elements, then the filters come in handy again. You can either specify a filter file that should be used to select the changes, or you can define a filter impromptu on the command line.

It is very important to maintain the Golden Master and regularly apply the changes. If not done, it means that over time the Golden Master and the actual output continue to diverge. At some point in time, the differences are to stark, so that the algorithm that assigns the individual elements from the Golden Master to the elements from the current version gets tricked, and will start to make mistakes. So using the CLI or GUI is mandatory in the long run. However, it also means that tests that were kept from becoming broken thanks to the Golden Master as explained above, will then break once the changes are applied. For instance, in the example above with a changed HTML ID, once that changed or deleted HTML ID gets applied to the Golden Master, the outlined mechanism will fail and the test will break. What we can use instead of the ordinary HTML ID, or any other single identification criteria for that matter, is using the retestId.

4. The retestId

The idea of the `retestId` is fairly simple: when creating the copy of the website (known as the Golden Master), we can insert additional attributes (say an ID) to each element inside of that copy. Since these attributes only reside in the copy, not on the actual website, they can never be subjected to changes. So if we ensure that these attribute values are unique, it means we just created a virtual constant identifier. This virtual constant identifier is added to every element and is called the `retestId`. The overall idea works essentially like outlined above: we find the element by its retestId in the Golden Master and then do a 1-on-1 assignment of all elements of the old to the new website. Then we use the element from the current website that has been assigned the retestId and return it to the underlying Selenium.

In addition to being constant, the retestId addresses another problem that is common in test automation: often enough, the element that one wants to addresse doesn't have a single unique identification criterion like an HTML ID, name, or CSS class. In that case, one is usually forced to use a XPath or CSS path as identification criterion, both being meaningless and hard-to-maintain. With the retestId, you can instead use a meaningful and short String that can be manually set to any value, as long as it's unique within the Golden Master.

5. Outlook

The reason recheck was created and is made open source is simple: It addresses one of the main challenges of a really interesting problem: The Oracle problem in AI-based UI-test generation. The Oracle problem is the very hard problem to predict whether a certain outcome of a software after a certain input is correct. Since problems are in the eye of the beholder, this problem cannot be solved in a general way. So instead, recheck circumvents the problem: the software gets manually tested *once*. After the outcome is determined to be correct *enough*, it gets frozen in the form of the Golden Master. From then on, only *improvements* are to be allowed—all other changes to the output should be rejected by fixing the underlying changes in the code

(regressions). This then essentially means that test automation has become an extension of change control or version control, further tying the above association with e.g. git. Think about it this way: version control governs static artifacts like code and configuration files. The dynamic behavior of the software is unfortunately defined by more (data, runtime system)—thus we need automated tests to close this gap. The current state in software test automation however, is woefully inadequate and only provisionally addresses this need. Recheck on the other hand consequently follows this approach up to the `recheck.ignore` file and can be rightfully called “Git for the GUI”.

6. Conclusion

In this paper, we have presented an open source tool that implements and demonstrates a different approach to software test automation than the current assertion-based one. We have also shown how well-known shortcomings of that approach can be addressed to make it applicable to real-world projects, and how it paths the way to AI-based test generation by addressing the dreaded Oracle problem.

References

Michael Feathers. 2004. Working Effectively with Legacy Code. Prentice Hall International. EAN / ISBN-13: 9780131177055

Approval Tests. https://approvaltests.com/. Accessed August 1, 2020.

Jest. Facebook Inc. https://jestjs.io/ Accessed August 1, 2020.

retest-web-example. ReTest GmbH. https://github.com/retest/recheck-web-example. Accessed August 1, 2020.

retest-web. ReTest GmbH. https://github.com/retest/recheck-web. Accessed August 1, 2020.

recheck documentation. ReTest GmbH. https://docs.retest.de/recheck/usage/. Accessed August 1, 2020. recheck CLI. ReTest GmbH. https://github.com/retest/recheck.cli . Accessed August 1, 2020.

Evolving Software Testing at the Pokémon Company International

Paul Grimes
p.grimes@pokemon.com

Abstract

How can you know that your services will handle the requests of millions of users a day? Or that making a fundamental change to one of your technologies won't break your user experience? By creating a phased approach to testing the right pieces at the right time that your entire team can use and build on. In the Pokémon Company International (TPCI) quality department, we are responsible for the Pokemon.com website, the software for tournaments played by 1000s of players, and the services used for logging into applications like Pokémon Go and Pokémon TV. Since the launch of Pokémon Go in 2016, our quality-focused department has worked to develop strategies that reduce the number and duration of customer incidents in the face of millions of daily active users. We will present the phases that our test engineers follow and the tools we use to ensure that the services we are delivering are capable of meeting our users' demands. From exploratory testing of our API's, to developing unit and integration tests, to deploying scalable performance suites, we will discuss the tactical choices we've made and how they affect our outcomes. This integrates with our web and mobile testing safeguarding the end-to-end user experience. By integrating testing early and doing the right work at the right time, TPCI is ensuring our customers have exceptional encounters as they interact with our brand.

Biography

Paul Grimes has worked in the software industry over twenty years. He loves technology and has worked in many vanguard fields including web services, game network engineering, automation planning and automation implementation. He spent the early part of his career at Microsoft working on Office, then shifted to work on PC and Xbox games. He also has varied experience from working at Barnes and Noble, Disney and various startups in the games and data knowledge industries. He currently works for the Pokémon Company International as a software development engineer in test.

1. Introduction

The Pokémon Company International (TPCI) is a wholly owned subsidiary of the Pokémon Company of Japan. It is responsible for the development, production, distribution marketing, and licensing of Pokémon products outside of Asia. This includes the Pokémon Trading Card Game, Pokémon video games, Pokémon animated series and live action movies, and Pokémon merchandise such as apparel, toy, and plush.

To support the brand and the many diverse efforts, TPCI has a dedicated technology organization. The tech org is responsible for both internal tools and external offerings. The different offerings are vast.

Pokemon.com is the official website for everything Pokémon which is available worldwide and translated in 12 languages. There are smaller "mini-sites" which are used to announce new video games or large offering such a new set for the training card game. Pokémon TV is where fans can watch their favorite episodes of the animated TV show or one of the animated movies. The Pokédex can help fans find information about their favorite Pokémon.

The Pokémon Trainers Club (PTC) provides user an online identity, which can be used to store and manage both adult and child accounts. PTC allows players to track their progress in tournaments for both the video game and the card game, sign-in to Pokémon Go - a game licensed to developer Niantic, play the Pokémon Card Game Online, or track which episode of the Pokémon Animated Series they are watching on Pokémon TV.

Our quality team inside the technology organization focuses on ensuring quality as we develop these and other upcoming offerings. We work with internal teams on the development of projects, work to improve the development process, validate releases, and try to make sure we are applying the right validation at the right times.

2. Quality Team Values

Our team is organized around six core values developed by our quality team and our leadership group. They help us inform our decisions. They have been amended and added to by the team as we have changed and grown. We recognize team members who demonstrate these values at monthly team meetings. Our team values are:

- **Great Triumph -** We believe every member of our team is working to deliver amazing, memorable experiences. Valuing everyone's opinions and viewpoints will help us reach our goal.
- **Customer First -** Using customer-centric practices in our work, we are committed to providing a quality product and positive experience to our customers and fans.
- **Continued Learning -** We strive to better ourselves every day. We will do this by continuing to learn new things, take on new tasks, and by asking questions. We're ok with trying something different and failing - I'll know what to do better the next time.
- **People Matter -** Our team is a family. It is super important to us to care for each other, even outside of work. We believe the people make the company great and treat them accordingly.
- **Transparent Communication -** We are honest and transparent. When discussing the quality of a product, we will use data to communicate the quality. Obfuscating the true quality of a product isn't productive.
- **Courageous Action -** We act without fear of impediments or dissenting opinions. We confront risks with prudence and tenacity even if they leave us vulnerable. We support each other because we trust that our actions improve quality for everyone.

3. Team Organization

Our team organization has changed organically. Our director has managers reporting to him. The managers handle people management tasks as well managing teams of four to eight people. Our director works with our managers to produce a vision for where the team is headed. This vision is then translated into the action by our steering committee, which is made up of the managers and selected individual contributors. They focus on issues such as inclusion and working direction to drive changes to make us more effective. The discrete day-to-day work of the quality organization is divided across the team into pods and Scrum teams.

Pods and Pod Leads. Pods are small groups of two to six individuals working on a specific product. For example, there are pods for organized play tools, pokemon.com, and Pokémon TV, and Pokémon

Trainers Club to name four. The individuals on the team may be from different managers. They are a mix of Software Development Engineers in Test (SDET) who work on tools, developing automation, and frameworks and Software Test Engineers (STE) who develop test cases and collateral and work on execution. A Pod Lead is chosen by the managers to own and drive the quality responsibilities for the pod. Pods can be scaled for the demands of a team and rearranged to best serve the business.

Scrum Teams. Scrum teams are assembled to work on a specific project that may be longer or shorter than the duration of a project. They use Scrum procedures with a scrum master, Product Owner (PO) and team members doing development. These teams tend to stay together so that estimating remains constant. The Scrum teams are typically 3-7 contributors, including the scrum master and PO. These Scrum teams focus on things like adding automated regression testing to legacy projects, developing continuous integration/deployment pipelines for projects where they are lacking, improving the quality team's data gathering and dashboarding capabilities, and performance testing.

Individuals may be part of a pod and a scrum team simultaneously. This structure allows us to share knowledge about projects across the group giving each individual an opportunity to see projects across the technology organization. Being a pod lead gives individuals a chance to develop the skills of owning a project and planning the work for a project without having to do career growth or people management tasks such as employee reviews. It also provides an individual ownership of a project and allows partners to know who to go to with concerns around the direction the pod might be taking. An individual's manager remains their advocate and helps them plan their growth. Managers also remain aware of projects throughout the organization because employees they manage contribute to projects across the organization instead of in a single focus area. The department can react to changes in priority because of the flexibility of the team composition. This structure allows individuals to remain focused on delivering quality and confidence to our partners while giving people the opportunity to develop the skills they wish to improve.

Here is an example of how this might look in practice. Our director's name is Klein. Klein has three managers, Adams, Baker, and Clark. Each manager has a mix of SDET and STE's reporting to them.

For a release of PTC we needed to replace the database structure. One of Adams SDET's, Davis, was chosen as the pod lead for the project. The demands on the team were high because they needed to guarantee both functionality and performance of the chosen migration. Another SDET from Adams' team was added to the pod, Evans. Frank, an STE from Baker's team, Ghosh and STE from Clarks team, and Hills an STE from Adams' team were also added to the pod. As demand for more automation became apparent, a third SDET, Irwin was added to the pod from Baker's team.

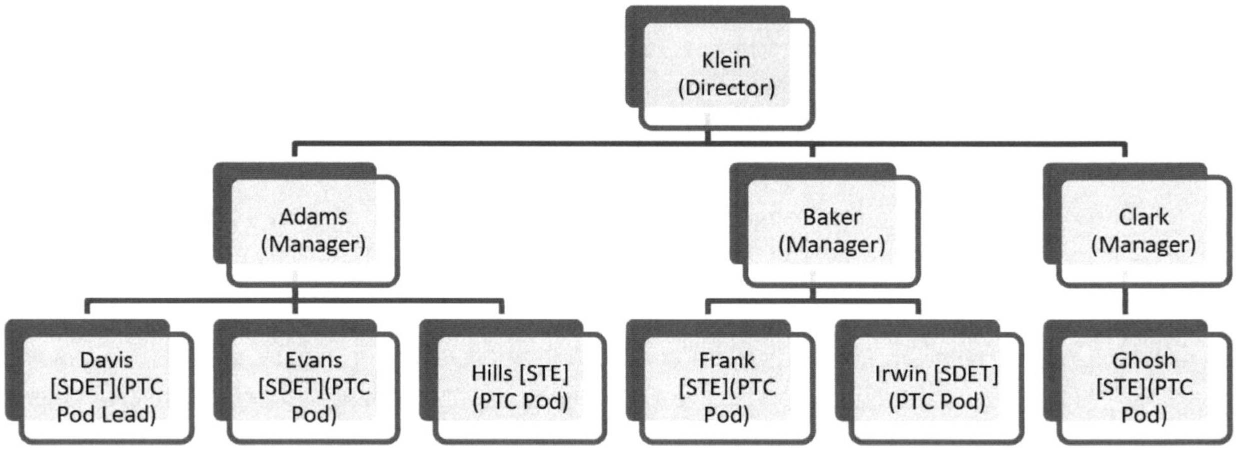

Figure 1. Example Org Chart

After shipping the database migration, PTC work drastically reduced. Evans became the pod lead for PTC pod, and Hills remained on PTC pod for continuity. Davis and Frank became members of a scrum team focused on automation regression (ART). Hills contributed to that scrum team as well. Irwin became a pod lead on PCOM, and Ghosh joined that pod. Frank began working on a separate pod focused on PTV.

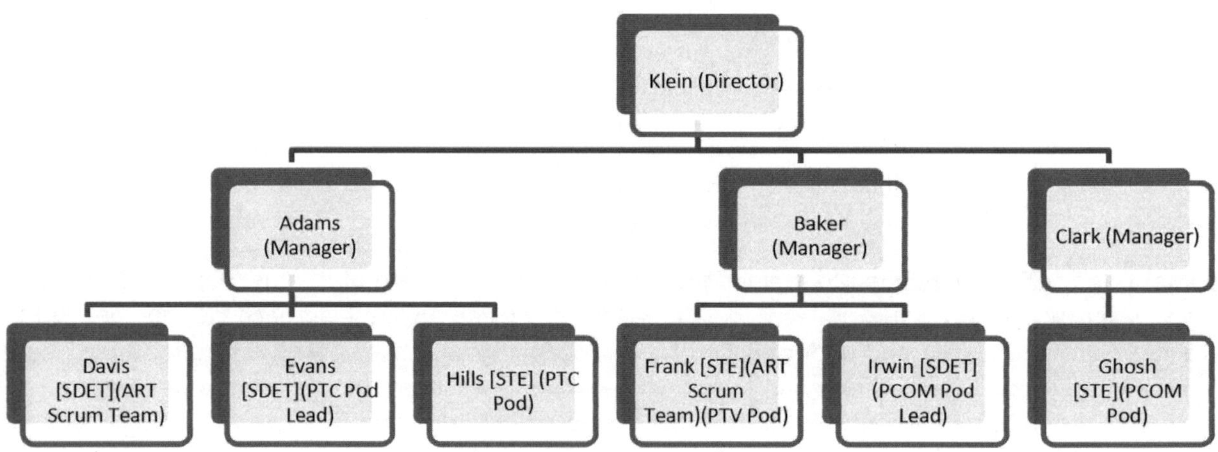

Figure 2. Org After Shipping

4. Approach to Quality

Inside each pod, there are a number of phases that each team may need to complete depending on the project. The pod lead will help derive the plan with input from the pod and the partners. Each phase when done in order allows the team to surgically address the most important issues at the right time. These phases tend to build on each other, so the work done in a previous phase helps inform the work of the next phase.

First, case development occurs in the exploratory phase. Next, the libraries or test runs are created during a test development phase. Automated tests and system verification occur in an integration phase.

The systems are stress tested and their performance determined in an evaluation phase. Finally, confidence and readiness are determined in the release phase.

These phases may happen seemingly concurrently during a sprint or take multiple sprints to complete. They may align to their own cadence or happen as tasks on a Kanban board depending on the team they are being done for but, by acknowledging which phase of testing is appropriate at the time, the pods and individuals can determine where a feature is and how much confidence the team has in its readiness for release.

5. Exploratory Phase

During our exploratory testing phase, we are discovering what the extent of the testing for a feature set may be. This often includes setting up a local development environment so we can replicate what the development team is doing. It may include setting up a test environment or performing testing against the first environment that the development team is using. Tools like the developer tools in a browser for web testing and Postman for API testing are invaluable at this time. Typically, test engineers are reviewing basic functionality, discovering edge cases, and evaluating implementation strategies.

For a recent PCOM release, an update was being made to the Pokédex. We decided to investigate if we would be able to use mabl, an automation tool, to develop a sustainable automation suite. We used the exploratory phase to develop reusable components in mabl called flows to determine if automating this task was feasible. In this case, the actual test cases had already been developed and we were exploring the ability to automate the cases. With some experimenting and collaborating with the mabl team we were able to develop working flows that would allow the development of an automated pass of Pokédex changes.

6. Test Development Phase

Once the basic shape of testing is understood, engineers can begin developing tests and organizing test suites. Discussions occur with the development team around where they have unit tests and how that testing is executed (locally, part of CI/CD). Test is involved in code reviews to determine where gaps may be occurring. Common test libraries may be explored or developed at this point to make developing automation easier. Many of our pods and scrum teams will publish libraries to internal repositories for common tasks such as integrating with CI/CD, publishing results of tests to information repositories so that other pods can easily integrate saving time and effort.

In a prior release, we had developed integration tests for the services that PTV uses. These services allow users to continue watching episodes when switching devices. As use of these services expanded, we determined that we should publish a test library for those services for reuse. In the test development phase the pod working on those services factored out the common functionality into a Python library, and then refactored the existing integration tests to use the library. That library was then published internally for other products to use as part of their integration testing.

7. Integration Phase

With cases in hand, the team will begin work on cases that address the entire system. Often the focuses of these tests are to ensure multiple components work together as designed. These help validate architecture choices made by the development teams as well as our devops team. These tests are often automated and run as part of CI/CD pipelines using Jenkins or Team City. Often the results of these and the unit tests are used to evaluate code coverage, highlighted by tools such as Sealights. Where it makes sense, teams will publish tests in Docker containers so that they can be run by simply executing the image and collecting the results. This allows these tests to be repeatable in multiple environments. The results of the tests may be written to a test case management system such as qTest.

The PTC team has integrated Python tests that cover 69% of their API. They have also incorporated mabl tests to cover the UI through the web client. By integrating both of these strategies into a single CI/CD workflow in Jenkins, each build has 86% or more total coverage per build.

8. Evaluation Phase

In the evaluation phase, the focus is no longer just functionality, but performance and stress as well. Using the libraries developed in the previous quality phases, stress and load testing can be performed to simulate the behavior of the system when thousands or millions of users are accessing it. Tools like Locust are used to create load on the system to simulate scaling events or determine starting parameters. Resources may be manipulated in stress tests to simulate running out of memory or database access issues. Estimates for the predicted number of users are sourced from business partners as well as historical data.

Using Locust, we were able to determine that we were seeing errors we didn't expect in the services used by PTV when the system was under large loads. We were able to determine that there were issues with replication of data across regions, and that best effort routing was not appropriate for our design because the data replication may not be as fast as user requests for data. To address the problem we changed routing from best effort to location based.

9. Release Phase

In the release phase we are looking to provide confidence to our stakeholders. The focus is on providing data that helps make business decisions around a products readiness. Often the team is answering questions such as "How many users can access the system at a time?" or "What monitoring will exist in production?". Often run books have been reviewed and checklists developed so support engineers know how to address incoming issues.

10. Conclusions

By taking this phased approach, many positives have occurred on the team. The quality team tends to possess very deep understanding of our products and services. We are often able to help make improvements to the development process such as continuous integration testing rapidly due to our experience implementing it at TPCI. We have seen dramatic reductions in the number of incidents in our legacy products because the goals and metrics are known and evaluated for prior to releasing to production. For the Pokémon Card Game Online, for example, we have reduced the number of incidents from around four to six per release (with 4-6 releases per year) to less than three incidents per year. The quality team is able to iterate rapidly, finding solutions to problems that may exist across pods and products and addressing them at their root. Most importantly, we have been able to measurably increase our customer satisfaction, both with internal customers and partners and consumers.

11. The Future

Part of our culture is to always be growing and looking for opportunities to make improvements. We are looking to create common methods for producing dashboards to make communicating project status with our partners even easier. This will focus on developing a common set of tools for collecting and accessing the data produced in our testing. We hope to continue developing our common libraries so teams that rely on internal services can simply choose. A tool instead of needing to develop one. We also hope to move teams towards CI/CD pipelines that automate much of the evaluation of new services and automatically publish all the way to production when applicable. We are also developing deeper ties with our customer service teams to try and understand where consumers are encountering issues, how we can address them and provide customer service representatives better tools to mitigate issues.

By constantly refining our processes and evolving how we approach challenges, our quality team is ready to tackle new opportunities.

References

Docker Inc. "Get Started With Docker." https://www.docker.com/ (accessed August 1, 2020)

Jenkins. "Build Great things At Scale." https://www.jenkins.io/ (accessed August 1, 2020)

Locust. "An open source load testing tool." https://locust.io/ (accessed August 1, 2020)

mabl. "Intelligent Test Automation for Everyone on Your Team" https://www.mabl.com/ (accessed August 1, 2020)

Tricentis qTest. "Agile Test Management for the Enterprise." https://www.tricentis.com/products/agile-dev-testing-qtest/ (accessed August 1, 2020)

Sealights. "Smarter testing means delivering high-quality software faster." https://www.sealights.io/ (accessed August 1, 2020)

Jet Brains Team City. "Powerful Continuous Integration out of the box." https://www.jetbrains.com/teamcity/ (accessed August 1, 2020)